Sir James Neville

Sir James Neville

War and Peace: a Norfolk Soldier Abroad and At Home

Sara Barton-Wood

First published 2023 by Poppyland Publishing, Lowestoft, NR32 3BB.

www.poppyland.co.uk

ISBN 978 1 909796 99 7

Picture credits can be found in the captions.

Typeset in Avenir Book 9.5/12.5pt.

Printed by Ashford Colour Press.

Front cover: Neville sitting in a planter's chair on the verandah of his bungalow, October 1925.

John d'Arcy / NRO Nev 7/34.

Back cover: top—Neville on leave at Sloley Hall with friends; middle—group of officers including Neville; bottom—South African Constabulary cart, 1924.

John d'Arcy / NRO Nev 7/32 (top and bottom), NRO Nev 7/34 (middle).

Frontispiece: James Neville on leave from Eton outside the family's house in Ecclestone Square.

John d'Arcy / NRO Nev 7/32.

Contents

Acknowledgements

This book has been a very long time coming, from conception in 2014 to publication this year. This is partly due to Covid restrictions when I was not able to go into the Norfolk Record Office, but also to my own personal commitments and tardiness! I had hoped to have it ready for publication at the very latest by 2018 to mark the centenary of the end of the First World War, and I apologise to John d'Arcy, Neville's literary executor, for my lack of diligence.

Mr d'Arcy has been very supportive of my efforts, and I want to thank him, JEH Neville's two daughters (Lindy and Janie) for their contribution and consent to this project, and Neville's grandson Simon Gorton and his wife Babs, for having us to stay at Sloley Hall as B and B guests in the summer of 2017. The Hall is now run by Simon's son Peter and his partner Jodie.

I also want to thank my husband Richard Barton-Wood for his enormous help with the photographs and for proof-reading my final draft. As always, he has been a huge support and great friend.

Sara Barton-Wood, 2023.

Aftermath of Disaster

In this opening chapter I introduce my subject, James Neville, who lived through the most momentous events of the 20th Century, often at the heart of the action as a soldier. His diaries and letters on which I have based this book are in the Norfolk Record Office, but I also met both his daughters Lindy and Janie, and his grandson Simon who now runs the family home, Sloley Hall, near North Walsham, as a Bed and Breakfast.
I have started with a quote from his journal, dated January 1925.

I feel that this year is going to be, or has got to be, a momentous one in my life. It boils down to whether I can start to make good, get my toes in or not. Anyhow I have the consolation of knowing that whatever happens, it cannot be so disastrous as last year. I am embarking on my fourth lustre—the 28th year—perhaps as Jane foretells, it will bring the beginnings of better days, but how it can, is at present beyond my comprehension.

Today I feel utterly finished. I sweat when I think of what the future will be, of the hell that has got to be lived through during this very year that starts today. If only the earth would open and swallow me up. If only I could go somewhere where I should never meet anyone I knew, I could live in a certain amount of peace. But that would be cowardly and henceforth my life is not my own.

What *had* he done? This was the first volume of James Neville's diaries that I opened and read with deepening interest as I came to the end of the first two paragraphs above. I say a little more later in this chapter, but you will have to wait until Chapters 12 and 13 to find out the details of what Neville had done!

Neville lived through most of the 20th century and was a compulsive diarist and sometimes a talented writer, though the quality of his work varies. He wrote almost every day in his journal (of which there are over 60 volumes in the Norfolk Record Office). He also wrote letters to his father and sisters, which they returned when he was abroad initially as a subaltern in the British Army during the First World War; then to Russia with the North Russian Expeditionary Force (to fight the Bolsheviks and try to stop them taking over that vast country); then to Ireland again with the Army, during the lead-up to independence in 1922. He left the Army and went off to the Sudan in 1925–6, where he worked as an inspector on the Gezira cotton picking scheme.

Neville (centre in striped jacket) with three friends, *John d'Arcy / NRO. Nev7/32.*

I came across his war letters at the Norwich Heritage Centre when I was researching a short article for the history column in the local paper, the *Eastern Daily Press*. The small volume of letters between Neville and his father and two sisters, while Neville was serving in France as an officer in the Great War, and subsequently in Russia, were published in 1931. This was a private publication (in those days known as vanity publishing), under the title *The War Letters of a Light Infantryman*. Only a dozen copies exist. But I was struck by his vivid descriptions

Sloley Hall from the garden at the rear.
Richard Barton-Wood, August 2016.

of the conditions of war on the front, and by his wealth of good humour and warmth. I made a mental note to return to the War Letters when I had more time. Five years passed. I finally decided the time was right and got in touch with Neville's executor, John d'Arcy.

Mr d'Arcy was enthusiastic. But he also asked me if I would be willing to write a biography of his first cousin (once removed) to go with the letters. I hesitated for a moment. There were an awful lot of volumes of his diaries from his adult life in the repositories of the Norfolk Record Office. But then Mr d'Arcy said something that made me decide to go for it.

> Jimmy (as James Neville was known) had a love affair with the wife of his commanding officer.' he said. 'I think it was in about 1924, long before he got married to his wife, Marie-Louise. They ran away together to South Africa and there was a terrible scandal. It did not work out and Jimmy had to come home and try and get on with his life in another job.

No journalist could resist a story like that! An army officer is supposed to be a gentleman. Honour is everything. My man broke all the rules, gambled and lost. I slept on it overnight then rang Mr d'Arcy back and said I'd do it. As I waded through the papers in the NRO I began to develop a real affection for James Neville, warts and all—and believe me, there were an awful lot of warts! He was selfish and emotionally unstable. He enjoyed picking a fight, perhaps a quality valuable in a soldier, but he lost friends and made enemies within his own family with this tendency. He was certainly brave and aggressive, and remarks over and over in his journals that he could not wait to get to the front to see a bit of action.

But I felt I knew him well. I understood his decision making. I noticed we had many of the same flaws—short fuse on temper, for example—and the same desire for fun and excitement. We both grew up in Norfolk and shared a love of sailing and swimming, family get-togethers, picnics and horse riding. We both enjoyed and understood the power of words.

Most of this biography is based on his diaries, but the War Letters section is an edited version of his own privately published book (1931). This exchange of letters between Neville and his father (and his two sisters) makes clear that the two men loved each other deeply. Neville senior always signed himself off with 'with love from yr aff father' and frequently entreated his son not to try to be a hero but to come home safe at the end of the war. The father also sent to his son while he was serving in the British Army during the First World War in France, copies of Shakespeare's plays, Greek poetry with advice on how to master the complex metre and a chess set, not to mention delicacies from the Sloley garden such as asparagus in May and strawberries in June. I have this mental picture of young Neville enduring the most horrific and gruelling of conditions in the muddy trenches of the Western Front, but in his spare time reading Hamlet, or Aristophanes, or being check-mated by his servant at chess, and feeding on Norfolk's finest. There is a rare sweetness in the letters and although the two men sometimes fell out (often over their women friends!), I am in no doubt that Reginald Neville was overwhelmingly a kind family man and his son wanted his father to be proud of him.

I met both his daughters, Lindy and Janie, and interviewed Janie. Both said their father was a 'difficult man'—charming and urbane with people he did not know well, but bad tempered and unpredictable with his own family. Lindy said she did not feel this had adversely affected her life, but Janie said she felt her father let her down. She burnt his letters and photographs a year or two before we met, in frustration that he had made so many broken promises, and wondered out loud if he had perhaps been bipolar, a condition not readily recognised or treatable in the early 20th century. Both girls went to boarding school, but after that their father would not spend any more money on their education ('A waste of money to educate girls', he was fond of saying, as well as 'A soldier's daughter does not cry' whenever Janie was in tears). They finished school at 16 and returned home to work on their father's farm at Frankfurt House in Sloley.

Reginald Neville's portrait in Sloley Hall.[1] *Richard Barton-Wood, August 2016.*

I also met his grandson Simon Gorton (Lindy's son) who now lives at the old family home, Sloley Hall, which he runs as a bed and breakfast with his wife Babs. Together they have restored the house to something approaching how it would have been in Neville's day, and it was a huge privilege to stay there for two nights and to see the original family portraits that line the dining room. Neville died when Simon was 25 so he has some memories of his grandfather, commenting that much of his behaviour

Simon Gorton, Neville's grandson, his wife Babs, and the dog, at the side entrance to the hall.
Richard Barton-Wood, August 2016.

above right: Sloley Hall.
John d'Arcy / NRO Nev 7/32.

below right: the dining room at Sloley with ancestral portraits hung on the walls.
Richard Barton-Wood, August 2016.

which would be considered abhorrent today (such as the use of the racist word 'nigger' or the expectation that his father would support him financially so he could live like a gentleman) was normal at the time. Simon also believed that the Great War had turned his grandfather from a decent human being into a bully. We shall never know the truth —nature or nurture?—and today we have a much greater understanding of why people behave in certain ways and are able to help when it becomes extreme.

This is the life and times of James Neville as recorded in his diaries, but keyed into a computer by someone who would really, really love to have met him. He died in 1982 at his home in Sloley, survived by his second wife Betty and his two daughters and their families.

Where I have referred to Neville recording or saying anything, it is always from his memorial (written at the age of 78 but based on the journal he wrote at the time), from his diary, his letters or his History of the 43rd Regiment. His two daughters were still alive at the time of writing and happily consented to a brief interview, so where I refer to them saying anything, it is in the interview. The recordings of the interviews, and a copy of the transcript, are held in the NRO Sound Archive.

Notes

1 Reginald was born with the surname White and was the son of James Sewell White, a Judge of the High court of Calcutta. He took the surname Neville by Royal Licence in 1885. Wikipedia, December 2017

Early Years and Home Ed 1887–1904

Neville describes his privileged family background, his family's life in London and Norfolk, his early instincts for a practical life in the army. As the only son in a family of three children, he was very close to his mother who seems to have been the only person in his entire life who could persuade him to calm down when he was in a temper.
He talks about his early education, firstly at home and subsequently at a small private school in London. Idyllic summer holidays were taken in Norfolk at the home of relatives in Ashmanhaugh, where the family enjoyed sailing and swimming on the Broads and in the sea on the east coast of Norfolk

James Edmund Henderson Neville, to give him all his names, was born in July 1897, the son of a London barrister and later Conservative MP for Wigan. His third name, Henderson, was his mother Ida's maiden name. She was an Australian and much admired for her beauty by her only son, and by many other members of his family and their friends.

His father, Reginald, a barrister and conservative MP, was made a baronet in July 1927. According to Who's Who, the family seat is at Sloley Hall near North Walsham, in Norfolk. Born Reginald White, he was the son of James Sewell White, a judge of the High Court of Calcutta, who assumed the surname Neville by Royal Licence in 1885. James became the second Baronet on the death of Reginald, and his much younger half-brother Richard (more about him later), became the third Baronet. Since there were no further male heirs, the title became extinct in 1994.[1]

Young James Neville was born at his parents' home at 15, St George's Road, Ecclestone Square, London SW1, a very smart address. The house was large and spread over several floors (at least three with six flights of stairs), with a drawing room on the first floor. The house was staffed by five women as well as his mother – a parlour maid, housemaid, cook, nurse and under-nurse. The family, mother, father, son and two daughters, were a tight-knit unit and took holidays together at Sloley Hall until the death of Grandpa Neville, who owned the Hall and surrounding estate, in 1912 and the Hall passed by inheritance to Reginald.

So young Neville was born into an upper-middle class family at the very end of the 19th century, in the year of Queen Victoria's diamond jubilee when England was at the height of her days of empire. He had two older sisters, Angela and Mary (known ironically as Plain Jane for her beauty). But it was the son on whom all the hopes of the family rested. He was expected to go to a

Neville's parents, Reginald and Ida, at Ludham, after a sailing trip.
John d'Arcy / NRO Nev 7/32.

Interior of the house at Ecclestone Square.
John d'Arcy / NRO Nev 7/32.

smart preparatory boarding school, followed by Eton, which is in fact what happened.

Whether or not he was expected thereafter to go into the army is not clear. His father was not keen for Neville to sign up at the start of the Great War in 1914. Like many politicians he was happy to send the sons of other families to war, but not his own. Reginald frequently took his son to his 'mysterious chambers' to watch him at work and might well have hoped that his son would follow him into the law and/or politics, though there is no mention in the diaries that young Neville was under any explicit pressure to do so. Reginald himself had followed his own father into the legal profession. But young Neville was 'bored stiff' by his father's chambers and persisted in his desire to sign up. At the age of 18 he was nominated for a commission at The Royal Military Academy, Sandhurst. And indeed, Neville seems to have had an instinctive desire to become a soldier. He records his earliest memory as crowds cheering soldiers returning after the relief of Mafeking in South Africa in 1900.[2]

He also recalls that during the funeral of Queen Victoria in 1901, he was 'taken to play (with toy) soldiers' by Nanny Violet, the nursery maid, at the London home of his grandfather Neville, while his mother and older sisters watched the funeral procession. Another early memory was the strong impression he got of the return of the 'volunteers' from the Boer War in South Africa. (A volunteer did not mean, at this time, someone who worked for no pay. A military volunteer is a person who enlists in military service by free will, and is not a conscript, mercenary, or a foreign legionnaire. Volunteers sometimes enlist to fight in the armed forces of a foreign country, for example during the Spanish Civil War.) All through his early life it seems that Neville was fascinated by uniforms, by medals on a manly chest (which he calls 'fruit salad'), and by the possibilities offered by serving King or Queen and country in the armed forces. To begin with he thought that he would like to go into the navy, but a slight astigmatism in one eye put him out of the running for that service, though apparently not for the army. Neville's home life as a youngster was a happy and privileged one. He records that he and his sister Angela, nicknamed Jelly, (he seems to have been much closer to her than to Mary/Jane) spent many pleasant hours sliding down the banisters at 15 St George's Road on a metal tray, or having pillow fights with her under the bottom shelf of their old nursery dinner wagon, which usually ended in tears from Angela until the pair made up with hugs.

His day started around 7am when he and his sisters were woken by their nurse, given breakfast in the nursery and then taken out for walks in Central London. While King Edward VII (who succeeded Victoria) had appendicitis, Nanny Griffiths would wheel their pram down the Buckingham Palace Road to read the bulletins on his health that were posted up on the palace gates, and then report back to the children's mother.

Sometimes they went to dancing lessons in Sloane Square, run by a Miss Cowper. The journey to Sloane Square meant travelling on 'a green bus from Elizabeth Bridge, over the Victoria railway line, or the underground from Victoria.' In those days he adds, 'The underground was not pleasant. The third-class carriages ... were dirty and the windows were opaque from accumulated smoke and steam.' Neville does not mention this, but the underground we fondly know today as The London Tube, was at that time using trains on some routes that were still drawn by steam engines as they had not yet been electrified. Young Neville was easily cheered up. 'The one redeeming feature of all these tortures was that sometimes we had sprats for tea,' he says!

Occasionally, and to Neville's great joy, their little group would see guards (he presumably means The Guards which change every other day in front of Buckingham Palace) marching from their barracks accompanied by a band. Once home from the walk, Neville was put back into his cot for a rest (having been carried up the six flights of stairs) and he remembers 'thumping the cot in time with the bass drum which I could still hear out in the street'.

Sometimes their mother, with nanny as reinforcement, would even take them to Green Park and would read *The Children of the New Forest*[3] by Captain Marryat to them under the tall elm trees. Beyond the railings of the park stretched a vast avenue of trees as far as Parliament Square where Admiralty Arch now stands. If there was no traffic, the children were allowed to bowl their hoops free from any interference from nanny or mother.

The children ate all their meals in the nursery, and as the dinner wagon had to be pushed and carried up so many flights of stairs, the food was often cold or lukewarm. The only hot item was tea, which was brewed over the nursery fire. The children's clothes were washed in the laundry room in the basement, but then dried over the fireguard in the nursery, which made the place stink. There was no dedicated bathroom for the youngsters, so a saucer bath was filled with tepid water for an all-over wash.

Their personal items were kept in a drawer in the large square table in the nursery, and under the table was THE BOX, a packing case where Neville kept his toy trains. More general toys, such as Lotto, spillikins, and snakes and ladders, were kept in the drawing room (possibly to stop the loss of the many tiny pieces, or perhaps to discourage the staff playing games when they were meant to be working). The children could only visit the drawing room after tea to be with their mother. To young Neville his mother was 'a goddess in face and figure, and a being to me of infinite beauty, kindness and love'. Only at weekends did they also meet their father in the drawing room.

Angela and Jane (Mary) (on bicycle).

John d'Arcy / NRO Nev 7/32.

Around 6.30pm the children would be sent upstairs to bed with one of the staff, and about half an hour later, mother would come up to say 'good-night'. In turn, the children would kneel with their heads in her lap and they would say together 'Gentle Jesus meek and mild, Look upon a little child, Pity his simple city (sic), Suffer me to come to thee'. Neville's vision of the 'simple city' was 'a landscape view with Jerusalem on the horizon', which appeared in an illuminated Bible. And when it got to 'The grace of our Lord Jesus Christ and the Fellow-ship of the Holy Ghost', Neville's mind would turn to what kind of 'ship' this would be—square rigged, fore and aft, raked or a modern version. So many of his mother's Henderson ancestors had served in the navy, that he 'had no other thought than following in their illustrious footsteps'. But the astigmatism in one eye at the age of eight put paid to that ambition.

Angela had a talent for story telling and while the three children were in bed before going off to sleep, she made up a tale about a little boy called Trousers (Neville) and a little girl called Nibby (herself). Nibby and Trousers had a magic horse-bus which had a new adventure every night. In later life Neville also tried his hand at fiction with moderate success and some of his short stories are in the repositories at the Norfolk Record Office (NRO). Neville liked words, was good with them and understood their power. He wrote in his journal every day as both his daughters confirm.

But Angela's health was a little delicate. The glands in her neck used to swell and the doctors thought she might have TB, in those days a killer. Angela was taken down to Broadstairs in Kent for surgery with a Dr Raven, and her mother and siblings went too. Broadstairs was thought to be good for the health because it was bracingly cold. Neville remembers the bleeding chilblains on his feet, though he did enjoy the summers on the sand at Dumpton Gap. But it was also there that he met and became great friends with a little girl called PooBah, the start of a lifelong friendship.

Neville may have had an advantageous start in life—good breeding, money, education, a loving family—but he had two character flaws which he never really came to terms with, though he acknowledges these flaws freely in his journal. The first was his susceptibility to the charms of women. He was tall, good looking and had a good sense of humour. He was a great charmer and women came easily to him. But he did not always understand how his actions would affect his prospects; let alone how they would affect other people. He was careless in his romantic relationships, did not think through how things might turn out and appears not to understand why some people disliked him. These days we would say that such a man has no emotional intelligence. In those days he was a bit of a cad. The second was his volatile temper, and it was this that alienated his two daughters perhaps even more than his inability to remain monogamous. His younger daughter Janie recalled in an interview that her father would fly into a rage, frightening his wife (Marie Louise) and his daughters, and would continue to sound off until he got what he wanted.

The only person who seemed to have been unmoved by his tantrums was his mother. Neville wrote in 1904, 'Mother called my tantrums "tomps", and would not speak to or play with me until I recovered my manners. She was never severe, but always unshakeable, determined and absolutely just. I believe I was much more horrid than the other boys I met of my own age.'

Everyone else seems to have pandered to Neville's uncertain temper, or made excuses for him. Friends would say it was because of his poor financial state in later life which made him irritable. Perhaps this or that was unfair. His daughters told me that their mother would beg him for forgiveness when she had done nothing wrong, just to try to get her husband to calm down; the two girls were too young and vulnerable to stand up to him until they were married with families of their own, and by that time it was too late. Neville had no sons of his own who might have put the father in his place. Whatever the reason, sadly, he never mastered these flaws. Nevertheless, Neville could write up quite a storm in his diary, in which he confided everything very frankly just as it occurred and he has given us a beautifully readable account of what it was like to be a boy, then a man, during the twentieth century.

Turning now to his early school days, Neville and his sisters had a governess as their first teacher at their home in London. Neville was taught to read while his older sisters did sums or writing. The three children had lessons in the dining room with a 'very sweet governess' called Miss Trennery. Lessons started soon after their father went off to his legal chambers. Young Neville's first idea of what money looked like was one of his father's paper briefs, tied up with pink tape, because he knew that his father went to his chambers 'to make money'. He also knew that the paper brief was worth rather more than the two pennies a week given him as pocket money by his mother, but only if he managed to walk nicely with his toes turned out!

Miss Trennery was a 'very patient' mistress, patient with the young children's school work and also patient with James Neville who had to read out in class the word 'behind'. He had been told by his mother and father that 'behind' meant 'posterior' and this was a word never used in polite society, nor anywhere else if possible. Miss Trennery had to deal with a 'tomp', but seems to have taken it in her stride. When young Neville started screaming with fury at the indignity, Miss Trennery told him, very seriously, that as soon as he stopped screaming and behaved like a man, he could go back to the nursery and that would be the end of the lesson.

Most of the summer holidays between 1900-1906 were taken with relatives at Ashmanhaugh Rectory in Norfolk, to be near Neville's father's parents at Sloley Hall. The Norfolk air suited Neville's mother better than anywhere. She used to say that she felt well while in Norfolk. She got excruciating headaches in London and had to retreat to her room and lie down with curtains drawn and take the drug Phenaceton.[4] She got headaches in Norfolk too, but not so badly or as frequently as in London. The only treatment that seemed to suit her was for a family member or close friend to sit beside her and stroke or comb her hair.

It is quite possible that it was the extraordinary and traumatic process of getting ready to go on holiday that brought on these headaches for his mother. When the law term ended, half a dozen trunks, packing cases, boxes, bags, dogs, cats, three children and five staff were loaded up into a private bus hired from the Great Eastern Railway Company. Even the roof was loaded with their belongings. The bus would accommodate several people inside, plus one on the box on the outside.

'I can see it now,' says Neville. 'Father riding behind us on a bicycle down the Embankment towards the bottle neck at the Mansion House. In those days of steam, the Cromer Express from Liverpool Street in London stopped only at Ipswich before arriving at Norwich, and we did not even have to change to go on to Wroxham. At Wroxham there was more pandemonium as we detrained where Bearded Ben, a friendly porter, always met us and got us loaded up for the final stage to Ashmanhaugh'.

Norfolk's more remote corners had opened up to 'invasion' from the south with the arrival of railways in Cromer in 1877. It immediately became a favourite holiday resort for the London set, not just the Nevilles who already had a family connection in Norfolk but also bankers (such as friends of the Frys and Barclays) and artists and writers. For a while Cromer had no fewer than three railway stations, one of which was extremely close to the beach.

Ashmanhaugh, pronounced 'Ash-m'n-hay' or 'Ash-manner', the destination for the Neville family, is a tiny village about twelve miles north east of Norwich. Its most significant building is the little 12th century flint-built St Swithin's Church with its distinctive round tower, the narrowest in England. This is where the Neville family had their own family pew and where James's religious education continued on Sundays. He enjoyed hearing his father read the

Ashmanaugh Church, exterior.
Richard Barton-Wood, June 2021.

lesson as he had 'a quite beautiful reading voice'. Odd bits of the Old Testament captured his imagination, such as the story of Jezebel, when John comes to the queen 'driving furiously'. But otherwise he found church 'boring and incomprehensible'. Perhaps for entertainment his gaze would fall on the colourful Resurrection scene of the east window's stained glass, the work of William Morris of Arts and Crafts fame, though he never showed much interest for either art or theology.

For church, Neville was made to wear a kilt and plaid socks in Henderson tartan, a doublet in black velvet and a Glengarry bonnet. He does not say if he protested against the outfit, only that he become the target of street urchins who threw orange peel at him. Neville wore this same outfit at an 'unforgettable' Christmas party given by a Mrs Powell where a magician was the main entertainment. The magician produced a number of miniature bagpipes from the inside of the handkerchief pocket of his doublet. Neville says that he still cannot work out how he managed that. The last time Neville saw his black velvet doublet it was hanging on the wall of Sloley Primary School in 1974 as an exhibit of bygone children's clothing.

The one time the Nevilles holidayed outside Norfolk during this period was in Littlehampton in 1904 and he remembers it with great pleasure. 'It was a lovely place,' Neville declares, 'with lovely glorious sands.' This was the time when Russia and Japan were at war, and since England had a treaty with Japan, England was very anti-Russian politically. Neville said he remembered hearing about 'pogroms', and harsh and brutal treatment of prisoners in Siberia. Everyone on holiday in England at the time would grab a deck chair at 6d a seat, and join in some rude song about Admiral Togo of Japan. Arthur Balfour was prime minister at the time and he also came in for some sensible advice:

If I were Arthur Balfour, I would I would
Give up my parliamentary life
And stick to golf and take a wife
If I were Arthur Balfour.

But even then, during the precious period of summer holidays in Littlehampton, the children had a governess called Miss Honey, nicknamed by the children as Miss Horrid. According to Neville she was a fiend. 'She ganged up with nanny against us', he writes. 'And on one occasion she threatened to drown herself which frightened Jane a lot. Angela and I tied ourselves together with string to outmanoeuvre her, but Hal (Stogdon, a cousin) let the side down by cutting us apart. Father came to visit us from London occasionally and when we complained about Miss Horrid, he said "You will have to bear it"'.

That year Neville's birthday in July was hijacked by this 'dreadful governess'. She decided that she wanted to be rowed up the river to see something she was interested in. Their lodgings backed onto the River Arun and Neville can remember longing to join in as he watched competitors have a go at 'the greasy pole' during the annual water festival. (The greasy pole is a large pole suspended over the water horizontally and then covered with grease. Young people would try to walk along it as far as they could until they inevitably fell off into the water/mud below. It's a fun activity still found in water festivals all over England today). And there was he, no doubt dressed in his smartest clothes for Miss Horrid's benefit, being rowed up the river to see some church or other worthy building that was of no consequence to him at all. For some misdemeanour, he was sent to bed that night without supper, but was so hungry that later on when everyone else had gone to bed, he came down and 'pigged the rind off the nursery cheese'.

Perhaps Norfolk was the place where they all truly relaxed for there is no mention of a governess for the summer holidays at Sloley. 'Ashmanhaugh Rectory[5] was a paradise for nearly two months,' writes Neville. 'The grounds contained a wood in a little dell where we made paths through the undergrowth. On the eastern boundary a little clearing was "home" (for games of *Last One In* or *Tag*), and from there we could look across the cornfields to the only shop in the straggling village where we could buy a bag of bulls' eyes for tuppence.' (These were globe-shaped hard-boiled sweets, usually in black and white stripes. Tuppence would be less than 1p in today's currency).

> Once a week we were driven by nanny in the ass cart to Hoveton for stores from Roys (of Wroxham).[6] This was a small triangular shop at the junction of the Tunstead and Stalham roads and I remember so vividly the buzz of flies on the fruit on the glass-enclosed entrance. No-one seemed to get ill from the lack of hygienic presentation. The ass, as usual, was very reluctant to move anywhere and my sister Jane rode a bicycle in front of the cart with a carrot tied to the back of her saddle. Someone also discovered that the ass did not like the sound of a box full of pebbles being shaken over his rear end, and that frightened him into a trot.

Roys of Wroxham (as it was generally known despite being located north of the river in Hoveton) was established in 1899 by the brothers Albert and Arnold Roy. The original general stores expanded over the years to become something of a Norfolk institution, a full-blown department store, beloved of Broads holidaymakers and advertised from the 1930s as 'The World's Largest Village Store'.

Another treat was to visit Mrs Norgates who loved children and would give them glasses of home-made mead and ginger biscuits, which made Jane wobble rather on her bicycle on the way home. Or rosy-faced Mrs Mason, the wife of the blacksmith, who gave them a dinner of a 'luscious dark thick soup with light Norfolk dumplings floating in it'. That was an end-of-holidays meal.

The Nevilles sailed dinghies on the rivers and Broads, took picnics to one of the many Norfolk beauty spots, went for bicycle rides *en famille*, went riding, walking, canoeing, played games on the lawn in the light of the setting sun, had friends to stay, and, for Neville probably the most important of all, enjoyed a spectacular freedom to try things out. For example, their Aunt Charlotte used a wheelchair and for some reason one day, it was available—in other words, its usual occupant was not around. It had a spade handle along the push-bar which activated a single small wheel. Two of the children would squash into the seat while the third pushed the chair as far as it would go towards a downhill slope. Then one of the occupants had to stand up to try to manipulate the steering gear. It crashed often, but the chair, Neville reports in his diary, 'stood up to the crashes very well.'

Ashmanhaugh Rectory.
Richard Barton-Wood, June 2021.

On another occasion Neville discovered some open pots of paint and a stiff brush inside the greenhouses. He was not usually allowed to 'help' with painting jobs. Before long the door on the inside of the greenhouse was daubed with many different colours which, to him, was 'very satisfactory', though not to nanny who 'bounced me off to bed

Three of the family in the pony and trap, a favourite summer pastime in Norfolk (James is on the left).
John d'Arcy / NRO Nev 7/32.

Friends pull faces for a 'funny' photograph. James in on the right. Sloley Hall, November 1914.

John d'Arcy / NRO Nev 7/32.

and closed the curtains after a hiding'. But this punishment did not serve any purpose, as Neville soon got bored and the bright sunlight through the curtains gave him enough light to play with nanny's toilet collection. He found scissors, paper, perfume and handkerchiefs. Oh dear!

The three children had each other to play with and many friends visited, but Ashmanhaugh Rectory and Sloley Hall were full of relations, many of them ageing. Aunt Charlotte (Granny Neville's sister) was 90. Granny and Grandpa Neville were also in their nineties. Aunts Amy, Kate and Rose, Aunt Charlotte's daughters, were Reginald's age, in other words in their fifties. (Even in the 1950s and 1960s, this author remembers teatime with the extended family where the children would have to be seen and not heard otherwise there would be complaints.)

Neville says that 'Visits to Sloley from Ashmanhaugh were not popular. ... We hardly ever saw grandpa. He and father would be closeted in the library while we had to meet the strictness and criticisms of the aunts. ... Only Amy was ever nice to us. Kate never forgot that Rose had given her measles when they were children and as a result, she was partially deaf. She never missed an opportunity to remind Rose of that'.

Their mother, Charlotte, sounds like the ultimate bad dream. He says 'All three aunts were handsome and accomplished. Amy was particularly gifted, a good classic linguist and no mean actress. Had she a less autocratic, jealous and spiteful mother she could have made a name for herself professionally. But all three were tied and dragooned by their old dragon of a mother.'

Old Aunt Charlotte, moreover, disliked Neville's mother Ida and showed it. Ida had tried to help the three girls to 'come out' in London by having them to stay and introducing them to her friends. And when Rose got engaged to a young man, Henry Stukely Leak, and was subsequently jilted by him, it was Ida who came to her rescue, had her to stay at the house in St George's Road and comforted her.

Notes

1 Who's Who entry. The Neville Baronetcy, of Sloley in the County of Norfolk, was a title in the Baronetage of the UK. It was created on 2 July 1927 for the barrister and Conservative politician Reginald Neville. He was succeeded by his elder son, (James), the second Baronet, who was the author of *The War Letters of a Light Infantryman* (1931) and also wrote under the pen-name of 'Gaid Sakit'.

2 The Siege of Mafeking was the most famous British victory in the Second Boer War, taking place over a period of 212 days in 1899-1900. Robert Baden-Powell, who defended the town and went on to found the Scout Movement, became a national hero. Wikipedia, November 2017.

3 *The Children of the New Forest*, published in 1847, is a children's novel set in the time of the English Civil War. The story follows the fortunes of four children who are orphaned during the war, and hide from their Roundhead enemies in the shelter of the New Forest where they learn to live off the land. Its great appeal lies in showing how young people can manage perfectly well without parents or any other authority, forage for food from wild plants and organise their social relationships without supervision. More or less guaranteed to fire young Neville's imagination!

4 Phenaceton was the forerunner of paracetamol, introduced in 1887 and was the first synthetic fever and pain relief agent on the market. It was discontinued when doctors realised it had carcinogenic qualities, and also tended to cause kidney damage. Wikipedia, November 2017.

5 Sold in 2018 for £1,200,000.

6 Wroxham is situated about eight miles from Norwich on the Norfolk Broads. Roy's of Wroxham still exists but is vastly expanded into a department store. My own Norfolk born and bred father Ben Rust of Aylsham remembers the early version.

Proper School 1904-10

Neville attended a small London school with his sisters for a year, and was then sent to a boarding prep school where the head was a bully. Neville then attended a second prep school for a year where he started to excel at sport. The family visited Switzerland during the summer holidays. Neville senior stood for parliament as Conservative MP for Wigan in the election of early 1910, but unexpectedly lost to the Labour candidate.

Graham Street

School proper began for Neville in 1904 when he was seven. Angela by now was 10 and Jane 13 and they all went to Miss Wollesley Lewis's High School for Girls in Graham Street, Pimlico.

The school had a reputation for Christian teaching and a strict upbringing, which is probably why it was chosen. Neville was in the kindergarten with one other little boy, and a form mistress called Miss Cookson. She was blond and Neville 'at once fell in love with her'. Miss Cookson left soon after Neville's start at the school to get married. She had a baby, but sadly she died in childbirth.

Neville was at Graham Street School for two years and says that he enjoyed his time there, but sadly does not say any more about the school's conditions. Much space is devoted in this part of his diaries to his feelings and thoughts about other members of his family and friends. His comments earlier about his three aunts and their 'dragon of a mother' is just one example.

In his handwritten memoir, drafted in his seventies, Neville devotes many pages to these years. Like many people approaching the end of their lives, Neville seems to have retained a clear and detailed recall of a singularly happy and carefree early childhood. He describes in loving detail many 'jolly japes' with the children at Beechwood, the eighteenth-century mansion where his Aunt, Mary McCorquordale, lived as well as various expeditions with his own family to Scotland where his father enjoyed hunting, shooting and fishing.

Boarding school—Norfolk House

In the spring of 1906 at the age of eight, Neville was sent off to Norfolk House in Beaconsfield, Bucks, a small preparatory feeder school for Eton and other leading public schools. As was typical of small private schools, Norfolk House was owned and run by a married couple, Cecil Thomas Marcon (usually referred to as CTM) and his wife Florence Neville Marcon. Florence was the sister of James's father Reginald and known in the family as 'Aunt Flo' and James had been a pageboy at their wedding in 1901. Not only that, but Norfolk House was part-financed by Neville's grandfather, and was thus the obvious choice for young Neville's first experience of boarding school, even though Grandpa Neville had concluded that CTM was 'a poor tool'.

Reflecting in later life on the experience, Neville recalled that 'It was very exciting to

Norfolk House at Beaconsfield, 1912
John d'Arcy / NRO Nev 7/30.

be rigged out in another suit and top hat at the age of eight and this, at the time, mitigated the loss of home. I can remember the overwhelming home sickness when I woke up on the first morning in a strange dormitory. Mother had taken me as far as Marylebone station (in London). Father's only advice to me as I was leaving was "If a boy hits you, hit him back".' He had been given cherished presents to distract him from the pain of parting – a pigskin writing case with a strap by his mother, a big stamp album by his sister Jane, and a silver pencil with black, red and blue leads. But he was miserable to begin with and the only thing he looked forward to was an occasional visit by his mother and perhaps one or both sisters.

Neville never protested about being 'sent away', as this was what all boys of his social standing could expect and to show unhappiness was considered weak. So, in London he was handed over to Mr Marcon and taken to Beaconsfield where the school was located in a Georgian building in the centre of the town. 'The schoolroom looked out onto the main road to High Wycombe' Neville says. 'I believe the complement was 10 boys, if that. I knew one of them, Charles Spackman, as he was the son of the rector at Sloley and about 18 months older than me. Charles said that he was not so ill-treated as other boys as the Neville wing shielded him.' And there was the rub. Marcon (CTM), the headmaster, was a bully and today would almost certainly not be allowed anywhere near a classroom. According to Neville he was 'impatient to a degree ... sarcastic, which the boys did not understand ...and a tyrant who terrified his pupils.'

Neville could read and write by this time and he could do simple arithmetic, but long division was a mystery. Nor was he clear on how to write numbers in letters. He was asked to convert 1001 into words, and CTM did not bother to explain what was required. Instead he started with sarcasm and moved on to shouting.

> CTM: 'Have you ever learnt anything boy?'
>
> Neville (in fright): 'I must have been badly taught, Sir'.
>
> CTM (shouting so all the boys in the class froze): 'Badly taught? Badly taught? Hahahaha. Young Neville here thinks he has been badly taught! Have you ever heard such a thing? Hahahaha.'
>
> 'He went on and on,' Neville says, 'until I wished I had never been born.'

And it got worse. Every day CTM scolded Neville for being a 'mother's darling', which he probably was, but that was not his fault. One pupil, Kenneth Corley, who joined the tiny band of young scholars in September 1907, had very large ears which stuck out. It was not long before CTM realised these were perfect targets for his rages. The boys were all sitting at their desks, and CTM asked Corley a question, which Corley tried to answer. The next thing Corley knew, CTM had grabbed one of his large protruding ears and flung him across the room to land in a howling lump against the opposite wall. Neville says he can remember shivering in fright at the battering the boy took, and covering his own ears in case CTM decided to have a go at him as well.

Another newcomer to the school, whose surname was Thorburn (first name unknown) was still not able to control his bladder at night. Thorburn was made to wear a truss in bed which seemed to make matters worse, not better. He got the usual 'merciless' treatment from CTM.

CTM was also an inveterate snob, and would commit the unpardonable sin of criticising a boy's family in front of his own. CTM's relations often attended the boys' midday dinner, and young Neville says he can remember that CTM would tell unflattering stories about his own Aunt Flo and other members of Neville's family. Also on such public occasions, CTM would ask the boys which senior public schools they were bound for. Marlborough was considered acceptable, also Westminster, Bloxham and Lancing. But not Charterhouse (Neville's father Reginald's *alma mater*) or, for some reason best known to himself, Eton which is where young Neville was to be sent when he was old enough.

CTM's monologue would go like this: 'I

can see you Neville, walking down Bond Street in a top hat, with a gold-capped Malacca cane under your arm—hahahahah!' All of this would be said in a tone of voice to make it clear that it was a sneer, nor a compliment. At the end of the first year (i.e. at Christmas 1906) young Neville was invited, as the newest boarder, to make a farewell speech, as was the tradition at the time. His father wrote it for him and the final words included wishing Mr and Mrs Marcon 'a happy holiday skating in Switzerland'. The words nearly made him choke.

The routine at Norfolk House was typical of a preparatory school at the start of the twentieth century. Cold showers at 7.30am, supervised by Miss Rowland, the matron, followed by breakfast of Quaker oats, cold ham, and bread and margarine. On Sundays they were also allowed an egg and a supper in the evening as well as a lunch. Butter in those days was a luxury and margarine had not yet reached the giddy heights of, at least according to the advertisements, tasting just like butter. So, as Neville says, 'It had a filthy taste!' On Sundays they were allowed four ounces of sweets. These were laid out on a slab outside the dining room. But CTM's two children, Ruth and John, were always there and always tried to cadge sweets off the boys, even though they already had plenty of their own from their father. Neville disliked them both intensely.

Lessons started at 9am and consisted of Latin prose and grammar, maths, history (of the British Empire) and geography (also of the British Empire), and once a week they had French and drawing classes. Neville was not a great scholar and found Latin both tedious and pointless. 'Caesar, what a swine he was for writing his commentaries to worry small boys nearly 2,000 years later!' he confided to his memoir (though oddly, later on, he learnt Greek and found it 'easy, and a flexible language'). Neville also had the opportunity to learn carpentry which fired him with a love of working wood with sharp tools for the rest of his life. In the winter term the boys were allowed to make items that their much-reviled headmaster CTM might want or need. Neville made a wheelbarrow, and a stool for his mother.

above: classroom at Norfolk House.
John d'Arcy / NRO Nev 7/30.
below: changing room at Norfolk House.
John d'Arcy / NRO Nev 7/30.

Sport was always important in prep and public schools as a supposed way of developing team spirit, leadership and 'manliness'. Neville did not enjoy cricket or football, at least not until much later, but he did enjoy hockey except for the fact that he suffered from chilblains in the winter months. Getting knocked around the ankles by an opponent's stick would burst a ripe chilblain. This was agony. 'Such small injuries would never force a player off the field in the way that a broken limb or concussion might,' says Neville. 'But the chafing of a sock or shoe on an open chilblain was like having sandpaper and salt rubbed over a fresh cut. If a chilblain got infected, then it might seriously threaten a foot – otherwise, the show had to go on/stiff upper lip/don't make a fuss about nothing, and so on'. Norfolk House had a purpose-built gymnasium where Neville did his best, but failed to learn how to circle over a horizontal bar or climb a rope. Not a great performance for a prospective army officer! However, he did learn to climb a rope much later during officer training at Sandhurst.

Sundays at Norfolk House were 'boring past description'. After breakfast, the boys had to learn and repeat the Catechism, 'renouncing the world, the flesh and the devil'. For most of the boys, including Neville, since CTM was the devil incarnate this stricture was not difficult. After the Catechism, they had a lecture (known as 'pie-jaw') from CTM on general subjects, usually moral behaviour, and more specifically on life at a public school. (Neville does not explain the specific derivation of pie-jaw, but as the holding device of a boring tool it may be an oblique schoolboy reference to their unloved headmaster.) The Sunday 'pie-jaw' lasted until it was time to put on their top hats and form up into a 'crocodile'—an orderly line in which they walked two by two down to the parish church where they sat in the same side pews every Sunday.

On one long-remembered occasion one of the other boys farted, loudly, in the middle of the sermon. It must have been a welcome relief to him and brought the rest of the boys some levity amidst all this Sunday seriousness. But CTM was not amused. Neville comments 'By the inquisition which took place on our return, the perpetrator, who luckily for him was never discovered, might have spat in the King's face.' Then it was lunch and after that, an afternoon walk, followed by tea and an hour spent writing letters home. Neville's mother was always 'superbly punctual with her letters' and she did her best to try to comfort Neville when he failed at something. 'Don't forget Jimmy that you cannot do more than your best'. To his father, Neville was a scholastic failure.

But there were good times also. One Sunday evening in the autumn, after letters had been written, Neville and Roger Ekin (who became lifelong friends) wandered outside, unsupervised, and fell to scratching the backs of CTM's pigs with their umbrellas. They were spotted by one of the staff, rushed back into the schoolhouse and made their way to the changing rooms, by now cold and dark. There the two boys swore a solemn oath to each other:

> I, *Roger Ekin/James Neville, solemnly swear that when I am a man, I shall come here and knock CTM down!*

Neither of them fulfilled the oath. By the time Neville became a man, he had other people to knock down such as the Germans in the First World War, and CTM was 'an unimportant and unpleasant myth'. But Neville never lost touch with Roger Ekin, who went on to Westminster School and thereafter to Sandhurst like his erstwhile school friend Neville, though apparently not at the same time. Then Ekin joined the 55 Cokes Rifles in the British Indian Army and served in Palestine in the 58th Vaughan Rifle Frontier Force. The two men both survived both the First and Second World Wars and remained friends until they died.

Another permitted leisure activity at Norfolk House School was collecting motor car registration numbers (a forerunner of train spotting, perhaps).[1] Motor vehicles were still relatively new and cost more than the average house, so sightings were quite rare even in a prosperous town such as Beaconsfield. Most cars were unenclosed and far from comfortable requiring special clothing, such as a flat cap and goggles. Neville's mother, like other women passengers (they were rarely drivers!), wore special motoring caps or bonnets with a veil tied under the chin to anchor them in place and keep the ears warm. The noise the cars made was loud, so their approach could be heard from afar. All the Norfolk House boys would rush to the windows to take down the numbers, and considered themselves fortunate if they saw as many as three during play time. The speed of the cars was at best sedate. The maximum legal limit on public roads had initially been set at 2 mph but was raised in 1896, the year before Neville's birth, to 14 mph and again in 1903 to 20 mph (which it remained until was abolished in 1930) so the boys had plenty of time to note down their numbers. The young James Neville obviously had a fondness for cars as they frequently appear in his early photographs taken with his prized box Brownie camera.

Norfolk House, according to Neville, had only ten boys in attendance plus a couple of newbies, so it was hardly paying its way. Despite having new facilities built—such as a gym—the school was faltering badly at this time, though it staggered on in business until the 1930s. Young Neville started Greek in the spring term in 1909 when he was twelve. As Greek was taught by CTM himself, Neville may have approached this new subject with some apprehension. But, to his surprise, he greatly enjoyed not only the language, but also the teacher, whose attitude changed, becoming 'unaccountably kind and accommodating'. Perhaps CTM responded positively to a pupil whom he had hitherto written off as a complete dunce.

Neville does not go so far as to say he was sorry to leave Norfolk House—his actual words in his journal are 'I was not sorry to escape his (CTM's) clutches and fiendish tempers'—but the change in CTM's demeanour perhaps left less of a sour taste in his mouth than he might have anticipated. In the event, and for whatever reason, James did not see through his prep school years at Norfolk House. Instead he was taken away after Easter 1909 and sent instead to another establishment to prepare for admission to Eton the following year.

Stoke House School, 1909-10

James Neville's new school, where he started in May 1909, was Stoke House at Stoke Poges near Slough. This was where his father had also been a pupil forty years earlier but it was still under the same headmaster, EH Parry, known as Ted. Neville senior had subsequently won a scholarship in 1876 to Charterhouse School, and later to Trinity College, Cambridge, and James was proud to see his name on the honours board as RJN White (he was born Reginald James Neville White but changed his name to Neville by Royal Licence in 1885, thus becoming RJ Neville).

Young James Neville immediately took to Stoke House, and his performance improved exponentially, especially in sport. The cricket and football pitches were 'a paradise'. 'The cricket field was bounded on one side by the high wall of the kitchen garden, and by a row of majestic cedars on the other. ... At the north end of the cricket ground was a swimming pool.' No doubt Neville's sporting endeavours received every encouragement from the head master EH (Edward) Parry who had been a noted footballer, Oxford blue and captain of the university team. In 1880 and 81 the Old Carthusians AFC won the FA Cup under Parry's captaincy (the football league and cup were still strictly for amateurs only until 1885) and he also played for England three times 1879-82, though they lost all three matches.

The Old Carthusians FA Cup winning side, 1881. EH Parry is seen holding the ball.

Unknown, public domain.

As Neville was still under 12, he was ranked as a junior and he won every single sports event in his first term—100 yards, 200 yards, hurdles, high jump, long jump and even the egg and spoon race! To his gratification his whole family, including his father, came to the event and were inordinately proud to see their son called out six times to receive prizes. Neville was also presented with a little silver cup with two handles as a permanent reminder of the school record he had made. Later the same term he started to enjoy cricket, winning school colours half-way through the term.

The cricket team at Stoke House, summer 1909. Neville is far right.

John d'Arcy / NRO Nev 7/30.

The summer holidays intervened and Neville spent time first at Sloley Hall with Angela, which they both hated as Granny Neville and the three aunts spent most of their time criticising the youngsters. Thus it was a relief, Neville wrote in his journal, 'to leave the restrictions of Sloley for the freedom of mother's home in Switzerland.' It was the first time any of the Neville children, by now all adolescents, had been abroad and to spend a month in Morgins (a ski resort in the Alps in southern Switzerland) .... well, any young person would find that thrilling.

The crossing from Newhaven to Dieppe went well. The water was flat calm and Neville rather wistfully records that he thought it would be a fine life to have been a sailor. But by this time the astigmatism in one eye had precluded any chance of such a career. The Neville family, including both parents, then continued on by train as far as Aigle at the foot of the Swiss Alps, travelling second class which meant sitting up all night. Neville was delighted by his first sight of the mountains at Lake Geneva and the train followed the lakeside for many miles going via Lausanne and Mouteray. At Aigle the family got off and the remainder of the journey up into the foothills of the mountains was by horse and carriage, but it was so steep that passengers sometimes had to get out and walk.

Their Swiss maid, Martha, went wild with joy at being back in her own country, picking wild cherries from the trees growing by the side of the road, but their hotel on arrival was 'somewhat primitive'. Things got worse. Mrs Neville tried to explain to the manageress that her husband was a vegetarian, which seems to have been unheard of in Switzerland at that time. All the guests sat at one large table for the evening meal, and just grabbed the food as it was put in front of them. If you did not grab, Neville records, you went hungry. The teenagers, horrid as ever, were appalled by one female guest who was obese and had a black moustache.

'She consumed vast quantities of ice-cream and we nicknamed her "The hairy boffin". Our line on her was "Here lieth the hairy boffin, destined to lie in a deep coffin". Then Neville senior developed a raging toothache, while Neville's mother got stung by an insect which made her legs swell up. There was no doctor closer than Aigle at the bottom of the mountain.

Well, 'the kids' enjoyed it! The weather was fine and warm, they walked and swam and practised speaking French. Young James decided he was going to study the butterflies, of which there were many in this part of Switzerland. He had already shown an interest in lepidoptery while staying at Ashmanhaugh in Norfolk where his father had shown him how to brush a mixture of sugar and rum onto the bark of trees then, after dark, collect moths with the light of a lantern.

The journey home, a month later, was a nightmare. James's sister Jane started to feel seriously unwell for unknown reasons, rushed for the *lavabo* on the train every five minutes and groaned all night with stomach pains. Once in Paris, her parents tried to get a remedy by explaining to a chemist in a drug store in their halting French what was wrong, and Jane bravely swallowed the potion offered to her by the chemist without the slightest idea of what was in it. They then boarded the train to Dieppe, where they took the boat to Newhaven.

But this time the crossing was extremely rough. Neville had thought that he would find the movement of the ship 'fun'. But after ten minutes of the ship pitching and rolling, he was running for the side and he was horribly sick the whole way back. So was Jane, who brought up the contents of her stomach, including the recently ingested French remedy, plus probably whatever had been ailing her. Neville's mother held James's hand as he also brought up everything he had. Only Angela and Neville senior escaped. But it cured young Neville of wanting to be a sailor! Curiously, he says, he was never seasick again, even though he endured rougher seas than that in later life.

Neville went back to school at Stoke House in September and found, to his satisfaction, that he enjoyed playing football. The trouble at Norfolk House had been that there were not enough boys to form proper teams. But at Stoke there were plenty of boys to choose from. Neville was placed on the wing where he was able to use his long legs to run fast and he performed well. He was moved to left-half at mid-term and won his school colours. He recorded in his journal 'Visits from mother were not nearly so important now because I was really happy among my school fellows.' His academic work also improved and he comments in his journal that he learned three times as much in a short period as he had done at Norfolk House.

The following year, 1910,[2] was one of political upheavals for the country and the reverberations were felt in the Neville household. James's father Reginald had long held an ambition to enter parliament for the Conservative (or Unionist) cause. He had already fought elections in 1892, 1895, 1900 and 1908 as Conservative candidate for Leeds South constituency but lost every time to the Liberals. When a general election was called for January 1910 he was therefore delighted to be selected for the Wigan constituency, which had been held by the Tories for 24 years and was therefore considered a safe seat. Neville had high hopes of success, not least because for the first time he was facing a Labour opponent, the Liberals having withdrawn.

January's general election was hard-fought and often acrimonious. Its aim was to resolve a serious constitutional crisis brought about by the House of Lords' refusal to pass the so-called 'people's budget' of 1909, brought before them by Lloyd George. This had introduced higher taxes on the land and incomes of the wealthy in order to fund new social welfare programmes for the poor which was always going to be unpopular among the rich elite. It was passed by the Commons in 1909 only to be blocked by the Lords who opposed on principle any idea of redistribution of wealth. Reform of the House of Lords (opposed by Reginald Neville), Irish Home Rule (ditto), tariff-free trade and the rights of working people were all points at issue. A series of colourful cartoon-like posters appeared in Wigan trumpeting slogans such as 'United we Stand—a Strong Navy and Secure Empire fed on British Products' or 'That Tory Loaf... there's nothing in it!' Strange to say, in this post-Brexit era more than a century later, similar issues of tariffs, Ireland, workers' rights and Lords reform are still near the top of the political agenda.

Young Neville travelled north with the rest of his family to support his father during the campaign leading to polling day for Wigan on 17 January. On New Year's Day (then not a Bank Holiday) James arrived to stay with an aunt and uncle in Derwent Hill, Keswick. By the sound of it, it was nothing short of an extension of the Christmas holidays! There was party after party, and young Neville records that he went to a fancy-dress ball representing 'Preston' wearing one of his uncle's hats squashed down to his ears (i.e. 'pressed on'). At another get-together a young man asked after his sister Jane saying 'Who is that pretty girl over there?' True to the Neville adolescent sense of humour, James replied 'That is a baboon!'

While in the north, Reginald Neville no doubt sounded out his brother Jack, who, with a flannel manufacturing business in Rochdale, had strong views about Free Trade. The customs' duties he had to pay on imported raw materials, even from India and Egypt (then part of the Empire) as well as America (a close ally) were seen to be hampering trade. On 4 January, Reginald left Keswick for Wigan, followed by the rest of the family ten days later when they had finished partying. Young Neville says he went to meetings addressed by his father which were 'very interesting', but does not say what his father talked about.

Constituencies polled on different days over a three-week period until 1918, because elections were sometimes very riotous, drunken affairs with only men over the age of 30 permitted to vote. Police had to be called in from all over the country to control the mobs which formed around polling stations so the big conurbations had to take it in turn—Birmingham policed by all forces in the Midlands, then Manchester policed by all forces in the north, and so on. Once women got the vote in 1918, polling stations became much less violent with the civilizing effect of females standing in line to cast their votes.

So Monday 17 January was polling day for Wigan and the Neville entourage got together with other supporters for the anticipated victory celebrations. Young Neville records the little song:

Has anybody seen Neville?
He's our new MP
Has anyone seen Neville?
Our member he shall be
He's fighting like a Briton oh!
Twist will soon be twisted oh!
Has anyone seen Neville?
Neville's the man for me!
(Henry Twist was the Labour candidate).

The count was in Wigan Town Hall, attended by Neville senior, his wife and oldest daughter Jane. Young James and Angela were not present to hear the shock result that Neville had **lost** to the Labour candidate, Henry (known as Harry) Twist, a local man and a former miner who had started work down the pits at the age of eleven. There could hardly have been a greater contrast with Reginald Neville, the Cambridge-educated barrister and country gent from 'down south'. It was a narrow victory for Labour—with a majority of just 510—and one that was to be overturned within the year (see next chapter). James Neville's mother collapsed at the news, probably from shock because everyone had expected her husband to win. Young Neville does not say much more about this election, only that immediately afterwards he and Jane went skating on the pond at the park at Beechwood, and he only saw his father on the day Neville senior took his son back to school for the start of the Lent term. Nationally, the election failed to produce any clear mandate with a 'hung parliament' in which the Liberals held onto power but only with the support of some Labour and Irish MPs. The Lords, however, bowed to public opinion and passed the Budget into law on 29 April, a year to the day after its introduction.

Young Neville soon settled back into school life where he developed an interest in hockey which he played 'just better than badly'. There were no school colours available in hockey, and he later wrote that he did not remember any matches against other prep schools, but it was a popular sport in the army and what little he learnt at Stoke Poges, he would use to its full extent later in life. Neville sat the Common Entrance exam for Eton over three days in March and heard a week later that he had gained a place at the school and would be starting there in May in the class called Middle Fourth. A week after Easter his father took him to the tailors to be fitted for his new uniform—a 'bum shaver' (a short-tailed jacket) and pin-striped trousers, stiff shirts and a top hat, and three pairs of new shoes. He concludes in his journal 'Thus my happy year at Stoke came to an end. I was allowed to revisit the school from Eton, though it moved from Stoke Poges to Seaford.'

He spent the Easter holidays at his parents' London home in Eccleston Square. His mother, having collapsed at the election, was having a 'rest cure' at a nursing home in Wimpole Street. She hated it and claimed it did her no good, nicknaming it 'The Dogs' Home'. Young Neville had swimming lessons in the mornings fully dressed, as he had to be able to swim in his clothes before being allowed to go boating on the river at Eton. He passed the swimming test with a couple of 'beaks' (masters or teachers) from Eton judging him on the morning of 3 May and thus became a 'naut' (as Eton boaters were known).

In the afternoons he was sometimes allowed to visit his mother, and from time to time, his father insisted he join him at his chambers at 7, Fig Tree Court in The Temple which was 'purgatory'. Neville was 12 years old and liked physical exercise and practical matters. Intellectual exercise was just not of interest to him. He had to listen for hours while his father dictated letters to his clerk Davidge or talked to other barristers. It was 'unutterably boring and my heart used to sink when father announced that we would go to his chambers before going to see mother'. But his mother soon came home, and life resumed its normal course, though she continued to get racking headaches, whose origin was never diagnosed. Neville joined in the craze for roller skating, several times going to the Empress Rooms in Kensington with Angela, where they met friends such as Roger Ekin, and Uncle Jack, who had a beautiful woman, uncannily like Mrs Neville, on his arm. (Neville realised years later that Uncle Jack, like many men, was half in love with his mother).

Notes

1 At the beginning of the 20th century, with the number of mechanically propelled vehicles increasing, and accidents occurring more frequently, it became clear that cars had to be easily identifiable. The solution was The Motor Car Act 1903. From 1st January 1904 it became compulsory for every motorcar to be registered with a number plate. The first mark to be issued in London was the simple, bold, A1 and this was registered to Earl Russell. He wanted the mark so badly he camped out all night to secure it, making him not only the first registrant but also the inventor of the idea of having a distinctive, personalised or cherished plate on a vehicle. Since then, the registration system has changed four times to accommodate the ever-growing demand for vehicle registrations. The first plates issued were dateless, that is, there was nothing to denote the year of issue. This system lasted for 60 years from 1903 until 1963. Initially, the marks were made up of a local council identifier code of up to 3 letters, followed by a random number, e.g. ABC 123. In the early 1950s, as numbers started to run out, the components were reversed, giving rise to registrations in the format 123 ABC. The numbers did not exceed 100, though this did not indicate that there were no more than 100 cars on the road. Speedyreg.co.uk/history, November 2017.

2 Elections in 1910. In those days the election system was slightly different from how it is now. A date was set by which all constituencies had to have held contests to choose their candidates. Polling day in each constituency was then set by mutual consent of the candidates and could be any day within a 10-day period. That meant that the campaigns covered about 10 days before the state of the parties was known. Manchester was usually the first to go to the polls. *Evolution of the British Electoral System 1832-1987*, by Martin Pugh, p.20, publ by The Historical Association 1988.

Eton 1910-1915

Neville attended Eton until he was 18. He enjoyed the sense of 'grown-up-ness' and the sport—he even enjoyed 'fagging' for senior pupils! But during his time there, first his grandfather died, and then his mother, by which he was devastated. Towards the end of his school years the war in Europe started and he was eager to get on to join the army.

Term at Eton was about to start, and young Neville went to Windsor with his father. Together they bought some furniture for his room – an armchair and an ottoman (a padded or upholstered seat, with no back or arms, usually used as a stool and chest combined). He and three other new boys moved into Gulliver's on Eton High Street, one of the school houses where boys lived under the care of a housemaster and 'dame'. Unlike most public schools where pupils slept in dormitories, Eton prided itself on providing every boy with his own study bedroom throughout their school years. James's room had a collapsible bed, a wash-stand with a basin, ewer and potty and a bureau with drawers and shelves beneath, as well as the extra furniture his father had purchased.

By now Neville was a seasoned boarder and well used to change. He describes the start of his career at Eton in Middle Fourth[1] in this way; 'To be a new boy at Eton was a supremely wonderful experience. The freedom, even for a lower boy, was exhilarating; everything was wonderful, new and exciting. Having one's own room, which I'd never had at home, meant having something of one's own—pictures, books, furniture and above all, privacy, though we were never allowed to lock our doors, nor was there a lock.' Initially his teacher in all subjects except maths and French was George Lyttleton who taught the Lower Fourth (Neville's form) in a schoolroom in the old college buildings that dated in part back to the 15th century. It had massive dark-oak pillars and rafters, and overlooked the school yard with its statue of the school's founder, King Henry VI. Beyond this stood the chapel which was only big enough to hold the older boys in Upper School as, by Neville's time, there were in total well over a thousand boys at Eton.

The view from Neville's window at Eton in his first year there.
John d'Arcy / NRO Nev 7/32.

Free of home-sickness Neville found his academic work surprisingly easy, and within a month he was promoted to the Upper Fourth where his teacher was 'Briny' Brinton. Briny was a very different character from Lyttleton. He walked with a limp and was 'awesome and irascible'. But he was a great teacher, and once inspired, Neville worked hard to keep up. Every day lessons started at 9am and continued until 12 noon. At 12, prep started in the room known as 'pea-hole'.

Neville was a pupil at Eton until 1915 when he was rising 18 and the Great War had been underway for nearly a year. Writing his memoirs towards the end of his life, he

opposite: Neville on leave from Eton outside the house in Ecclestone Square.
John d'Arcy / NRO Nev 7/32.

No. 1.

DATE March. 28th 1913.

NAME J. E. H. Neville. DIV. C.2.

Exercise sent up for Good.

Latin Elegiacs.

SIGNATURES.
Division Master A. L. Goodhart.
House Tutor
Classical Tutor Hugh Macnaghten

Neville's work in Latin Elegaics was so impressive that it was 'Sent up for Good', a system of reward that is still used at Eton today.
John d'Arcy / NRO Nev 7/32.

looked back on his time at Eton with great fondness. He rarely comments on his studies or academic record though there is, in the NRO, a slip of paper which shows that a piece of his work in Latin was 'Sent up for Good.' The College website for 2017 declares that if any boy produces an outstanding piece of work, it may be "Sent Up For Good", and the effort is then stored in the College Archives for posterity. This award has been around since the 18th century. A 'Sending Up For Good' is rare and the process is rather mysterious to many of Eton's boys. First, the master wishing to 'Send Up For Good' must gain the permission of the relevant Head of Department. Upon receiving his or her approval, the piece of work will be marked with 'Sent Up For Good' and the student will receive a card to be signed by House Master, tutor and division master. It was therefore quite an achievement by Neville to get this accolade.

The opposite of a 'Send Up' is a 'Rip'. This is for sub-standard work, which is sometimes torn at the top of the page/sheet and must be submitted to the boy's housemaster for signature. Boys who accumulate rips are liable to be given a 'White Ticket', which must be signed by all his teachers and may be accompanied by other punishments, usually doing domestic chores or writing lines. In recent times, a milder form of the rip, 'sign for information', colloquially known as an "info", has been introduced, which must also be signed by the boy's housemaster and tutor.

As for punishments for poor work or consistent lateness, too many high spirits or rudeness, one traditional form was to make a boy copy Latin hexameters. Offenders were frequently set 100 hexameters, or, for more serious offences, Georgics (more than 500 hexameters) by their House Masters or the Head Master. Giving of a Georgic is now extremely rare, but still occasionally occurs.

Neville has much to say about his sporting prowess and achievements—cricket, rowing, fives, and yet more cricket! More about the sport at the end of this chapter. Certain events, however, clearly made a lasting impression on him. The first was the death of Edward VII on 6 May 1910, shortly after he had joined the school. Neville writes 'Gloom descended on the whole of England and the Empire. Men and women went into deep mourning, and all festivities were cancelled.' Many people reading this will remember the premature death of Princess Diana in 1997, and the great outpouring of grief at her loss. But she was special, young and still beautiful. The death of Edward VII was more nearly like that of Queen Elizabeth, the Queen Mother, who was 101 when she died. Of course, the nation marked the death of the Queen Mother, but no-one could describe this time as a period of deep mourning. But in 1910 England was a world power and the King was also an Emperor. Royalty was far more important then than it is now, and the level of respect and reverence royal personages got, was immense. Ordinary people thought of the monarch as the father or mother of the nation, and the monarch thought of him or herself as godlike.

Neville continues:

> The school was very lucky to see the funeral procession from Windsor Park just inside the tall iron gates. We watched the phalanx of blue jackets enter the Park and then turn left towards the south face of the castle. (The new king) King George V marched immediately behind the gun carriage and behind him all the crowned heads of Europe and the President of France. It was the only time I saw Kaiser Wilhelm II of Germany in the uniform of a Field Marshall.

The second is Neville's attitude to fagging. This was the system of younger boys (known as 'fags' from a seventeenth century word for toil or servitude) doing small services such as shoe-polishing, cleaning and running errands for older pupils ('fag masters') in the sixth form.[2]

Reflecting on the issue in later life, James declared himself very much in favour. His rationale was that it was quite 'salutary' for a small boy to serve others, on the basis that not all families make their offspring do any jobs around the house, and many young children grow up thinking all the work has to be done by 'someone else'. 'No man can command others unless he has first learnt to obey,' Neville continues, quoting Oliver Cromwell. 'Having served as a fag, a boy in turn learns how to be fair, just and

above: at Eton. From left – Maurice Buxton, John Chaney, JH Neville.
John d'Arcy / NRO Nev 7/32.
below: Neville working hard at Eton.
John d'Arcy / NRO Nev 7/32.

sympathetic when he becomes a fagmaster. There are no rights without service.'

Fagging was still in full swing at Eton during Neville's time there. By the sound of it, he was never seriously abused by his fagmaster, though potentially he could be beaten for misdemeanours. Neville's fagmaster was Stephen D Gladstone, for whom duties included preparing tea on Sundays. After the final lesson, Neville and two friends sprinted back to their house, collected two slices of bread and a pat of butter each from their tutor, and went down to the kitchen to make toast. It sounds easy, but the toast had to be perfect.

> Each square inch of bread had to be browned, and burnt toast, however carefully scraped, meant a tanning for carelessness. The scrum round the available space for making this toast was grim.
>
> Some boys had more relaxed masters and were thus under less pressure. Having served our masters, we were free to go and 'mess' in our rooms. After tea we had to tidy our fagmaster's rooms, which on half-holidays meant collecting shorts, shirts, stockings etc, folding them and putting them neatly in the ottomans, which all boys had. On dog-potter days,[3] we also had to roll up puttees (a covering for the lower leg as seen on soldiers in WW1). At my first effort I nearly came a cropper by rolling them neatly and tying them with the tape. Gladstone showed me how they should be done—making a coil of the tapes first and rolling the puttees[4] round the coil.

Fagging was eventually abolished at Eton in 1980 by which time the beating of boys by boys had been abolished and corporal punishments of any sort were rare. In an unusually democratic move, the then Head Master, Michael McCrum, allowed the boys a vote in which only ten of the thirty-five houses opted for abolition. But democracy only went so far at Eton and McCrum did away with it anyway declaring, 'I am not in favour of self-indulgence of this sort.' James Neville would definitely not have interpreted it this way—and nor did most Old Etonians in 1980!

The third is that in 1910 there was another general election in December. Neville says that this was due to 'reasons only known to the politicians.' In fact, there is no mystery to this unusual occurrence—two general elections within the space of one year. The January 1910 election (when Reginald Neville had narrowly lost to Labour in Wigan) had resulted in a 'hung' parliament with no party having an overall majority. The Liberals, under Asquith, held onto power with the wavering support of some Labour and Irish Parliamentary Party MPs but were repeatedly defeated by Conservatives in the Commons. In calling another election, Prime Minister Asquith hoped to secure an outright majority for the Liberals. Unfortunately for him, the result was almost exactly the same with 272 Liberal seats (two fewer than January) and 271, Conservatives. The Irish Parliamentarians (aka Irish Nationalists) won 74 seats and Labour 42. Political stalemate seemed here to stay. However, with the Liberals at least tenuously back in power, the House of Lords withdrew their opposition to Asquith's Parliament Act and accepted that in future the hereditary peers of the Lords would not be able to permanently block legislation.

But for Neville senior, who had finally managed to get elected as an MP at his tenth attempt by winning back Wigan from Labour, it was the realisation of a dream, and the family were delighted. The only person, young Neville says, who was not all that pleased was his mother, for 'In those days political receptions meant much finery, and long and boring queues coming and going.' Nevertheless, when it came to coronations, being an MP had some perks. When George V was crowned King on 22 June 1911, Neville senior got a seat in Westminster Abbey, and young Neville and Angela were allocated to a stand in Palace Yard, from where they had an excellent view of the procession to and from the Abbey. The pair had recently taken up photography and had had some success with their No 2 Brownie box camera, costing half a guinea (52½ p, or 10 shillings and sixpence in pre-decimal coinage) They had also been given a developing tank with which Angela became quite skilful at processing their own photos.

'She would kneel on the floor enshrouded with a blanket and no light whatsoever,' Neville recorded. 'She rocked the tank backward and forward for a stipulated length of time, then opened the box and put the film in hypo-sulphate (a salt of hypo-sulphuric acid) to wash it. Not until then was she able to perceive whether any of the photographs had come out. Looking at my early photos, it is astonishing how adept she became. We timed the exposures, and her photographs of rooms at 15 St George's Road are very good. Printing and fixing were exciting, for until then the photograph was an unknown quantity.' Their photographs of the coronation came out well, but sadly there are none in the Norfolk Record Office. Nor are there any of the rooms at St George's Road.

The fourth matter concerns two deaths in Neville's family. The first was his grandfather, James Sewell White. Early in the new year of 1912, Reginald was called to Sloley Hall from London because the old man had 'trouble with his water works'. Reginald's wife did not go with him as she and Granny Neville did not get on. The old man had a catheter fitted, and when this failed to drain his bladder effectively, the pain became excruciating. He was taken into the Norfolk and Norwich Hospital where a surgeon operated on him for an enlarged prostate gland. The operation was pronounced successful and Grandpa Neville appeared to be recovering well. But he relapsed and died on 12 January.

Young Neville says:

> Grandpa had always been kind to us, if somewhat aloof. He had a gruff voice, but a merry twinkle in his eye and was a handsome old man—bald as an egg with a white beard and moustache.

The whole family began to gather in Norfolk for the funeral. James, his two sisters and their mother, stayed with Aunt Flo in Wroxham, Flo being the sister of Granny Neville. 'It seemed odd to me at the time,' Neville records, 'that there was no room for mother at the Hall. She was the wife of the heir to the whole property. Perhaps mother made the excuse that she had three children with her. I know that she much preferred Aunt Flo to her sister.'

The funeral was held on 20 January, and was the first young Neville had attended. His grandfather was wheeled on a bier to Sloley church by four of the men who worked on the estate. Neville and his father walked behind the coffin and behind them walked his Uncle Jack and another man, Cloudesley Brereton. Behind them were two cousins, Ralph and Herbert Neville, and the dreadful CTM (the headmaster from Neville's first boarding school, Norfolk House). The women—Granny Neville, Ida, Angela and Jane, and Jack's new wife Lillian (the girlfriend Neville had seen skating with Uncle Jack at the Empress Rooms), followed in a Sunbeam car. Reginald, whose reading voice was much admired and had won him a prize at school, read the famous lesson about death and resurrection from Corinthians Chapter 15, but young Neville does not relate any more of the service. Once the more distant relations had gone home, the family gathered in the library in Sloley Hall where Reginald read the very lengthy will. The estate, later proved at £210,000 (equivalent to about £21,000,000 at today's values) was to be divided mainly between Reginald and his brother Jack, but with bequests to Flo Marcon and three other women in the family of £17,500 each.

Granny Neville stayed on at the Hall for a short time, but bought a lease on a house in Mulberry Walk, Chelsea, where she would live once it was finished. It was one of a number of new houses being built there, and the plan was that once Sloley Hall was vacated, Reginald, Ida and their three children (including young Neville) would move to live in Norfolk. In the meantime, the family also moved from St George's Road to a much larger house at 25 Ecclestone Square. James later recorded:

> Mother seemed very proud of it. The main rooms faced south and were high and spacious. There was one more flight of stairs than at No 15—eight flights not counting basement to

hall. Father, being chairman of Brentford Gas, installed gas lighting ...oil lamps had to be used for reading and candles for bedside tables. We had hoped for electricity which was universal even at Eton at this time.

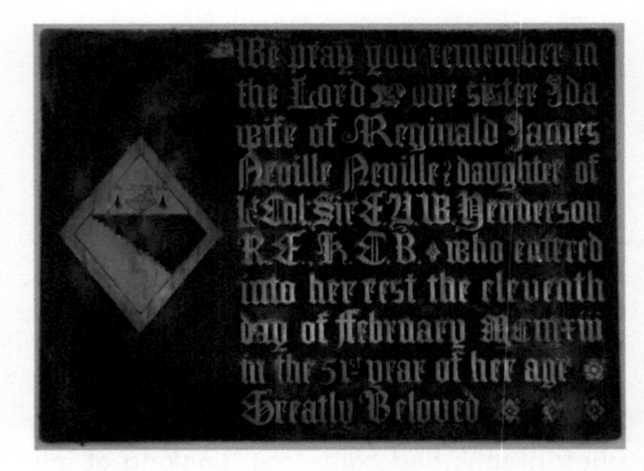

The plaque in memory of Ida, James' mother.
Simon Knott.

The second death in the family was much more devastating to young Neville now 16, as it was that of his mother. Ida was taken seriously ill during the summer holiday of 1913, and she took to her bed while the family were staying at Barton Rectory in Norfolk. She was practically comatose and did not recognise her family. Neville remembers that Jane sat with her all day, and everyone had to tiptoe round the house as poor Ida was so frail that she could not tolerate the slightest noise. This lasted about two days. She recovered enough to supervise the move to Sloley Hall, which needed a very thorough clean, at the end of October, and by Christmas she was well enough to celebrate the festival in the usual way.

Neville went back to Eton in January 1914, but returned home (to their London house in Ecclestone Square) soon after when Ida discovered that he had been exposed to chickenpox. He was there for about 10 days and 'had mother all to myself'. He even got to escort his mother to the doctor in nearby Victoria Square which made him feel terribly proud, as though he were already a man. Ida asked her son not to tell Reginald about the visit, as it would only make him worried. Neville did not ask, and was not told, what the health problem was, but suspects it was 'some dope to ease the dreadful headaches.' Neville again returned to Eton in early February, but on the 12th, which was a cold, very misty morning, he was called out from chapel by his tutor to say that he had heard Neville's mother was extremely unwell. Neville was told he should at once go to fetch some clothes and be ready to be collected by car. Beset by anxiety, Neville was picked up by his Uncle Jack's chauffeur, driving horribly slowly through the thick fog. Eventually the fog lifted, and they met Jack just outside Hemel Hempstead. Neville switched cars, and asked his uncle for news.

Sloley Church where James' mother was buried after the funeral there.
John Salmon.

'Jim,' said Jack. 'You must be very brave. Aunt Ida died last night very suddenly.' Young Neville burst into tears at once. He begged Uncle Jack to tell him that there must be some mistake. He was too young to lose his mother; she was the one person in his life that he could completely trust. Sadly for Neville, there was no mistake. The rest of the family were at Beechwood (I think this must be the home of relatives of either Reginald or Ida, but no-one in the family has been able to confirm it) gathered in the billiard room, and Neville says that his father 'looked as if he had been knocked on the head by a cosh, and was still dazed and unbelieving.' This was, after all, a second serious bereavement for him within the space of a few months. Jane was 'very brave', but Angela's eyes were red and swollen. They told him that Ida, who had been staying with one of her sisters at Beechwood to have a break from household chores after Christmas, had taken her dinner in bed.

Nanny Griffiths had been looking after her, and Ida had called out to her after she had finished eating. Then she had coughed slightly, and died.

Ida was 52 when her life ended. In 1913, the average life expectancy for a woman was about 57 (though possibly much higher for the rich, like the Nevilles), so she was not taken all that prematurely. Young Neville was allowed to go to her room and see her one last time. Nothing, he confided to his diary, would ever be the same again. A horrible blankness lay ahead. In tears again, he kissed her on the cheek. Ida was taken to Sloley, the place in the country she had loved, to be buried alongside Grandpa Neville. The church was packed with people from the village for her funeral, as she had been much loved, 'a real lady' as one villager put it. Reginald read the same verses from Corinthians as he had read only a few months earlier for the funeral of his father. The family returned to London the following day, where Uncle Jack took Angela into the garden and told her that she would have to be the oil in the family's engine now that her mother was gone. Apparently, Jane had been 'a bit of a trial to mother, and sometimes I (young Neville) did not get on well with father'. Ida had had to smooth things over when tempers flared.

Neville returned to Eton about 10 days later, but the rest of the family decided to continue their mourning on the French Riviera, as was common among wealthy people in those days. Granny Neville and Aunts Amy, Kate and Rose were already there at Beaulieu mourning the death of Grandpa Neville, so Reginald and his daughters joined them. Neville, at Eton, says that everyone was very kind to him at school, but it cannot have been much fun knowing that everyone else was enjoying the sunshine. However, his father came back to get him at Easter, and young Neville was able to be with his family for a short while. He says he remembers his bedroom window at San Remo (where the family were staying, about 30 miles to the east over the border into Italy), and also picnics in the hills behind the coast.

It was a black year in every sense. Angela and Jane wore nothing but black, as did their father and brother. Reginald had taken to 'wailing' after his father's death. Thinking no-one could hear him in his room, he would let go and cry noisily at night. The death of his wife made him 'wail' even more. Young Neville hated the sound. 'My room was on

above: Dr Foster and Reginald Neville in San Remo, in mourning for Reginald's wife Ida.
John d'Arcy / NRO Nev 7/30.
below: Jane, Reginald and James picnicking.
John d'Arcy / NRO Nev 7/30.

the same floor and I found his wailing very depressing. Such an outward show of grief also seemed to me to be unmanly.' A stiff upper lip was the accepted behaviour of the day for men, an ethos which Eton College upheld and which Neville absorbed to the hilt. Even so, it would be deeply upsetting for a young lad, not even a full developed adult male, to hear his father expressing his grief so noisily.

The three Neville children, now without their mother, wanted to be close to each other. One of the aunts, Maud, had rebuked Jane for allowing her brother James to go into her bedroom at Beechwood, which had upset them. Their father, not endowed with much emotional intelligence and very much a creature of his generation, had no idea how to treat his offspring in grief. He started to criticise, to the extent that his daughter Jane seemed to be able to do nothing right. He also, disloyally, complained to Maud about the behaviour of his children. He seemed to think that both his daughters were behaving like 'tarts'. As a result, all three children were alienated from their father at the very time when they needed him most. For a while they relied on another aunt, Mabel, but when she also died in August 1913, they turned to Molly and Jock who invited the children to stay at their home on The Hoo Peninsula in Kent. (Molly and Jock were probably family friends. No-one still living in the family knows who they were). They treated the three children with great kindness, and consequently all three of them started to regard The Hoo as home.

But they had to go back to Sloley Hall for Christmas when 'we all missed mother terribly. We (the three children) were a tight little bunch, but we could never anticipate father's moods. He wailed at night in his dressing room which was next to my room at night… My mum had been everything to me, and I'm quite sure I should not have made the fatal mistake of 1924 had she lived another 15 years.' (Neville is referring to his affair with the wife of his commanding officer which led to the two of them running away to South Africa together while Neville resigned his commission. Neville seems to

H. MACNAGHTEN'S Esq.

HOUSE FOOTBALL CHOICES.

1913.

G. H. Austen-Cartmell

C. S. Egerton-Green
J. Grahame-Stewart

R. F. Heyworth-Savage
H. J. R. Brierly
J. N. Cheney
V. A. C. Harbord
A. W. M. Baillie
J. E. H. Neville
E. H. Macnaghten
J. D. Simpson

R. Farquhar, (12th. man).

The list for the football team, including Neville.
John d'Arcy / NRO Nev 7/32.

think that his mother would most definitely have disapproved and advised him not to take this career-ending step. And she would have been right).

And so to sport at Eton. Young Neville says he was not much good at football, but he played in his house football team as goalie, with Hugo Austen-Cartmell as captain. Neville liked Hugo a great deal partly because he had flaming red hair, and was short and stocky, unlike many of the other 'sporty' boys who were tall, lanky and fast. Both of them hated the flannel knickerbockers everyone had to wear to play the game. The garments fastened below the knee with a two-pronged buckle which could injure a leg with a deep graze in collisions with other players, a regular occurrence during the game. Neville was much better at fives, an exclusive game played at just a few public schools in Great Britain, and he played for the school team, with John Chenay as partner. Their tutor also had a 'great reputation' at fives and always had one of his best players in the team. Neville names Jack-Johnny Bevan as one of the finest players—he was senior keeper in 1913 and won the House Fives with Micky

Lawrence. John Chenay also excelled at cricket. A left-handed bowler and at the same time a right-handed batsman, he was 'a very useful cricketer'. He stayed with the Nevilles for a week during one vacation at Sloley Hall, and fell for Neville's sister Angela, as had many other friends such as Roger Ekin, Tiger Wyld, Toby Sturges and Dick Warren. All of them regarded Angela as a 'magnet' (ie. a babe magnet.)

In July 1914 Neville had to sit his 'School Certificate' examinations, the predecessor of 'O' levels which were in turn replaced by GCSE exams, usually taken at the age of 16. He later recalled, 'I spend hours and hours learning the conditional clauses in Greek … and I was instructed to read the Liberation of Italy for history. My tutor in history, Sheekay Martin, fired me with a love of history which has never left me. On one occasion he gave each of his division a part to learn and act as a particular character at the Congress of Vienna in 1814. I remember the way he cued me in. "Now Neville, this is where Tallyrand comes in, and you Chadwick, must answer as Metternich." It was very exciting. At the end he opened an envelope and announced "Gentlemen, Napoleon has escaped from Elba". He was chosen to teach the future Queen Elizabeth history and was knighted for his work.'

By the end of 1913 sabres were rattling all across Europe as a prelude to the start of the Great War in August 1914. Young Neville noted in his diary 'I watched a battalion of infantry march down the road from Slough and wheel onto Agar's Plough (a playing field at Eton). It was the first time I had heard a band and bugle march. The regiment was the 52nd Light Infantry (Neville's own regiment later on) and … it was an impressive sight. The next morning the regiment marched through Eton and down the High Street to Windsor with band and bugles playing and regimental colours flying. What more could one wish for?'

Back home for the holidays at Sloley, August 1914 was to be a memorable last summer of high jinks at Sloley for the younger Nevilles and their friends, even if it was memorable for the rest of the world as the month when WW1 started. James recalled that his father was seldom at home and 'always had the excuse of the House of Commons, though his ladylove probably had a stranglehold over him.' (They only learned of Reginald's new partner much later on.) Jane, as the eldest, was nominally in charge 'with the unenviable task of trying to do the impossible: keep us all in order!' He records games of hockey, played on the lawn with walking sticks, that were 'furious to a degree' and parlour games after dinner that at times were 'far from friendly' and ended in riots. Father, when he learned what was going on, was not amused at such boisterousness and told Jane, 'You rode rough-shod over your mother and now you want to do the same to me.' James was appalled and wanted to confront his father, but was dissuaded lest it make her life intolerable.

In our age when even nursery-age children know the 'facts of life', Neville's comments about 'the love stakes' seem quaintly innocent. With the Fosters and other young people staying at Sloley, James records that once the after-dinner high jinks were over they would all change into pyjamas and nightdresses (known in fashion advertisements as 'slenders'), take a candle each (Sloley Hall had not yet been wired for electricity) and process up to their respective boys' and girls' bedrooms. The girls used the 'trunk room' (so-called from its barrel-vaulted ceiling) and the boys in the 'porch room' where they would make a fire and talk for hours. Inevitably, girls were a regular topic of which James (despite being 17½ and having two sisters!) was surprisingly ignorant. He later recalled:

> I only knew there was a difference between male and female but not what it was until John described to Robert and me how he had been seduced by an aunt who inveigled him into her bed and introduced him the facts of life. This was naturally very intriguing for I had no idea of a man's role… Anyhow, John told us he had great fun!

Everyone was talking about the coming conflict in Europe. Neville's family hung a big map in the billiard room at Sloley Hall ready to pin flags on it to show various positions of the Allies and the enemy. About the middle of August (1914) they heard that the British Expedition had landed safely in France under the Navy's escort and was advancing into Belgium. 'But after the encounter at Mons,' Neville writes, 'it was depressing to have to move the flags back and back, past Valenciennes, Le Cateau, St Omer, St Quentin etc. The road to Paris seemed open, until Marshall Joffre struck at the right flank of von Kluck's army on the Marne. At last the flags could be advanced.'

James's father Reginald spent much time touring the neighbourhood round Sloley to address meetings, explaining the causes of the war and calling for recruits.[5] Neville junior recalls that he used to go with his father when he was not at school and remembers the under-gardener at the Hall volunteered to serve, along with three other local lads. Young Neville took their photographs, and the next day they all went off to Norwich to enlist. They all died in the war. The casualty lists after the defeat on the Marne were 'catastrophic'. 'Every day the *Times* named friends and acquaintances,' Neville writes:

> And the regiments they had served in. Later when security tightened, the regiments were not named. I was 17 and I considered myself old enough to serve. I was afraid that the war would end as forecast before Christmas, and then I should have missed having a go. When I got back to Eton, I discovered that all the boys in my House in the year above had gone off to war.

Neville was depressed. Nothing seemed to him to have any point—not the academic work nor even the games. The casualty lists for the boys from Eton were 'horrific'. Before prayers on Sunday evenings, Neville's tutor used to read out letters from Old Etonians at the front. They varied but 'all praised the stubborn bearing of the men of the finest army which ever left our shores.'

Before long the reality of the conflict hit Neville in a personal way. In November 1914 Neville's adored Uncle Jack, his father's younger brother, was wounded at Baillend, while serving for the 5th Field Company Royal Engineers, and later died in hospital. Neville was devastated at the loss of his favourite uncle.

> Unlike Father, he was decisive, made up his mind and acted. He was clever, even ingenious, full of fun, natural, kind and interesting to a little boy like

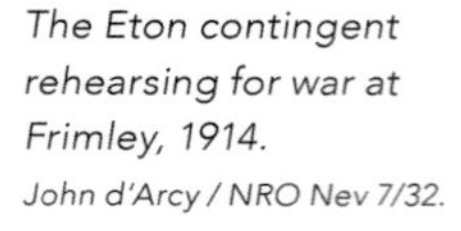

The Eton contingent rehearsing for war at Frimley, 1914.
John d'Arcy / NRO Nev 7/32.

me. He was also my godfather and I was very proud of him. He never shilly-shallied, procrastinated or allowed events to decide for him. He was so unlike father that it is a wonder they were born of the same parents.

By his mid-teens, James had formed a less than favourable opinion of his father, and the fall-out from Uncle Jack's death hardened his view. Jack's widow, Lillian, wanted him to be buried in France, but Reginald put 'intolerable pressure' on her to have the body brought home so that he could lay on a military funeral, complete with gun carriage and regimental band at Sloley Church. Neville describes Reginald's behaviour as 'extraordinarily callous and tyrannical' and notes that she only revisited Sloley once during the forty years of widowhood that followed.

Profits from the Post Office went to fund a new battleship every year and the British Fleet, renowned throughout the world as the finest, was said to outnumber the entire combined fleet of any two other Western European powers. The army however was seriously underpowered with just 700,000 men, all volunteers until conscription was introduced in January 1916. The principle of conscription was the subject of agonised debate at the time as it was seen as an unprecedented intrusion on the liberties of citizens. The pressing need for soldiers won the day and conscription for single men aged 18-41 was introduced in January and from June 1916 for all men of that age. Had our army been stronger, young Neville mused, would the German Kaiser have been more cautious in starting this war? The causes of the First World War are a matter of scholarly debate to this day. Suffice to say that Neville probably held a black-and-white opinion that Germany, led by the Kaiser, was entirely responsible and that the British and allies fought in defence of the high ideals of democracy, freedom and the rights of nations. But he was only a teenager, and teenagers very often hold strong views which become softened with age.

At the outset in August 1914, few had expected the war to drag on beyond the end of the year. When Christmas approached with no end in sight, James's determination to 'do his bit' strengthened and he resolved to leave Eton and join up at the earliest opportunity. Reginald, however, would not countenance this. Undeterred, James and his friend John Foster from Cambridge hatched a plot to return to Eton via Cambridge, sneak into the recruiting office and join up giving their ages as 18½ (rather than 17½). Unfortunately, Jane, who was 'thick with John', discovered the plan and told their father who was furious. Reginald summoned him to the library at Sloley, told him that he was 'now the only man in the family' and that his first duty was to the family, and absolutely refused to allow him to leave Eton before he was 18. 'I told him that he and I had nothing in common,' James records. 'He was furiously shocked and refused to speak to me.' When he returned Eton the following day, his father refused to say goodbye and Jane journeyed with him as far as Cambridge to ensure that he really did get on the London train!

Notes

1 In the early 20th century, there were Lower, Middle and Upper Fourth forms, with the last of these being designated Upper Fourth/Fifth.

2 Fagging was widely, though not universally, practised in public schools from the 1600s to the 1990s and was always a controversial issue particularly for its potential for physical or sexual abuse. The poet Shelley, who was an Eton schoolboy a century before Neville, described fagging as 'brutal and degrading' and famously organised a rebellion against fagging, not that it won him the praise of most of his fellow students! Other writers who have described fagging experiences include Thomas Hughes ('Tom Brown's Schooldays'), CS Lewis, Roald Dahl (who described warming toilet seats for his fagmaster at Repton School) and PG Wodehouse whose school stories frequently feature fags.

3 'Dog-potter' is probably a nickname for some kind of school military regiment, perhaps a form of Home Guard which the boys were encouraged to join up to as a try-out for the real thing. WW1 was coming and many of Eton's pupils signed up as officers when they finished at school. An email to Eton College revealed that the Eton College Volunteer Corps started in 1860, became the Eton College Officer Training Corps in 1908 and in 1948 it became the Eton College Combined Cadet Force. But the College archivist emphasised that 'It is only a guess that 'Dog-potter' refers to this.'

4 'I am fairly sure that the puttee referred to would tie in with a definition from the Encyclopaedia Britannica, namely that it was a "covering for the lower leg consisting of a cloth or leather legging held on by straps or laces or a cloth strip wound spirally around the leg. I have seen these on photographs of World War I soldiers. Such puttees were first worn by members of the Anglo-Indian army in the late 19th century. During World War I they were worn by U.S. and British infantrymen.' Eton College Spokeswoman, March 2018.

5 Between 1914-1915 the British Government called for an extra 100,000 volunteer soldiers to come forward. They got 750,000 men by the end of September, and by January 1915 more than 1 million had joined the armed forces voluntarily. By mid 1915 volunteer numbers were falling fast and the National Registration Act was created. It was a list of all the men fit for military service who were still available. Conscription was introduced in January 1916, targeting single men aged 18-41. Within a few months World War 1 conscription was rolled out for married men. Wikipedia, December 2017.

From Eton to Sandhurst 1915–16

Neville and a few friends nearly drowned during a swim at Sea Palling which brought home to him the peril he was about to face in the war. His few months training at Sandhurst were no hardship – he spent many weekends at parties and theatres in London with friends. Neville joined the Oxford and Buckinghamshire Light Infantry. He underwent further training and was about to go off to war but fell sick. A few months later he re-joined his unit in France.

Reluctantly back at Eton in January 1915, Neville found himself at 17½ the oldest boy in his house, though not house captain which honour fell to Osbert Peake (later a member of Churchill's post-war cabinet). Being appointed Captain of Fives might have been a small consolation, but when his partner John Chenay was taken sick, they lost the finals, and his last chance of gaining school 'choices' (the Eton word for colours) in any sport was thwarted. James was outgrowing school in more ways than one—at Easter he noted that he had put on six inches and was now six feet tall—only three more months and he would turn eighteen and qualify as a 'boy-patriot', as 18-year olds were known.[1]

He was not alone in feeling restless to get out and join up, something the Eton authorities understood, but not at any price. The immediate impact on Eton of the Great War was that 150 boys, who would have stayed on to the end, left to fight, some of them only seventeen or even sixteen, worried as Neville was that they 'might be too late for the war'. The younger generation of boys were sent to the front as they were the fittest, and consequently it was the younger boys who bore the brunt of early death.

Neville later recalled how one day a recruiting band arrived uninvited, disposed themselves in a semi-circle round the 'burning bush' (a Victorian gothic lamp in florid wrought iron which stood in the middle of the road outside the school hall) and struck up martial airs and songs. 'All boys within earshot simultaneously left their desks and rushed out to watch, sing and cheer. I can see even now that exceedingly clever and witty boy Henry Dundas going round the crowd of boys with his topper in hand. Copper coins jingled as he shook his hat. Having collected a respectable sum of beer money he went up to the recruiting sergeant with red, white and blue ribbons in his cap and told him where to find likely recruits of military age.' These included a particularly unpopular temporary 'beak' (teacher) known to the boys as Fornication Ford, to whose classroom Dundas led the sergeant. Several hundred boys cheered as the Sgt asked 'Fornic' to enlist. After this 'the recruiting band only came once more before steps were taken to immunise us from its blandishments.' Henry, sadly, was among those killed on the Somme just six weeks before the Armistice in November 1918, but not before he was awarded an MC and bar for extreme bravery on the field of battle. A tribute to him was published by his father and is now online. It includes a chapter on his time at Eton and references his 'ribald sense of humour that found unholy delight in shocking people.'

At the end of the Lent 'half' (as terms are known at Eton), Neville succumbed to a German measles epidemic and was obliged to remain at school. The sick bay was full and the boys were cared for by 'M'Dame' (i.e. the Housemaster's female assistant or matron). As a junior boy, James had thought her bit of a dragon, but now she showed a different side and was not only sympathetic

opposite: in uniform with Jane and Angela.
John d'Arcy / NRO Nev 7/32.

Neville at the wheel of Howling Herbert
John d'Arcy / NRO Nev 7/32.

but great fun and he became very fond of her, noting her distress at the loss of so many young lives. Fifty-three boys from Neville's house were killed in the war.

After this delayed start to the holiday, Neville finally set off to Sloley Hall which he now considered as home—'Eccleston Square was only a dumping ground for kit and the odd spree in London.' To his great delight, his Aunt Lillian passed on to him Uncle Jack's two-cylinder Swift motor car. 'Can you imagine my pride and joy in the time I spent polishing and fiddling with it?' he wrote, learning to drive by trundling 'round the oval and down the loke and back'. Angela christened the car Howling Herbert and it was his pride and joy for several years to come.

To his disappointment, James was not allowed to sit the entrance exam for Sandhurst in March, but his tutor promised him a nomination for a place instead. To this end he taught himself Morse code which he and Angela practised at Sloley by setting up a signalling line between their two bedrooms. Back at Eton for his final 'half' (as Eton terms are known) he was in rebellious mood 'and a great trial to 'M'Tutor' (i.e. Housemaster). Risking another confrontation with his father, he flatly refused to continue with Classics and instead chose to specialise in History, French and German 'which might be useful in France.'

Neville was, by his own admission, no linguist. He struggled with French and from the start hated German, finding the Gothic characters in which texts were written more difficult to read than Greek. As a beginner he was placed with mainly younger boys and taught—horror of horrors!—by 'Fornication Ford'. 'What a sod the man was,' he wrote, 'taking it out on me in front of small boys.' One day he asked 'Fornic' for help but was only ignored, so he cheekily said, 'Thank you, sir, for answering.' Ford 'got up in a paroxysm of fury and threw an ink pot at me which missed its target. All the small boys in the mixed class were enjoying the fun. I was not.' So he left the room to complain to his tutor who 'told me in his lisping, sticky voice "Don't worry, Neville, it's Mr Ford again. I will deal with him." And he did—but I often wish I knew how.'

During his final term at Eton, Neville found it hard to apply himself, even to sport. He enjoyed racquets, but he was a 'dead duck' at cricket, not good enough for the Upper Club and the Middle Club he found 'farcical'. He felt that the 'stupendous importance' of the war was not recognised nationally, complaining that the troops were ill-equipped, guns fell silent for lack of ammunition and 'the flower of England's youth was being slaughtered'. He left Eton as soon as he turned eighteen, not waiting for school to break up.

James Neville may now have been a 'boy patriot' but he had one last summer holiday to savour in Norfolk before going up to London to sign on. A number of friends came to stay at Sloley Hall including John Foster, Hilda Leach and his Granny Neville, now living in her new house in Chelsea. John Foster, by now a soldier serving with one of the Suffolk regiments, fell in love with Neville's sister Angela, but this met with great disapproval from their father. 'Father was extremely hostile and showed it,' Neville says. 'John was good-looking but not all that physically fit and suffered from a weak chest.' Nevertheless, their father still believed it was his sole prerogative to give or withhold approval before either of his daughters could become seriously involved with a man. In those days, especially in families such as theirs, that was the custom. Angela and Jane had joined the Voluntary Aid Detachment (VAD).[2] (Made up of both men and women, the VADs carried out a range of voluntary positions including nursing, transport duties, and the organisation of rest stations, working parties and auxiliary hospitals.)

The two sisters proudly wore Red Cross uniforms and put in many hours at the Gurney Convalescent Hospital for soldiers at Ingham, eight miles by road from Sloley. Their regular mode of transport, Neville records, was the 'dog cart' with 'fat and slow old Gertie in the shafts.'

The day before Neville was due to go up to Burlington House in London for his medical on 21 August, he and his sisters, plus John and Hilda, decided to go for a swim at Sea Palling. Norfolk beach enthusiasts will know it well and it has not changed much since those days. Anyone who does not know the beach at Sea Palling, some 20 miles south-east of Cromer, has missed a treat, but the rip-tide is notorious. That day the beach was deserted. The girls took it in turns to undress in the *batheesi*. The group were aware of the danger from draught ways (strong currents), and the breakers were quite big and heavy, so they stayed in their depth, allowing the waves to break over them.

Neville was the first to feel the cold and tried to come out after being flattened by one wave, but to his surprise he discovered suddenly that he could not stand, even though he was no more than 15 feet from the shore. As the next wave came over him, he tried to dig his fingers and toes into the sand, but found he could not even feel the sand let alone get a grip, and he felt the suction dragging him further out to sea.

Badly frightened, he swam frantically against the strong tow out to sea. After about five minutes he was able to get enough of a grip on hard sand to haul himself onto the beach where he lay, completely out of breath. Then he heard Angela shouting 'I can't get in'. With one foot on hard sand, Neville was able to reach out and get a handhold on his sister. Jane and John were just behind her, still struggling against the vicious current. Angela caught hold of John and Jane latched on to him, and as the next breaker shot up the beach, Neville hauled them all out of the water.

But Hilda was still beyond the breakers. With great aplomb, though also in great danger, she was floating on her back and facing out to sea, rising and falling with the crest and troughs of the waves. Neville was the strongest of five weak swimmers, but he was 'scared stiff'. 'I had no intention of going in again just there,' he wrote in his journal. 'But there was a boat on the beach a few hundred yards away, so I set off to try to find its owner with the idea that I could then launch it to save Hilda. I thought that so long as Hilda kept floating like that, there was hope we could get to her.

'But then from behind me came a shout. I turned and saw Hilda being propelled up the beach like a plank of timber. A large wave had caught her and sent her flying to safety. I cannot tell you how relieved I was. I have never since bathed, or allowed my family to bathe, where there are breakers, wind and an ebbing tide. It was terrifying.' Quite an experience, just before he was about to face death time and time again as a soldier in the Great War. Interestingly, he says he does not mind admitting that he was scared, though as a soldier, fear was not allowed at all.

The next day his father took him up to London. Along with other young men, Neville stripped for his medical examination. To his great joy he was passed fit. (His

above: Jane in VAD uniform.
John d'Arcy / NRO Nev 7/31.
below: Hilda and Angela (in the batheesi).
John d'Arcy / NRO Nev 7/31.

grandmother had been hoping that he would not pass the medical, and said so in so many words. Her sentiments were probably shared by all mothers, wives, grandmothers, aunts, sisters and even daughters across the whole of Britain. You can hardly blame them).

His next hurdle was Sandhurst, where he went about a week later and was posted to L Company in the old buildings. 'It was like starting at Eton all over again,' he writes. 'Strange faces and places, and stricter discipline than I was used to. We were quartered three to a room, with one soldier-servant to look after us. I made friends with Ben Cherry who had been at Eton, and who shared my room.' Neville and his band were known as gentlemen-cadets (GCs), and to begin with they paraded, as inconspicuously as possible, in 'civvies'. Their sergeant-major, RSM Wombwell of the Coldstream Guards, known as 'Thunder Guts', would pick on anyone unlucky enough to differ in any way from others in the ranks.

One young hopeful wore a Glengarry (the traditional woollen Scots cap) of the Highland Light Infantry. Thunder Guts bellowed at him. 'That gentleman wearing a scorch (sic. Scotch) cap in the front rank of company, stand still, Sirr'. His voice was so loud it could be heard from the firing range. Even when the unlucky GC discarded his 'scorch' cap, Thunder Guts did not miss a chance to bawl him out. 'That gentleman who wore a scorch cap yesterday, press on your butt, Sirr'. The RSMs were allowed to use any language, though not abusive words, provided that they finished their criticisms with 'Sir'. Even King Hussein of Jordan, who trained at Sandhurst, had the misfortune to be told by his RSM that 'You are the idlest King I've ever had to suffer with—Sirr!' Other fond forms of address included 'You are the most 'orrible, idle spring of the haristocracy,' and 'Your mother, Sirr, I hope is fond of you, but you make me want to vomit—Sirr!'

Heavy horses at Sandhurst.
John d'Arcy / NRO Nev 7/31.

The routine at Sandhurst, at least to begin with, consisted of lots of drills for the beginners. Starting at 0700 hours, the new recruits paraded up and down the parade ground in their civvies, except on Saturdays when only those men who had uniforms and army boots were allowed to parade. When not being drilled, they were in the gymnasium, walking the bench, climbing ropes and running miles cross-country. Young Neville had never been fond of gymnastics at school and for the first two months at Sandhurst, he dreaded the sessions in the gym. One particular exercise required the recruits to stand under a shelf, jump up and catch the edge then pull themselves up onto the top. Eventually Neville got 'the knack' of circling up onto the top of the shelf, but he hated having to jump down again without falling over.

The hours were long, but the training for battle, with hindsight Neville says, was 'minimal'. 'We went out on bicycles on map-reading schemes, dug trenches, practised shooting with a rifle, and once a week had a riding lesson'. Neville felt sorry for the horses who probably knew more than the recruits, having gone over the same exercises many times before. They practised jumping with stirrups crossed over the necks of the horses or bareback with arms folded. Two of the horses had nicknames—Jumping Jesus and Farting Philip!

They also did a lot of singing, mostly slightly obscene songs such as *Sammy Hall* or *Not a Sound was Heard as the Ottoman Shook*, and parodies of hymns. But it all felt full of purpose—to get a commission and to get to the front line and start actual fighting as soon as possible. But only one of the company officers, Captain Jeffries of the 29th Regiment, had any battle experience. So when 'Coochie' Hume came back from the front to get a commission, he knew more about the war than the officers. Understandably, he was intensively interrogated by Neville and the other recruits.

In the evenings, they studied. Neville found it 'very tedious'—military law, pay and mess book keeping, company accounts, theory of war by numbers. They also got lectures on the absolute necessity of knowing their men, their individual characteristics, their strengths and weaknesses, their anxieties, backgrounds, and their families so that they would know exactly what each man was capable of.

Cadets were allowed to keep motorbikes at Sandhurst, but not cars. Despite this rule, Neville took along his beloved 'Howling Herbert', and the officers in charge turned a blind eye. He went off with friends for weekends in London (forty miles and a slow drive in pre-M3 days!) in Howling Herbert, and had a great deal of fun, but leave for weekends away had to be obtained by handing in a 'letter of invitation'. Many cadets had got into trouble by writing their own such letters, so it was decided that 'letters of invitation' had to be in an envelope which had been through the post. Neville's sister Angela came to visit him one day, bringing with her a letter which his other sister Jane had 'forgotten' to post. Neville posted it to himself in Camberley, the nearest town to Sandhurst. The next day, instead of receiving the letter Neville was 'warned for Orderly Room' before Stallion Parade on Saturday morning.

Neville appeared before a senior officer, who threw his 'letter' down on the table and said 'Is this your writing?' Neville said it was not. It was his sister's. But when compared with the writing on the application for leave, which was indeed Neville's, the writing was the same. 'How do you account for the writing being the same?' said the senior officer. Neville explained that he and his sister had copied their father's handwriting. The senior officer was incredulous. Neville could not think at first how to prove his case, then suddenly remembered a silver cigarette case which Jane had given him for his 18th birthday on which she had engraved his name and the date in her own handwriting. The senior officer, who happened to be Irish, 'looked at the cigarette case and at me with a sour, malicious Irish eye'. Then he said 'I suppose I must give you the benefit of the doubt. Dismiss'. Neville got his leave, and he did not get any more trouble from the senior officer.

James and his Sandhurst friends had many cheerful evenings in London going to the theatre, musical comedies, and music halls, none of it serious or high-minded. They had to be back by Sunday evening 23.00 hours. If they were late, there were penalties such as cancelled leave. Neville nearly always had three friends in his car—two on the front seat and one on the dickey behind. The only lights were two oil side lamps and one acetylene headlamp. All of them wore goggles for motoring, turning up the collars of their great coats for extra warmth. Cadets without private transport took the train to Waterloo. Those without enough money for the fare would jump on and then hide in the lavatories, which meant that no-one could use the toilet during the journey.

At Christmas (1915), Sandhurst cadets had three days leave and on January 26, 1916 Neville received his order to report to the 3rd Regiment Oxfordshire and Buckinghamshire Light Infantry at Cambridge Barracks, Portsmouth. Before leaving Sandhurst all the new officers were issued with an officer's kit paid for by their parents. A valise, fleabag[3] (army slang for a bedroll or sleeping bag), housewife (pronounced 'hussif'—a sewing kit with needles and thread, buttons, etc. in a cotton pouch[4]), belt, sword, three pairs of boots, and two suits of service dress uniform. His pay at Sandhurst was 5/- per day (five shillings in old currency or 25p), which Neville spent entirely on 'messing' i.e. food and drink bought in the mess. His pay went up to 6/- when he got his first commission.

This was the end of Neville's training and he was soon to see enemy action. He says that his most abiding memory of Sandhurst was the crop of chilblains on his hands and feet. One evening he slipped and caught his heel on the edge of a stone step and ripped the chilblains open. He reported sick, and the doctor said he could be excused wearing boots for parade, which he attended wearing only shoes which promptly filled with water.

With hindsight, Neville says that he thinks he and his fellow cadets were slightly better-trained than those who went straight from school into the New Army battalions. They were also treated with a little more humanity than the temporary officers who had volunteered for the duration of the war, and were given the right to choose which regiment to serve with. At that time, as far as the regiment was concerned, regular officers were posted either to the 43rd or 52nd. The Territorial Battalions recruited their own officers and men and had their own reserve battalions, so the regulars and the territorials did not mix, which to Neville seemed lacking in vision. Later on, in World War II, the two merged, which the territorials resented as they lost their identity, but Neville says the regiment became much more integrated.

A Commissioned Officer

Neville immediately got ten days' leave, once he was commissioned, which he spent at 25 Ecclestone Square in London. This was his chance to say goodbye to his family and there were many tears as there was a fair chance he would not be coming back, except in a coffin. Even his father was there, taking him to Waterloo for the train to Portsmouth, fully equipped with valise and sword (which he kept till the day he died). But he does not say whether or not his father showed any emotion as he went off to war.

His first experience, once he was settled in at 3rd Battalion of the Oxfordshire and Berkshire Light Infantry at Cambridge Barracks[5] at Portsmouth (closed at the end of the war and now used by Portsmouth Grammar School), was to parade with recruits for drill. 'This seemed to me a sheer waste of time,' he wrote. 'After four and a half months at Sandhurst, I reckoned I could compete with the best at it. How wrong I was!

Cap badge and motto 3rd Battalion.
John d'Arcy / NRO Nev 7/32.

'At Sandhurst, all movement was at 120 paces to the minute. I found myself stepping off at 140 to the minute with my rifle at the trail (i.e. balanced in one hand parallel to the ground). There was no stamping of feet. Every detail was done quickly and quietly. Instead of the lengthy ritual of fixing bayonets in the Guards' manner, the best man was the one who fitted the bayonet the quickest. The motto was 'You whip it out, and pop it on'. The same applied to unfixing bayonets; best man was quickest man.

> When marching in file, we shouldered arms, otherwise the rifle was always held at the trail, and only with fixed bayonets did we move. There were several other rifle drill movements peculiar to light infantry, which I had never done at Sandhurst, such as fixing and unfixing bayonets on the march, which was extremely difficult to carry out in unison.

Every morning they marched out to Southsea Common, performed ceremonial and manoeuvre drill and guard duties and more. As a subaltern,[6] Neville then had to attend company orderly room to learn how to dispose of charges brought against delinquents, to understand the duties of the orderly office and procedure in a court martial. Once a week Major HT Donell-Brown lectured on regimental history in the billiard room, something Neville became very interested in later in life when he wrote a two-volume history of his regiment, still in print.[7] He and a friend, John Vidal, did a musketry course on Hayling Island which they both passed 'first class'.

In the spring of 1916, the 3rd Battalion moved out of Cambridge Barracks and marched up to Fort Widley on the Downs behind Portsmouth. Neville was detailed to carry the regimental colours, which he did, and deposited the flag, as instructed, in the Guard Room at the Fort. He was then 'respectfully informed' by the colour-sergeant that it was the tradition that the officer who carried the flag for the first time stood a round of beer to the sergeants' mess. Neville did as he was asked and footed the bill—only to learn later that this tradition only applied when the colours were carried 'uncased' ie. flying. 'I was had for a mug,' was his only, affectionate, comment.

At Fort Widley, much to Neville's disappointment, all officers above the rank of captain messed together in the Fort, while subalterns were relegated to a marquee. This arrangement meant that the officers never really got to know each other and, as Neville points out, encouraged division rather than the brotherhood which should unite any army. 'All are equal, save the commanding officer,' Neville complains in his diary. At the end of May came the Battle of Jutland (Denmark) the largest conflict between British and German battleships in the First World War. Although there was no risk of injury to the people living in Portsmouth, hardly a single family did not have a son or a husband serving in the Royal Navy and the place 'hummed with rumours' during and just after the battle as people waited on tenterhooks to hear if their families were safe. Neville himself met the sole survivor of the battle cruiser HMS *Queen Mary* which blew up and sank with all hands but him. 'He was a sub-lieutenant in the forward gun turret and all he could remember was the whole turret with its twin 12-inch guns being lifted complete into the air,' Neville writes. 'He escaped because the turret turned upside down on falling, and he was able to reach the surface where he was picked up by a destroyer.'

Naval Zeppelin in flight. *Library of Congress: LC-DIG-ggbain-14642, public domain.*

Zeppelins were intermittently raiding England at this time and Neville recalls how the Navy 'was itching to have a crack at one, boasting that none would pass inland over Portsmouth. 'One night, after lights out, the alarm was sounded and we bundled out of our tent. We assembled on the reverse slope of the Widley Down. Searchlights were quartering the sky and eventually one picked up a Zep. It came flying majestically towards the dockyard until thunderous gunfire from every ship in harbour was concentrated on it. It seemed to be right overhead, before taking avoiding action. It then put its nose up at an angle of about 30 degrees, and in a few minutes was out of range of the navy's low-angle guns.

'I don't think warships were equipped with anti-aircraft guns at this time,' Neville writes. 'But in any event such guns, known as 'Archies', had a poor reputation in the army. It was said that the three most useless things in the world were 1) tits on a man 2) balls on the Pope 3) Archie'. (This nickname was first used by Royal Flying Corps pilots and derived from a popular George Robey music hall song about a useless and hen-pecked husband called Archibald.)

Over the summer Neville continued training for his career as a soldier, specifically

Neville can be seen in the back row, sixth from the left.

John d'Arcy / NRO Nev 7/32.

for action in the war, but in his view it was severely lacking.

> I can remember one night-(training)-operation to repel an enemy raid, but none by day. Field craft was unknown, tactical handling of troops and formations were neither taught nor practised. We dug trenches, we were lectured on trench discipline, administration and sanitation. No-one had any thought beyond a trench. Static warfare was the mode of fighting and both sides stuck with that. What we learned came later, from experience under fire.

In June a large number of officers and men were posted for draft for the coming Battle of the Somme on July 1, 1916. This battle, one of the biggest and bloodiest in recorded history, lasted until November the same year and over 1,000,000 men were either wounded or killed. Britain suffered 60,000 men wounded on the first day alone, of whom 20,000 died. General Sir Douglas Haig, commander of the British forces, has been criticised ever since for his handling of the battle, for the human cost and the failure to achieve the territorial gains which were anticipated. Neville was warned for draft in September, but to his disappointment he fell sick and was taken off. 'I had the sad experience of seeing my best friends off from Cosham Station—Toby Sturges, William Giles, Rupert Blackwell, Philip Booth and Vivian Fanning,' he writes.

Knowing that he was 'missing all the fun', Neville spent a miserable autumn in Portsmouth at Fort Purbrook, one of the line of Victorian-era defensive forts on the hillside behind Portsmouth. The only relief to his misery was that he got to share quarters with Harry Spurge, a young man about five years older than Neville. The pair became good friends and eventually served together in France. Neville says of his friend, 'Harry's dad had been a senior naval officer and his upbringing had been very austere. He got to know the meaning of poverty and hunger. Yet he was never bitter, always upright and compassionate and helped me vastly with my disappointment at being taken off the draft.' (Harry was promoted to Captain but killed in September 1917, aged

25.)

Neville does not say what had been the matter, but in November he was passed fit and was warned for draft on 29 November, the date inscribed on the signet ring given him by his father. This time the draft, which included Neville, Spurge, Dowson, Chevallier, Cope and Dick Warren, went ahead and at this point Neville's war letters take over as the chief source of information about this stage of his life, save for a few comments about his social life in his later memoir. He does not say on what date he actually left for France, but his first letter home, from Rouen is dated 7 December, 1916.

We tend to remember, rightly, the horrors of war. Neville is quite matter-of-fact about death in armed combat, and appears to have greatly enjoyed the camaraderie of army life on active service. It was, after all, a very intense, unique way of living, never quite knowing if you would still be alive tomorrow and therefore you had to make the most of the moment.

Another issue which Neville mentions frequently is his 'fear of showing fear'. Bravery, especially physical bravery, was highly valued. Neville says that he much admired Bingo Baines because of his gallantry under fire. 'I remember once,' he writes, 'when we were at Witherval at the north foot of Vimy Ridge behind Arleux and Oppy, seeing him walk through a barrage of whiz-bangs (small calibre high-explosive shells so-called for their speed) with as much concern as if he were crossing Piccadilly. He, like the colonel, seemed to bear a charmed life'. On the other hand, cowards, especially those who wilted or ran away in the face of the enemy, were despised and could be shot for desertion. A medically fit young man who was not in uniform at this time was assumed to be shirking the fighting, and could be offered a white feather as a mark of disgrace. Pacifists and conscientious objectors (usually on religious grounds) who refused to fight once conscription came into force in March 1916 were widely reviled. Some were imprisoned and others drafted into non-combatant roles such as medics or stretcher-bearers.

Neville need not have worried. Like many men of his age, he was longing to have a go at the Germans whom he refers to disparagingly as 'the Hun' or 'the Boches'. He was a brave man and a good soldier, whatever his personal failings may have been, and while he was certainly scared from time to time, particularly on his first experiences in the trenches, he was never paralysed by fear. By August 1918 Neville was so blasé about going into battle, along with an American battalion (the Americans entered the war in April 1917) that he writes:

> I was excited, yes, and overawed by loneliness, but by now a fatalism was in my pocket. If my number was on a bullet or shell, nothing I could do would wipe it off. No matter how long we had to wait for the hands of our watches, there was never time to think of loved ones, home and beauty. I think my overriding prayer was that I should be spared being maimed for life. How lucky I was to lose only the full use of my right elbow. I still have my AB 136, stained with my blood, which contained the company roll and my diary, written during lulls in the battle.

And here the War Letters take over.

Notes

1 Boy patriot—Neville uses this term about himself, but it was taken from a novel of the same name by Edward Sylvester Ellis (1840-1916). Ellis was an American author who was a major author during the era of inexpensive fiction of the nineteenth century (dime novels). Because he wrote under dozens of pseudonyms, as well as under his own name, it is virtually impossible to know exactly how many books he wrote, but it is believed to be in the hundreds. fictiondb.com, December 2017.

2 Voluntary Aid Detachment—County branches of the Red Cross had their own groups of volunteers called Voluntary Aid Detachments (often abbreviated to VAD). Voluntary Aid Detachment members themselves came to be known simply as 'VADs'. Made up of both men and women, the VADs carried out a range of voluntary positions including nursing, transport duties, and the organisation of rest stations, working parties and auxiliary hospitals. Wikipedia, December 2017.

3 Flea bag—a sleeping bag. His valise may even have been a tent valise, which incorporated a sleeping bag. He could dispense with the tent portion if not required. Tent valises were carried with the baggage and originally only officers were allotted space for them. Great War Forum, December 2017.

4 A housewife or holdall pouch contained all that a soldier would require to carry out any repairs to his clothing when necessary. Inside it would contain a

thimble, two balls of grey darning wool (for socks), 50 yards of linen thread wound around card, needles, brass dish buttons (for battledress) and plastic buttons for shirts. The 'Housewife' was often contained within the holdall and stowed within the man's haversack. Imperial War Museum, December 2017.

5 Cambridge Barracks no longer exists. In Neville's day it was situated near Portsmouth. List of British Army installations, Wikipaedia, February 2018.

6 A British military term for a junior officer below the rank of captain; these days the term lieutenant' is more usual. Google dictionary, February 2018.

7 Neville wrote a history of his regiment, *History of the 43rd and 52nd (Oxford And Buckinghamshire) Light Infantry In The Great War Vol I, The 43rd Light Infantry in Mesopotamia and North Russia* published by the Naval and Military Press, original publication date of 1935.

The War Years 1916–17

At the start of the 20th century Europe was dominated by three large power blocs. Two of these, Germany to the north and the Austro-Hungarian Empire to the south, formed the core of the Central Powers. The third major alliance, the Triple Entente, was between Russia, Great Britain and France (known as the Allied Powers during the war). These alliances were meant to keep the balance of power so that no one country would dare to upset another in case it started a war.

Sadly, not only did these alliances fail to resolve the differences between the great powers, they also wove together such an elaborate web of treaties that when the crisis came, each of the major powers was drawn into the war by the treaties that were intended to protect it. Russia had a defence treaty with Serbia, Germany with Austria-Hungary, France with Russia, Britain with Belgium and France, and Japan with Britain.

Thoughts of an Armageddon in Europe had been in the air for many years prior to 1914. Britain had by far the biggest empire. This caused a good deal of jealousy among other countries in Europe, which had smaller pieces of the action in Africa, South America and the Far East. Everyone was jostling for position and power.

The three principal monarchs of the age, Kaiser Wilhelm II of Germany, King George V of Great Britain, and Tsar Nicholas II of Russia were all cousins with each other: Wilhelm and George were first cousins, George and Nicholas were also first cousins, and Wilhelm and Nicholas were third cousins. The three men, all of whom descended directly from Queen Victoria, liked to meddle in politics and, according to some historians, may have exacerbated the volatile situation.

The Kaiser was vain and posturing, determined to believe that he was an English gentleman, and compensating for his stunted left arm by flamboyant, militaristic gestures and rhetoric. The Tsar was henpecked by his wife, trying to strike an autocratic pose without the character to back it up. George V lacked the charm and royal presence of his father Edward VII, and was a domestic tyrant who caused his son Bertie (the future George VI) to stammer with nervousness. Both the former (the Tsar and the Kaiser) had real power and could actually declare war. George V had little authority, the British monarchy being largely symbolic. Nevertheless, the three men tried, and often succeeded, in making outrageous, secretive treaties with each other some of which may have been binding, some not, which exasperated their governments and almost certainly contributed to the inevitable outcome of war in Europe.[1]

The scene thus laid, the spark to the tinder was the assassination of the Austro-Hungarian Archduke Franz Ferdinand by Serbian terrorists in Sarajevo (the capital of Bosnia and Herzegovina) on June 28, 1914. Ferdinand was the heir to the throne of Austro-Hungary, and his death at the hands of Serbian terrorists led to a diplomatic crisis. Austro-Hungary, which wanted to weaken Serbia's hold on the Balkan states, attempted to humiliate Serbia with unacceptable demands as a form of apology – or it would declare war.

Serbia refused to accept the demands, and Austria duly declared war. Serbia's ally Russia declared war on Austro-Hungary in order to defend Serbia. Germany was forced to go to war with Russia, according to the terms of the treaty it had signed with Austro-Hungary. Germany assumed that its war with Russia would almost certainly entail a war with France according to yet another treaty between the Allied Powers.

The main first step Germany took to defend Austria was to attack France and Belgium

Archduke Franz Ferdinand of Austria.

Library of Congress: LC-DIG-ggbain-07650, public domain.

(though neither of these countries had officially entered the war). Germany decided to try to capture Paris as swiftly as possible, in the hope that it could take France out of the war before Russia could mobilise. The quickest way to Paris lay through Belgium, and so German troops flooded through the country which was trying to stay neutral. The attack on the Belgian city of Liege (condemned throughout the world as German soldiers behaved atrociously towards the civilians) brought the British Empire into the fight as Britain had an obligation to uphold Belgian neutrality which had been agreed in return for concessions in central Africa.
And so, within a month, Europe was tearing itself apart starting on Britain's doorstep.

James Neville's war started pretty well. He was drafted to the 52nd Battalion which was very different in atmosphere from the 3rd, so different that he wondered at times if the two battalions were in fact part of the same regiment—the Oxfordshire and Buckinghamshire Light Infantry. For example, the mess in the 3rd was organised so that only officers of the rank of captain or above were allowed to speak, and subalterns disappeared quietly as soon as the meal was over. In the 52nd, everyone was known by his first name or nickname, except for the Commanding Officer (CO) Richard Crosse and the fun was 'hilarious'.

'The noise and laughter was exhilarating,' he wrote. 'Table manners were unorthodox. Rolls and pellets of bread flew across and down the table. The mess sergeant Payne with Privates Talbot and Arnold managed to serve courses somehow. As soon as dinner was over, there was always a "rugby". This was often begun by the CO who, as soon as we were all in action, used to slip away to the orderly room with his adjutant.'

Lots of young men at the start of the 20th century thought war was a great adventure, and the announcement of hostilities invoked a mood of national celebration in Britain. Queen Elizabeth, the Queen Mother, (who was at the time only 14 and not yet a member of the British Royal Family) remembered being at the theatre on 4 August (her birthday, coincidentally). The theatre manager came onto the stage during the interval to tell the audience the 'good news' that war had been declared, to which the audience responded with applause![2] Philosopher Bertrand Russell records that he 'walked about Trafalgar Square horrified, discovering to my amazement that average men and women were delighted at the prospect of war … the anticipation of carnage was delightful to something like 90 per cent of the population. I had to revise my views on human nature.'[3]

Neville was no different. In his first letter home on 12 December 1916, he described a great send-off from Cosham Station with all the officers from Purbrook and Cambridge Barracks there to wave goodbye and good luck.

He wrote:

> Some of the soldiers were a bit blotto, no matter. All is well here (in Rouen, Northern France), and we are as gay as could be.... we are doing a six-day course of everything I have been doing for the past 10 months (at Sandhurst). We are accommodated in so-called huts which are less waterproof than tents. There is no room to put one's kit except on nails on the walls and the rain drips through and on to one's breeches and shirt.... Huts are only made of canvas nailed to uprights. It's very cold here and abominably wet, but I manage to keep dry in my trench coat and my big boots are an absolute godsend. We work from 8am to 3pm with an hour's break for lunch.
>
> You would laugh to see us—Dick Warren, Dowson, Harry Spurge and me—sitting in pools of water trying to open a tin of bully beef and picking sardines out on the end of rusty penknives.

It is no wonder that many men, including Neville later on, went down with a variety of severe stomach upsets and blood poisoning. Everyone had regular tetanus injections.

Obviously, the conditions were appalling and it is astonishing that Neville could write home that he and his friends were 'gay as could be'. They were at least three feet deep in snow with no proper shelter from the weather. They ate tinned beef and fish off the end of a rusty penknife. They would soon be on the receiving end of enemy fire and all this would go on for months, if not years. But they were at the start of a big adventure—a few years on, Neville was not so keen!

Neville wrote this introductory letter from his base, 55 Infantry Base Depot, Rouen. Although he came to France to fight, he was not beyond a spot of sightseeing.

> The cathedral (in Rouen) is incomparable and the perpendicular arches are the best that I have seen, I think. But somehow Roman Catholic churches lack the air of quiet solemnity which is so characteristic of ours. I can't abide the different coloured candles and the ugly confessionals. It's all too tawdry. I suppose the spire is an addition, isn't it? Put on later like the pots on Lupton's tower.[4]

So the letters, while they mostly describe the living conditions and military activities during the second half of the Great War, are also littered with references to the things which interest Neville, such as the political situation at home and how his father was faring as an MP, Greek poetry, music, literature and of course, his sisters.

Neville senior's letters by return are extraordinarily warm and concerned for his son. He might not have been good at showing his love for his only son in person, but his letters are full of encouragement and praise, asking the son to look after himself so that he will come home from the war alive and in one piece. The son's letters were so well written that his father often congratulated him on the clarity of his writing, and passed them round the family so that everyone could see the quality of the reports.

On December 21 Neville arrived in Fontaine-sur-Maye where he was reunited with his men of the 52nd Light Infantry. The whole regiment was to be stationed there until the first week of the New Year. His letter to his father records the following:

> We are billeted in a typical French village, all the houses of which are made of mud and lath and most of them are falling to bits like the blacksmith's shop at Sloley. In fact, within a mile or so of here, the Black Prince scuppered the French under Jean of Luxemburg (in the Crécy campaign of 1346).[5]
>
> We rode over to Crécy this afternoon and I stopped and had a look at the monument. The countryside is very dull and resembles Norfolk, but there are no oaks to break the skyline. You can see nothing but open fields for miles with the occasional hay stacks and now and then a big plantation. Today the Regiment paraded for a Brigade stunt—an attack scheme with airplane co-operation. We assembled, but then the weather was too bad and the whole scheme was washed out.

Another letter, again to his father, dated on Christmas Eve described vividly the countryside at night just a mile or so from the front:

> The sky and inky trees were lit up every other second by yellow flashes coming from far away. Flash, flash, flash, yet not a single sound to disturb the stillness of the night. And then I seemed to realise that probably each one of those flashes might mean that some poor man, friend or foe, was being blown to bits.

Between his arrival in France and Christmas 1916 there was little for him to do. Most of the day was taken up in riding over to a nearby village to watch football, sports or racing. He had 'one of the happiest Christmases since mother died' that year, and in the afternoon, he and another soldier went for a walk over to the battlefield of Crécy. Chevallier (a friend of Neville's in the regiment) had mugged up the history and they walked up the slope to the English position and rested on the spot from which King Edward III watched the battle.

'You were rather a scholar in history as far as I can remember,' Neville reminded his father. 'So you would know all about the battle of 1346. A quarrel was settled there in a few hours, yet we have been fighting for over two years, and still not decided it!' At this stage Neville had still not tested his nerve in battle. He had either an instinctive feeling that he was going to get through this alive, or the beginner's self-belief that he was indestructible. Whichever it was, he was able to write home with this:

> Never be anxious on my account because I know I shall come through all right. It is no worse for me than it is for you at home. You have the anxiety where I have the fun, and however unpleasant the conditions may be, they are all good fun to look back on. The only thing I am not certain about is that I may get the wind up and show it. I am afraid of being afraid. If I can control myself, I think all will be well, but that is my misgiving and a natural one. I know we are going to have a stiff time, but all the better.

As January 1917 progressed, the battalion was edging very slowly forwards to the front line. Every day, everything had to be packed up in order for the men to move on another two miles. But when they stopped, the first thing to be unpacked was always the gramophone, and one of Neville's favourites was Rachmaninoff's *Prelude* which reminded him of Sloley.

> It always plays out of tune, but it makes things very cheery while we make camp yet again. I was warned today that I shall probably be attached to the Royal Engineers while the division is in the line. Sapping (the work done by the army engineers such as building bridges) must be very interesting work ... the choice lies between Warren and me, and the Colonel has still to make his decision.

On 14 January he was at Ovillers-la-Boiselle where he and Harry Spurge spent the morning in a little *estaminet* (a small café) where they bought lots of liqueur chocolates followed by an omelette. But that evening he was close enough to the front line to see the flashes of the guns which lit up the whole sky. He was stationed in a hut just behind the old German front line of 1916 at the side of the Albert Road.

Just as I sent off the message, an

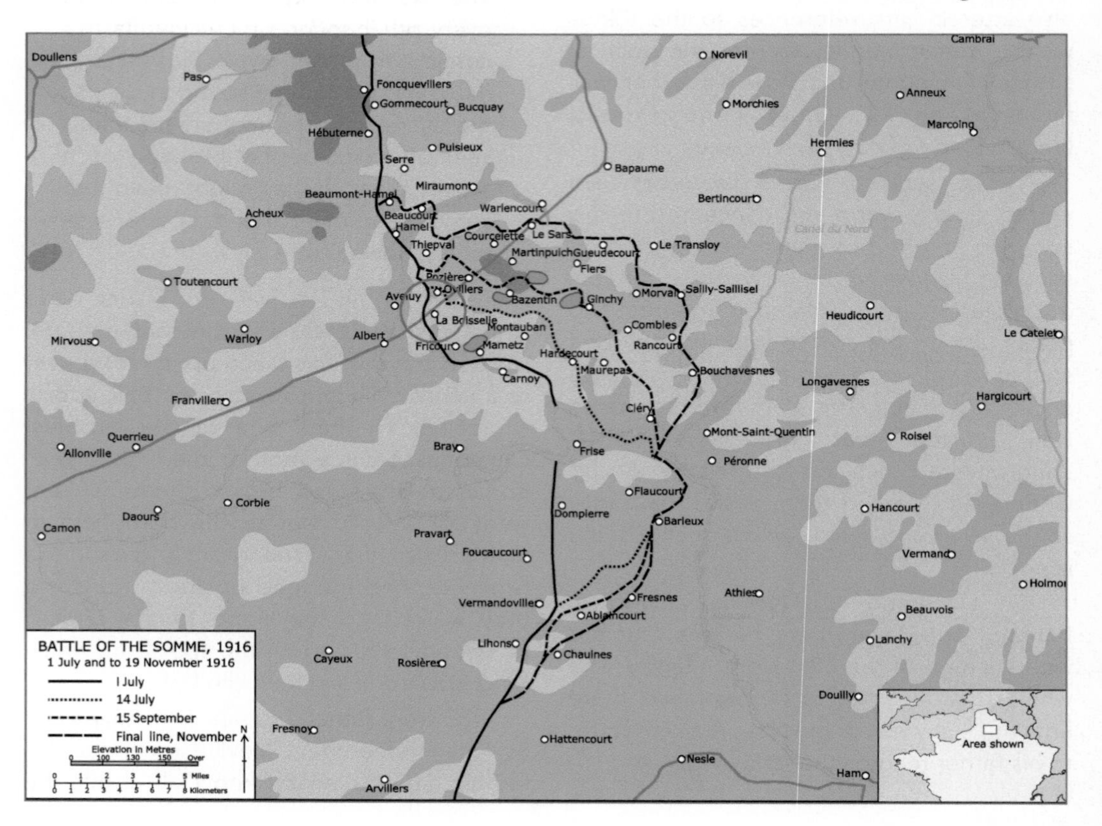

Map showing Neville's position in January 1917. The dotted line shows the German front line on 1 July 1916 and the long dashed line (final line, November 1917) shows where the front would have been in January. The Albert Road is shown in grey

redrawn from a map by The Department of History at the United States Military Academy, public domain.

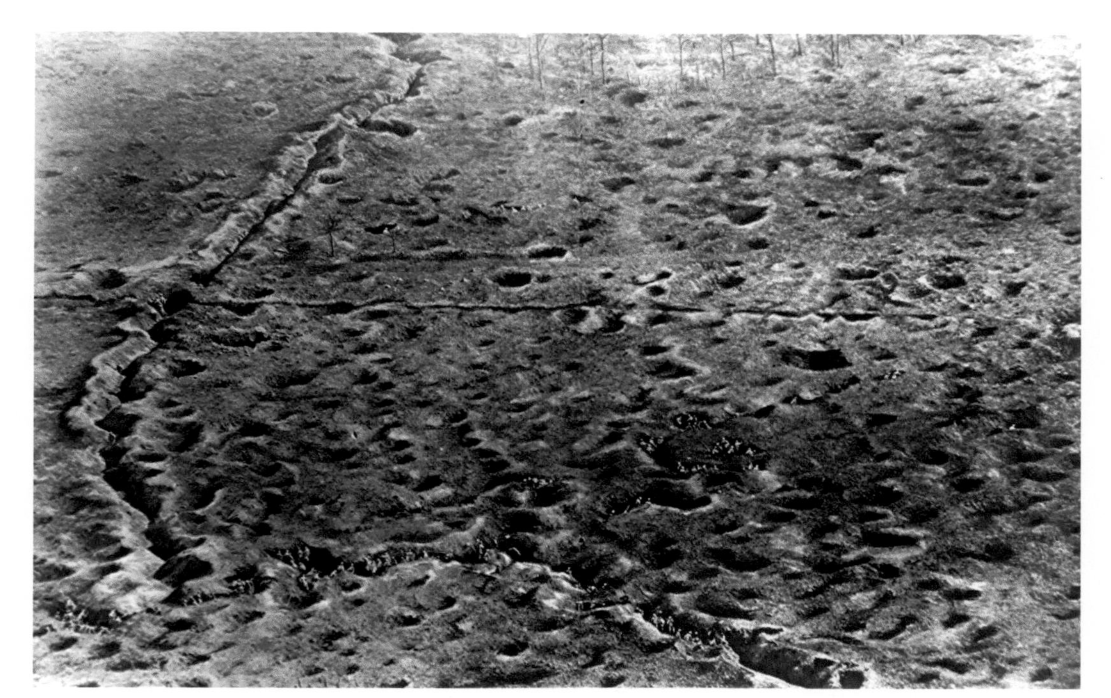

Photograph shows a battlefield on the Somme front in France during World War I, with French troops moving through trenches and shell craters into an area formerly held by the German army.
Library of Congress: LC-DIG-ppmsca-40796, public domain.

> officer descended the dug-out sweating from every pore. I have never seen anyone in such a malt. He had been caught in our barrage and he said that our guns were dropping shells 200-300 yards behind our front line, and he had crawled the whole way from shell-hole to shell-hole until he struck our post. Then I got a message to say that gas was being let off to our right.

Life became quite a lot more real for young Neville from that day on, and he spent most of the rest of the Great War in that part of France where millions of men died. He missed the Battle of the Somme by just a few months, but he saw heavy action in the Second Battle of the Somme, which marked the start of the end of the war.[6] The following morning, he had to wash in shell-hole water.

> I don't think I have ever experienced such cold. The whole place is simply torn up into a mass of shell holes. The ground all round is littered with shell cases—bombs, grenades and duds of every kind, and here and there a little wooden cross marks some poor chap's grave. As I was returning from my sight-seeing, I saw a boot sticking out of the ground. I kicked it and then saw a piece of khaki puttee attached to it. It gave me rather a funny turn.
>
> There goes another shell on its mission of mercy. I wish it was not so close. There he goes again. Bang-z-z-z-! Fizz! Like an underground train going out of a station. The whole hut rattles when it goes off. We are now in support huts not three miles from the front line. Griffiths-Williams and I made a tour of the battlefield and found a few stumps of trees marking a coppice of days gone by, a few ruins where a village once stood, a great many wooden crosses and here and there a boot and leg protruding from the ground.... We also had a look at a derelict tank which I tried to get inside, but my shoulders were too broad. Next, we looked at the crater of the mine which was blown up behind the German line on July 1. It took 10 months to make and I am not surprised, and so far it holds the record for the biggest mine exploded in this war. We reckon that it was 120 feet across and nearly 80 feet deep. The ground outside the mess is torn up by shell holes which are water logged and the mud has to be seen to be believed. The whole landscape is

> utterly desolate and, although very interesting, also very sad.

On 20 January, the battalion was at Bouzincourt. Neville writes:

> We marched up to a hut near Poziéres to draw thigh gum boots and on the way, we were shelled with lachrymatory gas (tear gas) which had no ill effects except to make our eyes water and cause a choking feeling and to make breathing uncomfortable. We had to wait while another regiment passed us and while we did so, a man fell into a shell-hole full of water. Being heavily equipped and having all his rations to weigh him down, he very nearly went under. We left the duckboards (wide slats of wood placed on the bottom of trenches to stop the feet of soldiers getting wet and then contracting trench foot) at "C" dump, and until there the going had been quite easy. But as soon as we got off the duckboards, it was nothing more nor less than hell. The gum boots had no grip on the ground and we went along floundering up to our waists in mud, slipping up and falling into shell-holes full of water, and all the while my ankle boots swung in between my legs and the ration bag grew heavier with every step.
>
> More than once the men had their gum boots sucked off in the mud and had to continue in their socks. Every time a man fell into a waterlogged shell-hole, his rations went with him and these often went to the bottom.

A report from *The Times* (April 15, 1917) tells how plucky British soldiers had 'in places to fight almost to their waists in mud, but nothing checked them'.

Still in Bouzincourt a few days later, Neville recovered enough to find his sense of humour and write home.

> The Hun always relieves the front line by day and saunters along with his hands in his pockets from post to post. A party of them came quite close to us and waved their arms, and at one post they asked our men to come and have a drink by holding a bottle of beer over their heads so we could all see. They seem quite genuine in their invitations because they are never armed. I simply longed to have a shot at some of them to pay off old scores, but it only meant that we would have been sniped at or taken prisoner on our lone visits to the posts at night. I believe that if you were lost in this sector, the Hun would lead you back to your own line-up.

At this point Neville seriously wondered if his nerve under fire would hold. He was fine.

> The only time I felt at all funny was at 6.30am on the 17th. We had had no sleep all night and the Hun started shelling and our guns replied. The strafe lasted three quarters of an hour. I had a shivery feeling and, try as I would, I simply could not control that shivering. Harry said "It's very cold isn't it?" and I said "Yes, I can't keep warm." We both had the wind up, but I don't think we betrayed it.

Neville's main first job was to equip British troops on the front line with supplies. A small railway mounted on duckboards had been set up behind the line, and trolleys were loaded with revetting material (such as stone or concrete used for shoring up defences). A working party, including Neville, had to push the trolleys along the line.

> The ground is frozen hard as iron and the snow on the surface has been trodden into ice,' he wrote in a letter to his sister Mary (Jane). 'Needless to say, to make the night more exciting, the railway line is shelled at odd intervals. Pushing these damned trucks is hard and exhausting work and the men loathe anything in the nature of a fatigue. But the stuff has got to get to the forward dump for the men in the front line. Poor devils, I do pity them in this weather.

On 2 February back in Ovillers-la-Boiselle he was still pushing trolleys, sometimes half the night. He wrote in a letter to his father

Trench railways near Arras, 1917.
US National Archives and Records Administration: 16576822, public domain.

that:

> I was out last night from 6pm to 3.15am. Each truck was stacked with 40 duckboards and pushed by six men. The ground over which the bloodstained railway runs is undulating and these heavy duckboards took a lot of pushing to get up the incline. Then about every 200 yards the damned trucks came off the line and the duckboards were shot off like a pack of cards. That meant restacking them all over again, and this sort of thing happened all through the night. We were all dead beat by the time we got in. It is colder than I have experienced before. My boots are frozen stiff every morning, the beer and water are solid at meals and the condensed milk like ice cream. I always go up to the line with a fleece under my British warm, a balaclava helmet pulled down over my ears and wrapped at the bottom with a camel hair scarf. Sometimes in the middle of the night it is so cold that a dew-drop on the end of my nose freezes into an icicle.

Neville had told his father that he had lost his compass and another one arrived for him in the mail of 4 February, together with 1000 cigarettes which he shared with his men. Also in the same package was a copy of the *Times Supplement* which Neville enjoyed reading, along with Hamlet and Richard III!

But more was to come on the same day. Two more parcels from his family! The first contained Devonshire cream—frozen solid but it was successfully thawed out with the juice of some tinned strawberries, which were served hot as pudding for lunch. And the second had in it some plums, peppermints and chocolate. Neville was delighted and wrote back that he would keep these stores as emergency rations.

And now back to the war.

On 12th February Neville got his first experience of coming under fire. His first night in the trenches on 11 February was quiet but the following morning, guns from the British side began to strafe the enemy with 'some big stuff and shooting with good success' though Neville does not say what, if anything, they hit. During the evening of the same day, Chevallier, the Lewis Gun Officer and the Brigade Intelligence Office came to see him with another officer called Giles, to warn them that they might be raided during the coming night. This information had been extracted from a German prisoner.

Neville wrote to his father.

> Shoveller, as we call Chevallier, talked so loud that I thought the Kaiser in Berlin would probably hear him, and as the posts are very close to the Boche, it seemed he wanted them to hear as well. We prepared at once for the worst and got out bombs and all manner of ammunition. The suspense was awful and around quarter to eight Giles decided to visit the other posts which left me in charge, and at 8pm the barrage began on our left. We couldn't see much as the night was black as pitch and it was very foggy, but then I saw the rocket go up to tell our gunners to open fire—I was mightily relieved to see that. It seemed all hell was let loose on the Germans. I looked over the parapet and saw our first shell burst, most beautifully timed. But the second… I saw a trail of fire go straight into the right-hand corner of our trench with a fizzing noise. Shrapnel!
>
> The next thing was a long-drawn out groan of agony and I knew that some poor devil had gone. Later I discovered that that was our two servants. They had been killed in the right corner of the trench. My servant was a gem and looked after me like a father. It was his first time in the front line, and the first time I had seen a man killed. Sadly, it was a shell from our own guns, not five paces from me, and yet I was not touched. Two more of our shells burst over the same corner so I told the men to edge down to the left-hand end of our post. While we were moving another of our shells burst right over my head, I was knocked absolutely flat and my tin hat rolled down the trench. Luckily there was a dug-out in our post, and I told the men to take cover while I and the Lewis Gunner waited at the top and had a peep over the parapet every now and then. It seemed unlikely that the Boche would come our way as well and if they had, our guns would have given them worse hell.
>
> On the other side of the trench was a little shelter that Giles and I had occupied earlier. I heard the shrapnel ripping it up and the bits rattling like guns. As the shelling got hotter, I thought I had better do something about it, so I sent through a message on the power buzzer to say that our guns were firing short. I thought that the barrage had been blasting us for an hour, but when I looked at my watch, I was dumbfounded to see that it was only 8.15! All through the bombardment I was as cool as a cucumber. I was quite surprised at myself, but then we had no time to think of anything, and I felt frightfully excited and wished I had a rifle instead of an automatic. The bombardment ended at 9pm and we all got into the trench where I found Giles whom I had never expected to see again. The raid was easily repulsed; only about 12 got into our line, of whom six were taken prisoner. The raid started 70 strong, and the enemy lost about 30 all told, so it was a failure from their point of view.

Albert in 1918.
Library of Congress: LC-DIG-ggbain-26255, public domain.

All was quiet for a couple of weeks, and he wrote to his father again on 4 March, this time from Albert:

> On 23 February we paraded at 5.30pm for the line, (i.e. and then went up to the front line), an 8-mile march. Then we took the damned duckboard track on which I experienced the worst journey since I have been out here. Men were falling into shell-holes up to their armpits in wet mud, from which it was a labour of Hercules to extract them and caused much delay. The mud was indescribable. I took over from a King's officer, who was nearly off his head from being alone for six days under a piece of corrugated iron with nothing to eat but bully beef and biscuits.

At 5.15am Neville went over to the Company HQ to find the place very excited. News had come through that the enemy was retreating—which meant Neville and his men could go after them and see some open warfare. A gunner went forward to lay a telephone wire and the news came through that they could occupy the enemy second line. 'Huge excitement!' Neville wrote:

> Eagle and I started off in daylight at 5.30pm. We got through the wire and were going along the Pys road when the Hun, who had obviously spotted us advancing, put down an awful barrage. We left the road and got into a shell hole, but we had to wait for about an hour before the shelling diminished. Gradually we went forward to try to find this trench which no-one had seen before. By this time, it was pitch dark. I took two platoons forward (a platoon is comprised of between 20 and 50 men and commanded by a lieutenant such as Neville), but we got lost, so I thought it would be best to try and strike the road and adjust my bearings. With the compass I found the old German front line which we followed until we found the Pys road. Thus, I was back where I started from! On the road I found a messenger who said that we had to return to our old posts.

Neville's letters also dated 4 March now cover the last few days of February. The exchange of fire between the British and German guns continued without a break for the next few days. Neville had to relieve the 74th but the route to doing so was well known by the Germans. He said in his letter to his father:

> My guide told me that they had a rifle laid on the track to and from the forest. We wasted no time crossing the crest and then descended into the valley, crossed a stream and so reached the communication trench. The Boche knew all about this little bridge over the stream because rifle shots cracked like whip lash at odd intervals, and put the fear of God into me! ... This was the first continuous piece of trench system I had been in, and the Company HQs were established in a dug-out with about five steps. The 74th were not sorry to quit!

The bombardment from the Germans continued relentlessly. On 29 February he wrote:

> It was awful. The Hun runners were able to enfilade our bit of trench and they did so with excellent effect. Shrapnel bullets were falling all round us. I had one man killed in my platoon, concussed to death, and rather a nasty sight. We were all a bit shaken after 12 hours of it. The two platoons on the left near the stream had the worst of it and had one man killed, two wounded and a sergeant shell shocked.

On 1 March Neville thought he was about to get some hand to hand fighting. A gunner popped his head over the side of the trench and said:

> They are coming over! We were up those steps like rats, but in the shemozzle Fritz (Eagle, a British soldier despite the German name), pinched my automatic by mistake and I did not know where his was! As I got to the top step, two shells burst just over my head in an orange glare that lit up the inky darkness. Star shells[7] were sailing

Burying the dead from the trenches.
Library of Congress: LC-DIG-ggbain-14642, public domain.

up in the air all round, in fact the Germans had got the wind up badly and must have thought that we were coming over. By the light of each star shell, I peered into the night, but could not see any sign of a moving thing. From our side, not a single Verey light (a flare used for temporary illumination) was fired, so whoever thought that the Boche was coming must have been seeing things. But I was almost in a panic when I could not find my automatic. I had visions of being unable to defend myself.

The following day Neville said that he spent the day burying Canadians killed five months previously. The bodies had been frozen during the winter and now were thawing out. 'Some were a horrible sight,' he wrote. 'Thank God their dear ones cannot see them like this.' This was the end of eight days in the front line and Neville returned to Albert, where he said he was going to try to forget the past week. But only two weeks later he wrote again to say:

> This is the last opportunity I shall have of writing to you for a long time, so that you can guess what we are going to do. If it is all successful and I come through unscathed, I hope I shall soon come home on leave. The suspense and anticipation is the worst of it. I am sure that once we are on the move, it won't be so bad... Well *au revoir*. I hope I shan't be a coward. It will be over by the time you get this. I will write again as soon as I can.

It looked as though Neville expected to be called on to go into some serious, close-up fighting and indeed a footnote on the same page of the War Letters (4 March, 1917, Bruce Huts, Ovillers-la-Boiselle) says that the 52nd had been warned to attack Loupart Wood (west of Bapaume) on 15 March. The enemy, in the end, retired on the eve of battle.

He was not therefore, called upon to go back into battle, and even had a little time to do a spot of sight-seeing with his friend Dick Warren. March 9 saw the pair in Amiens where Neville had time to admire the inside of the cathedral, with statues and tombs completely surrounded with sandbags in the event of a direct hit. They tried to hitchhike back in the late afternoon, but none of the British staff cars would stop for them. He had a reasonably long rest, a good two weeks, during which time he wrote that he thought the war would 'not last much longer'. That had been the line from every soldier and every politician from the start of the war, and they were always wrong. He also reported that he had heard a wild rumour. 'Turkey has thrown up the sponge and Austria is treating for an armistice. There might be some probability in the former.'

All through March the German retreat continued, and Neville commented that he thought it was a 'very careful and systematic retirement.' Bapaume was set alight and left to burn to the ground, and all the dug-outs were destroyed. They also laid traps for the foolish or inexperienced. Souvenir hunting was common among soldiers and civilians—indeed, Neville himself was not above searching for quirky little items. He wrote that 'Souvenirs of an attractive character have been found to be attached to explosives such as artificial flowers,

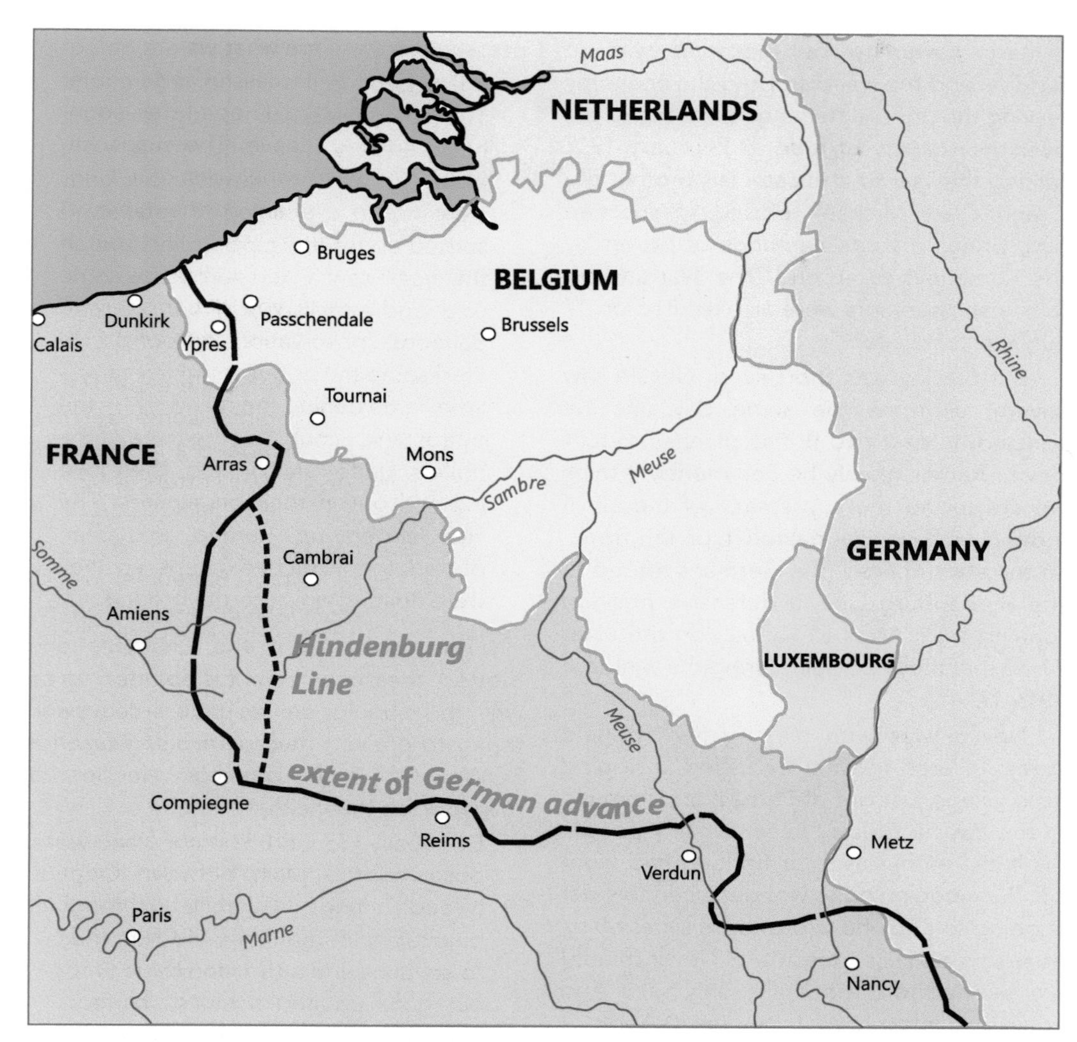

Map showing position of the Hindenburg Line.
redrawn from a map by The Department of History at the United States Military Academy, public domain.

evergreens, even nose caps and bits of dud shells.'

And then suddenly on 17 March came the news of revolution in Russia. An uprising had been expected for some time. The news cheered up Neville and his men no end, though I have the feeling they must have misunderstood its significance. The Russians had not been faring well against Germany but they had at least been a distraction on the Eastern Front. With the uprising in its own country, Russia was obliged to withdraw from the war altogether, leaving its allies (France and Great Britain), to finish the job alone. The Allies were weakened by the Revolution, not strengthened by it.

There were essentially two Russian revolutions in 1917, or at least two important phases. The first in February 1917 saw the overthrow of the old Imperial government under the Tsar. During the second, in October the same year, the Bolsheviks under Vladimir Lenin seized power over the whole of Russia.

The bond between the Tsar and the people broke during the bitter Russian winter of 1916-17. The Tsar's government was corrupt and highly inefficient, and the Tsar himself (Nicholas II) was reactionary and at times erratic. For example, in 1905, he dissolved the Duma (the Russian parliament) without consultation or agreement. The Russian Empire also had many ethnic minorities which had grown restive under the restrictions placed on them by an intolerant government.

But it was the inefficient way the old regime had organised the Russian effort in the Great War that finally brought revolution. Poorly equipped and led, the Russian army suffered defeat after defeat against Germany. Russia was clearly no longer a military power to be reckoned with in Europe, and the war disrupted the economy leaving the people starving. Riots broke out over the scarcity of food in February 1917 forcing the Tsar to abdicate. His brother the Grand Duke Michael refused to succeed him, bringing three centuries of power by the Romanovs to an end. The Tsar and his family and servants were all executed on 17 July the same year.[8]

But the joy was short-lived. Neville saw several air-fights the same day and he spotted at least two British planes brought down. Rather glumly he comments, 'I think we are losing the supremacy of the air, if indeed we have ever gained it, on this front.' At the start of April, the Germans retired to the Hindenburg Line, a defensive position running from Arras to Laffaux on the River Aisne that they had built during the winter of 1916-17.

Neville was with his regiment behind Arras, billeted in what he called 'a ripping little village just out of Pernes' (a commune in the Pas de Calais). As with many people his initial enthusiasm for fighting had worn off. 'I am beginning to wonder when this war is going to end,' he wrote to his sister Mary. 'It seems endless, doesn't it? Never mind, I am wedded to the one and only 52nd.' And again, in a letter to his father on 10 April:

> The Boche is getting an awful hotting as you will have seen in the papers. Five thousand men captured! At last the end of the war is in sight, the Boche has no stomach for the fight now.

Neville was a bit fed up with being left out of the action as he was the officer left behind in charge of the reserves. But on 20 April Neville was finally called for, so he and another officer marched with their men to join the regiment north of Arras. It took them three days, and the army had neglected to provide for them—no cookers, no rations, no mess for the officers which meant that they had to forage for food. 'The whole thing was carried out in true British Army style,' he wrote. 'No-one knew we were coming and nothing was arranged for us.'

Neville found the 52nd in good spirits but the regiment had been put under severe pressure by the German guns.

> It had been in the line for a fortnight. The companies had to dig in under heavy artillery fire and many men were blown up and buried while our guns were not in a position to retaliate. I started up for the support line and on the way, I saw a Hun aeroplane come over and attack one of our Sausage Balloons (observation balloons). He fired some tracer bullets which carry a little flame behind them and ignite the petrol tank. I could see the trace of the bullets quite plainly and then two jumped out in their parachutes. The Hun circled up, turned and then potted the wretched chaps as they were floating down to the ground.

(This reads as if the Germans shot 'potted' their own men. It is not clear to me why this should be so, unless they were trying to prevent their men being taken as POWs. Or it is possible Neville has misreported the incident).

> Eventually I found B company and we observed the plain between Oppy (Wood) and Gavrelle through binoculars. Three times the Hun tried to advance and attack and three times our guns opened a hellish barrage. Then a train came up to Neuvireuil and as the German soldiers were getting out, our heavies opened up. You could see the men falling. They had a terrible gruelling.

But so did Neville's side.

> Oppy Wood which had been in full leaf and thick at that when I last saw it on the 26th, had been distinctly thinned by shell fire,' he wrote on 30 April. 'The enemy opened on our front line at 5.15 and never left us alone all day. They were crumping all round our dug-out but not actually on it, as luck would have it. There was no communication open with HQ so David Barnes sent off a carrier pigeon to try and get our guns to do a bit of counter battery work, and also ask for stretcher parties to come and remove the wounded still lying out. The

candles in the dug-out were blown out every five minutes and we had to stand to with matches!

German U-boats upped the ante during this month as they decided to attempt to starve Britain into submission by sinking US merchant ships carrying corn and other food supplies across the Atlantic. The Allies had been trying to persuade the US President Woodrow Wilson to support them in their war effort and this move by Germany sealed the deal. Wilson asked Congress for a 'war to end all wars which would make the world safe for democracy', and Congress voted to declare war on Germany on 6 April, 1917.[9]

But in spite of all that, Neville's platoon had no casualties until the evening, when orders for their relief came at 6pm:

> While we were preparing for it, our guns put over a Chinese bombardment.'[10] The enemy in retaliation blew in our dug-out. One man was buried and when extricated found to be dead. Two orderlies were also wounded. The rest of us were untouched. A composite battalion relieved us all at 11pm and never have I been so glad to get back in all my life.

Oppy Wood and the nearby village was lost and retaken three times, and two more attempts were made to take these objectives with the help of the 99th Brigade, but they remained in the hands of the Germans. According to Neville, they brought in 'tremendous reserves' to defend the place, which must mean that they saw this as a hugely important, even decisive, moment in the war. Losses on both sides were heavy. Spring 1917 was now well under way in the Pas de Calais.

Neville wrote to his sister on 10 May from Camblain-Chatelaine:

> The wood is heavenly now, carpeted with a mist of wild flowers, cowslips, blue and white violets, blue bells and a few buttercups. How I wish that there was no war on! We are now in a topping little village with very good billets. My billet is heavenly and so comfortable that I almost imagine myself at home when I wake up in the early morning. We are having a most awfully good time like a pre-war holiday and it is good to be alive to enjoy it all. Bruay is just over the hill and we make jovial parties to go in there to see the show which is the best I have seen out here. After it we have a cheery dinner at the Hotel Cerniclet, a very nice little place. We are being allowed two nights out of billets, so Grover and I have applied to go to Paris. Bingo Baines and Giles went today and we shall probably go next week. It ought to be good fun although we shall not be able to see much in 48 hours. However, I hope to be able to get to Versailles.

So it was not all ghastly.

Group of soldiers, Bruay, France, May 1917. Neville is back row, left.
John d'Arcy / NRO Nev 7/33.

Neville's father wrote often encouraging his son in the efforts he was making, and like most fathers took great pride in his son's achievements. On 22 May he wrote, 'I rejoiced to see in today's Times an extract from the *London Gazette* dated 19 May, stating that, with another, 2nd Lt JEH Neville, Oxford and Bucks Light Infantry, has been promoted to Lieutenant from Jan 1, 1917. I congratulate you dear boy on your promotion and wish you all success and happiness.' And in a touching aside he asks, 'Is it any use sending you out asparagus? It is just beginning at Sloley.'

24 May, Queen Victoria's birthday. was Empire Day and at that time an official national celebration (until 1958 when it was rebranded as Commonwealth Day). Neville senior wrote:

> I send you a few Eton clippings which may interest you. I see in today's *Times* that one of the battalions of the Oxford and Bucks has had 18 casualties—a bad business. Take care of yourself dear lad, with best love always, your affectionate father.

Of course, as spring advanced the weather warmed, bringing torrential rain instead of snow and ice. On 30 May Neville wrote that he, and B Company, were completely flooded out of the dug-out, and he had gone out to reconnoitre ground for a new trench—and incidentally to scupper any 'Boche', who might be around. One very unpleasant effect of the warmer weather was that soldiers killed months ago in the depths of winter and whose bodies had lain frozen in No Man's Land, now thawed out and the stench of death and decay filled the air. 'The whole of No Man's Land was carpeted with Canadians killed in the attack of 2 May,' Neville wrote. 'The stench was something frightful.'

There was a period of leave then for Neville and he went home to Sloley for 10 days to see his father, though he does not say what he got up to. A letter dated 14 June from Neville senior to his son tells of the lasting affectionate bond between the two men. He wrote:

> It was sad work parting from you on Victoria platform (in London), I saw your great red hand the last thing as the train took the bend. I hope you are all the better for your short, all too short, ten days, and that you will get over with your gallant and cheery spirit the inevitable reaction after your return to the dreary everyday weariness of life at the front.... God bless you my dear son and keep you safe and well. I can't tell you what pleasure it gave me to see you again, and talk to you, though I had not much of that or as much as I should have liked. And there are dozens of things I meant to have asked you but of course forgot. Here's to our next and speedy merry meeting, my lad!

Neville wrote back on 26 June from the Village Line, Canal Right Sub-Sector.

> We are in the line opposite La Bassée. The Canal is on our left. We were rushed away from the Vimy Ridge area in buses to come up here and take over from the 66th Division (which, according to rumour, was lost in England for two years!)

This was a far better position than Neville had been used to on active service. He and his men were actually due more rest time than they had been allowed, but he did not mind that much as the danger was so much less.

> 'This part of the line is an absolute rest cure compared to any I have been in so far. There are communication trenches right up to the front line. Up to now I have been accustomed to relieve over the top. I don't mind how long we stay here. On the night of 23rd we were warned that the enemy might make a raid on the regimental front. As Giles is on leave, I am in command of the company. We stood to arms all night, but no raid was attempted. They would have got an awful hotting if they had tried... I am amazed at the absence of shell fire. There are however certain things to beware of, for example "minnies", rifles grenades and "pineapples". It is possible to have 15–20 in the air at the same time,

but our Stokes Mortars can have more than that.

The most trouble he got was from rats, which thrived on the dirty conditions and grew to an enormous size, sometimes as big as a cat. 'The shooting stick is a great novelty,' he wrote to his sister. 'I am going to take it into the trenches with me and try to shoot some of the insolent rats which sit on the parapet and positively laugh at me as I go my rounds at night.'

His father meanwhile had his mind on higher matters, recommending more literature to his son:

> And how are you dear Laddie? I hope strong and well. In that awful welter of war, you want a "patient and enduring courage like old Odysseus." I wonder whether you would like Butcher and Lang's translation of *The Iliad*. After all, no-one has so thoroughly expressed the eternal characteristics of soldiers so well as Homer, and the shift of scene and the flavour of memories of Eton classrooms and sunny boyhood may be refreshing to you in the weary battle ground.[11]

And again, his father signed off with the tenderest emotions.

> My little son, you are on the threshold or your twentieth birthday. You do not know—how should you?—how you represent to me your dear mother's greatest gift, and what love and sympathy she showered on your boyhood, that love and sympathy which is your most priceless treasure. May God give you many birthdays laddie, and save you safe and unharmed from the hell of war, to be a joy to yourself and to us and to others. With best love, yr aff father.

He also sent a bottle of fine French brandy.

The weather in the trenches was dismal at the end of June and Neville found himself wading up to his knees in liquid mud. He was issued with thigh gumboots which kept him dry—very necessary as the tunnel that connected the trenches was at or below water table level. He spent a great deal of time wandering around the trenches trying to get a sense of direction.

He wrote to his father:

> You can imagine how hard it is to tell the direction of the enemy when you emerge from the tunnel into the posts,' 'You cannot possibly tell which way you have travelled underground. No-one seemed to know the exact direction of the Hun trenches, so I spent my time wandering about trying to find out posts over the top, and fell into countless shell holes full of water and mud.

Neville was about a thousand feet from the front line, but he was close enough to see some 'dazzling' displays of gunfire:

> I watched a marvellous firework display last night. Our guns were bombarding the Boche on the left with our new blazing oil shells. I expect you have read about them in the papers. It was quite dark and we could see the shells burst into gorgeous flame which sent a long arm of fire shooting to the earth. Others burst and shot the flaming liquid in a fan of fire, while others burst producing the effect of a fountain of fire. The whole sky was lit up and it was a lovely sight to watch. The troops were tickled to death with the show. I heard a man say 'That's drumming Jerry up not 'arf'. I only hope the Boche has not got any stuff like it for us.

People had been saying the war would not last long—famously, many said it would all be over 'by Christmas' 1914, the year it started. How wrong they were! But now Neville senior, a barrister and MP, predicted the end of the war in 1917, with a

Neville had been prepared for gas attacks during his Sandhurst training in 1916 where he took this photograph of a fellow cadet.

John d'Arcy / NRO Nev 7/33.

reasoned assessment of the situation. (He was wrong of course and the British Royal family were right to take the precaution on 17 July of changing the name from Saxe-Coburg, a German name, to Windsor, to avoid being seen as 'the enemy' by the British public.)

He wrote to his son:

> For the first time during this war, I think I begin to see light and an end approaching. The internal condition of Germany, the greater shortage of food and raw materials owing to the tightening of the blockade by the US, the revival of the Russian offensive, the arrival of a preliminary contingent of Yankees, the active cooperation of Greece, the political unrest in Austria, the difficulty of getting food into Germany from Holland, Scandinavia and Switzerland, the knowledge that the submarine campaign, though inflicting enormous damage, has failed to starve us out, the necessity of shipping gold from Germany into Holland in order to support the mark, are all together putting a pressure on the Germans at home, which is nearly as effective as the military pressure of the allies at the front. A member (of Parliament) told me this week that he was told in conversation by Lord French who had in turn been told by Sir Douglas Haig that the war would be over this year. I sincerely hope it may be so. The Germans will have to be desperately quick if they want to make peace before the full weight of the American troops makes itself felt, which will be beginning within 3 months from now.

Cosmo Gordon Lang, Archbishop of York with Major Crawford Stuart and others, c.1918.
Library of Congress: LC-USZ62-127642, public domain.

But the war was far from over for Neville junior. Back on duty in the front line at Le Quesnoy he wrote to his sister on July 13:

> Last night the Boche tried to kill us all with gas shells and it was my turn for duty too. They started popping them over about midnight. The cry came down the trench 'Gas'. B Company was in immediate support with gas sentries on duty, whom I had to visit during my tour of duty. The shelling went on for half an hour and I stumbled round the trenches wearing my gas mask, running into the traverses and barking my bare knees on the revetting. It was pitch black and doubly hard to see with a respirator on, but I found all the men wearing their respirators and joking with each other. There were only four casualties at the time. A shell burst right outside a dugout and the gas went straight down the stairs and gassed our stretcher-bearers and sanitary corporal, who were the oldest soldiers in the company. One has since died. When I saw them in the Air Post, one poor devil was coughing and spitting his very soul out. How I blessed the box respirator. I have just returned from having a swim in the baths at Bethune.

And he wrote again to his sister on 24 July from Cambrai, when he confessed that he might not be cut out for work in the army:

> The last two nights I have spent on patrol which does not amuse me much. It's too exciting. Our wire is most awfully hard to negotiate and I get hung up and torn unmercifully. I was never made for a boy scout to crawl on my belly, for my displacement

> is too great. Patrolling would be good fun if only the enemy had no rifles, bombs, or machine guns which take the interest out of the whole affair. I fear that I am no soldier; the longer I stay out here, the more I seem to reverence the Boche and his ways and his shells and his rifle grenades and bullets. We are living the life of rats who only venture forth at night, and the whole thing is horribly monotonous. The weather has become perfectly glorious which makes this life more irksome, because I feel that I was not make to live like this in glorious sunny weather. The trenches become as hot as ovens and flies are breeding as only flies can. Never mind, it will be over soon.

Neville was less than impressed when a personage no less than the Archbishop of York, Cosmo Gordon Lang (and later Archbishop of Canterbury), came to take a service for the fighting men at Bruay-la Buissière to the northwest of Lens.

He wrote on July 28 to his father:

> I happened to sit next to an officer in the 52nd Canadians, General Horne, the Army Commander who introduced the Archbishop. I was not very impressed by his lecture. I was sitting right at the back of the theatre and he seemed to lower his voice at the end of every sentence, which is a criminal fault in a speaker. He laid great stress on self-discipline and the duties of an officer after the war, and said that he thought the men who had done the fighting would have the first word in everything which, to my mind, is impossible. He spoke for an hour and when he had finished Horne got up and said in five minutes all that it had taken an hour for the archbishop to say.

Back at home his father, while not worried to the bone about his son's chances of survival, seemed to understand that his son's life was no picnic. I' fear you must be having a horrible existence in those sweltering trenches,' he wrote on 28 July. 'I suppose gunfire thunders away all day and night, and midges and mosquitos add to your discomfort. There have been reports of raids both by our men and the enemy in the neighbourhood of La Bassée, but it looks as if you are fighting at night and that the push is made further north. Your sector will be engaged all along the line. I have heard the thunder of the guns in Flanders after traffic has died down, and the German communiqués mention that the intensity of the gun fire in Flanders is greater than on the Somme.'

Neville senior also mentions a report in *The Times* about the origins of the war and its timing. In the same letter he wrote, '*The Times* today publishes an interesting account of a secret meeting between the Kaiser and the Austrian Archduke and the heads of the German, Austrian and Hungarian staffs and Foreign Offices on July 5th 1914, when the ultimatum to Serbia was deliberately planned so as to force Russia and France into the war, and that probably the order for mobilisation was given in Germany about that time, more than three weeks before the declaration of war, though the Kaiser on July 6th 1914 rushed off for three weeks yachting in Norway to put everyone off the scent.' An interesting theory.

By contrast Neville in the trenches (Robertson's Tunnel, July 30) asked in a letter to his father whether he had watched a fight in Palace Yard between two MPs, Noel Pemberton Billing and Colonel Archer-Shee, of which there was an account in the paper. 'What an exhibition!' he wrote. 'I should fancy that Pemberton Billing is pretty unpopular in the House now. I see that he had challenged Archer-Shee to a twenty-round boxing match in aid of charity and that the Colonel declined, retorting that he is at present engaged in fighting Germans, which Pemberton Billing ought also to be doing. Nasty one for PB, he has made himself pretty notorious lately, hasn't he?'[12]

It is unclear whether Neville senior was indulging in another spot of wishful thinking, hoping that the war would suddenly end and his only son would then return to England, but yet again he expresses a view that the end—i.e. victory for the Allies, cannot be far off.

He wrote on 31 July :

> The German news is that … they are enduring a worse bombardment than anything yet felt whether on the Somme or Arras. They are nervous. The morale of the German regiments (according to members of Parliament back from the front) is rapidly diminishing and they think that the real debacle is about to begin, when the elite Storm Troopers depart. The French have held their own and have badly dented the German belief in their own invincibility. The prospect of a fourth winter campaign must depress them, especially as the strictness of the American blockade makes it clear that they cannot draw supplies from abroad.[13]

And again, he rather sweetly asks his son if he still has his chess set.

> Shall I send you out another set? You know how highly I look upon chess as a pastime for employing weary hours. My father found it a godsend on board ship in his journeys to India.' (His father James Sewell White was a High Court judge in Calcutta). Best love little son, and God bless you my dear, dear boy, always yr aff Father.

The month of August starts with Neville musing to his sister Angela in a letter about the meaning of this war, which had nothing to do in his opinion, with 'avenging Belgium', which had been invaded and taken over by Germany in the early days of the First World War.[14] Some of the men under Neville's command seemed not to have 'the foggiest clue' about what they were fighting for, and others either did not know or even care that much.

> 'People at home, from what I gather, seem to be obsessed with the idea that the army will fight to the death to avenge Belgium. Nothing is further from the truth. We shall go on fighting until we are told to stop.

> The men here do not hate the Boche because they are the Boche. They hate them as an enemy and for what they have done, or are supposed to have done. Belgium and her rights, the occupation of Serbia, never enter anyone's thoughts at all. We are fighting for those at home to save them from the fate of Belgium and Serbia.

There is then a gap for a full four weeks, so the next letter, again to his sister, this time from Braddell Castle near Cuinchy is dated 4 September. By this time Neville had been fighting on foreign soil for just over six months, though it seemed a great deal longer to him. And he complained that he had heard nothing from his family since 25 August (though it does not appear that he has written to them either).

He wrote:

> I am waiting for the mail to come in. Thrice blessed mail, the soldier's only joy or one of the few. Here it comes, hurrah.

> No letter from home, as usual. Only a pass book. What is the matter with you all? Can't you find any pens? I enclose a Field Message form for you to write to me on. Just sign your name.

Dear Neville, what a sense of humour! He also reported on a nasty mosquito bite. 'The swelling on my face has gone down,' he wrote, 'but I fear that this will leave a scar like the one caused by that loathsome boil.' His father wrote back with sympathy. 'I am sorry to hear you have had a virulent gnat bite. I know what it is and shall carry to my grave the mark of the beast that bit me on the cheek in 1911 at Barton (Broad), since when I have always had mosquito curtains at Sloley. You will have to be careful about it and get it clean and well: when mine was all cleaned out I had a hole in my cheek as big as a sixpence.' Blood poisoning from an infected bite could lead to death in the days before penicillin. Lord Carnarvon, of Tutankhamen fame, was bitten on the neck by a mosquito in Egypt and died just six weeks later.

At this time Neville's military life was fairly quiet. There was always the possibility of an attack, but the action seemed subdued. According to newspaper reports, it had not moved elsewhere, but the whole of the Western Front was nothing like as busy or dangerous as it had been the previous year (in the Battle of the Somme June 1916). Neville wrote that he was enjoying an early morning swim most days in the nearby canal which was 'dirtier than the River Ant at Irstead!' (on the Norfolk Broads). He also kept up with world news and was horrified by what was happening in Russia as that country geared up for the (October) Revolution. He wrote to his father on 12 September, 1917, from Cuinchy Barracks to say:

> Civil war between Kerensky (a lawyer and key political figure) and Kornilov (a top military man in the Bolshevik army)! Whatever will happen now? Altogether the war is most depressing nowadays, there is nothing to cheer us up except the Italian offensive,[15] which although very fine, will not make any material difference to the length of the war. Peace seems further off than ever, but I suppose we shall have to stick it until someone at home thinks he had lost enough out of it.

What did eventually cheer Neville up was listening to a vivid account of the retreat of the 10th Irish Division through Serbia by an officer, NG Clarke, posted to D Company.

> I was simply amazed at what he had been through while his platoon was rearguard to his regiment', Neville wrote to his sister on September 13.
>
> He was cut off twice by the Bulgars and completely separated from the rest of the British Force. Yet he managed to evade the enemy. He landed at Salonika in Mesopotamian kit and then had to go through Balkan winter in shorts, with the temperature 20 degrees below zero. I heard how on one occasion he took a sentry off the fire step and the sentry left his feet in his boots, frozen to the ground. He saw the Scottish nurses who had retreated all the way from Belgrade sleeping by the roadside, marching with the men, leading their pack mules, in the fighting line with the troops enduring all their hardships and yet not giving in, their kit torn to ribbons, no hats, no skirts.
>
> And this officer who had been attacked, surrounded and who had charged with the bayonet because the bolts of the rifles were frozen, has got no reward. No honours list has come out for that campaign: a great retreat, terrific cold, only one field gun in support, boots worn out, clothes practically non-existent and yet no official recognition. He told me how he saw some Zouaves (a class of light infantry regiments in the French army) attack and carry all before them, knifing the Bulgars and slitting them up, how they re-formed and charged again. In the last lap of the retreat he was in command of the rearguard, left behind to hold a pass for four hours at all costs. He retired at the end of the four hours and marched until his men could go no further. Then he formed a square and slept until dawn. On waking up he saw Bulgars in his rear, so each man of his party picked out one of the enemy and they fired together. The Bulgars blew bugles and beat drums under cover of which commotion he was able to slip round a spur and eventually reached Greek soil. Apparently, he only lost five men out of twenty. I have never heard a more vivid account of fighting. He was under orders to join the 43rd when he transshipped and landed at Salonika.[16]

On 16 September Neville wrote from Cambrin to his father saying there was little of excitement to report, but in the same letter he mentions, almost casually, that one of his men (Platoon Serjeant Boddington) had been sniped through the head while looking over the top (of a trench) at two Germans who had just thrown a bomb, and a fellow officer (Ames) had had a leg blown off by a 'pineapple' which burst right at his feet. Both survived, and crucially for Brits, retained their sense of humour. 'The serjeant lost a lot of blood,' wrote Neville. 'But seemed quite cheerful when I bid him goodbye at the Aid Post. And I found Ames lying stretched on the fire-step. All he said was "Isn't this bloody!"' A few days later he wrote to his sister Angela from Le Preole, where his regiment was taking a rest, saying, 'We are having a topping time, riding, swimming etc'. By this time everyone was so used to the awful conditions of the war that the only way to survive was to ignore it or make a joke out of it.

Neville's family were on tenterhooks at the end of September. *The Times* had reported that the Germans had made a raid west of La Bassée, very close to where young Neville was based, and at the same time he was due for leave around 2-3 October. His father was hoping that his son would be home to enjoy the lovely Indian summer in Norfolk in Sloley where the estate had produced a fine crop of grapes. 'Not only many bunches but also very fine berries,' he wrote. 'We shall soon be gathering apples and pears, and potatoes have done better than Billham (the gardener) ever remembers, good sized heavy tubers with clean skins and no disease.'

Notes

1 *Royal Cousins at War*, Andrew Marr on BBC1, September 2017.

2 *Grandmother of a Nation, Queen Elizabeth the Queen Mother*, by Sara Barton-Wood, Hodder and Stoughton, 1999.

3 As quoted in *Great Britain's Great War* (p.32) by Jeremy Paxman, Penguin 2013.

4 Lupton's Tower at Eton College, built in 1520 by Henry Redman, is part of Lupton's Range which provides accommodation for the Head of the College (the Provost). Roger Lupton (1456–1539) was an English lawyer and cleric who served as chaplain to both King Henry VII, and to his son King Henry VIII, and was appointed by the former as Provost of the College. Eton College website December 2017.

5 Edward of Woodstock, known as the Black Prince, was the eldest son of Edward III of England. He participated in the early years of the Hundred Years War but predeceased his father and so never became king. In 1346 Edward commanded the vanguard at the Battle of Crécy, and was named the Black Prince after the battle, at which he was said to be wearing black armour. Wikipedia, December 2017.

6 The Second Battle of the Somme, 1918, was fought during WW1 on the Western Front from late August to early September, in the basin of the River Somme. It was part of a series of successful counter-offensives in response to the German Spring Offensive, after a pause for redeployment and supply. Wikipedia, December 2017.

7 The use of slang terms for various types of ammunition in WW1 was wide and fascinating. A Minnie was one name for a heavy trench mortar, about five feet long and which shot a shell with ninety-three pounds of high explosive, with a range of well over 1,000 feet. Even though no shell fragments might touch a man, the explosion was so powerful as to cause severe concussion which would burst his insides like a kernel of popcorn causing instant death. A Minnie was also known as a Flying Pig (because it was shaped like a pig with a curly tail), a Sausage or a Rum Jar. A Pineapple, so-called because its body was serrated into tiny chunks, was a bit smaller being a German mortar shell eight inches long with a hollow stem which would be slipped over a gun when fired. It had fish-tail shaped wings and was also known as the Fish Tail. Firstworldwar.com, December 2017.

8 The Russian Revolution, Wikipedia December 2017, Britannica.com, December 2017.

9 American entry to WW1, American-historama.org, December 2017.

10 Chinese bombardment—this was a preliminary artillery bombardment which signalled to the enemy that an infantry assault was probable once the bombardment finished. Firstworldwar.com, December 2017.

11 Homer's Iliad is the famous description, set during the mythical Trojan War, of the quarrel between King Agamemnon and the warrior Achilles. Written in ancient Greek, it is an epic poem in dactylic hexameter often studied at A level by students of classics. Wikipedia, December 2017.

12 Noel Pemberton Billing was a highly eccentric MP, notable for his bombastic speeches, who became known as 'The Minister for Air', as 'the air' was the focus of most of his speeches. His other focus was treachery, or rather conspiracy theories. Despite his own wife being half German, he lobbied for all those of German extraction to be interned or deported, along with Jews and homosexuals. He founded a right-wing newspaper called *The Imperialist* to spread his views. Sir Martin Archer-Shee was a Conservative politician, currently serving as Lieutenant-Colonel commanding three different battalions, including the Gloucester Regiment, the Yorks and Lancaster Regiment and the King's Own Scottish Borderers. Wikipedia, November 2017.

13 American ships took up positions with the British Royal Navy for a blockade of the North Sea to prevent the German High Seas Fleet from operating. It lasted even after the armistice into 1919, but was completely uneventful. Wikipedia, November 2017.

14 The treatment of Belgium by German soldiers is considered disgraceful. It became known as 'the rape of Belgium'. Germany went so far as to claim that resistance by the Belgian army was 'illegal' and there were mass executions of both civilians and military personnel which were entirely gratuitous. Wikipedia, November 2017.

15 The Italian Offensive to which Neville refers is a series of battles fought on the border between Italy and Austro-Hungary. Italy had entered the war in order to gain territory in Austria with a surprise offensive. But their efforts quickly got bogged down in trench warfare not dissimilar to the Western Front, but at high altitudes and with very cold winters. Much of the civilian population was displaced by the fighting. Wikipedia, November 2017.

16 The Macedonian Front of WW1, also known as the Salonica Front, was formed by the Allies to try to help Serbia against the combined attack by Germany, Austria-Hungary and Bulgaria. But the aid was too late and in insufficient force to prevent the fall of Serbia, and was complicated by the internal political crisis in Greece. Nevertheless, a front was formed, running from the Adriatic coast at Albania to the Struma River. The Macedonian Front remained stable, despite local actions, until the great Allied offensive in September 1918, when Bulgaria and Serbia were liberated. Wikipedia, November 2017.

The War Years 1917–18

October 1917

Neville's father continued to plan enthusiastically for his son's forthcoming leave, asking him in a letter dated 2 October, 1917, if the two of them could expect to travel down to Norfolk together from London. Would the son like a day shooting pheasant with Edward Cubitt (a neighbouring farmer), and another day shooting duck with Jack Cator at Woodbastwick? Or even a day with Major Jary at South Walsham?

Neville's last letter before his leave, 4 October, 1917, was written from Cuinchy. 'Thank you for the lovely lavender enclosed in your last letter,' he wrote. How wonderful to have a father who will send you a sweet-smelling herb when you are in the middle of the disgusting hell of war! Young Neville commented in the same letter that he had had a bath for the first time in two weeks which was 'very necessary as for the first time I found crawlers in my clothes'. Sadly, there is no reference to what he got up to on leave. I'm guessing it would be shooting, partying and visiting family and friends.

Neville game shooting while on vacation from Eton.

John d'Arcy / NRO Nev 7/33.

By the end of October he was back in France and feeling, understandably, very low. 'I am beginning to despair of this filthy business ever having an end,' he wrote to his sister on 2 November from Marles-les-Mines.

> Italy has bitched things so badly. Germany has had wonderful luck in her autumn campaigns: Belgium in '14, Serbia in '15, Rumania in '16 and Italy in '17, while we and the French hold on like grim death, giving help to all the allies in turn.[1]
>
> The situation is not convincing of victory for us. In theory we may be winning but in practice we seem a long way off. The Boches know that they cannot win against us and so strike at our weaker allies. The result seems good as far as they are concerned.' His father tried to put a positive spin on things, saying the situation was not 'irretrievable.

If it draws the Italians together and extinguishes the lamentable political intrigues which have cursed Italy for so long,' he wrote, 'then it will unite their nation as it has never yet been united. All through her history, England has never been so near her victory and her triumph as when externally things looked blackest—and so I trust it will be now.

November 1917

Neville was on leave again at the start of November in Marles-les-Mines (though this time it appears he was still in France), moaning to his sister in a letter about how he despaired of the war ever coming to an end. But on 6 November, leave came to an end and Neville and the regiment marched 15 miles to Les Ciseaux. He said it was 'quite pleasant' but the weather was closing in for winter now.

> Mud and water reign supreme once more; discomfort begins afresh, the same as last winter all over again and, I suppose, next winter too'

The march continued until Le Nouveau Monde, where Neville developed dreadful toothache, but there was no such thing as a proper dentist's surgery and a soothing anaesthetic before a tooth was extracted. Men were men in those days and Neville describes the procedure in this way.

> This is the third day of continuous aching. I got the doctor to yank one out while I sat on a soap box perched on a midden outside the Aid Post. Unfortunately, it was the wrong tooth! It was a perfectly good one and must have been aching from reflex action. All the farm hands watched the operation and laughed like hell'

The correct tooth was finally extracted by an army dentist at Poperinghe (about 30 miles away in Flanders, some seven miles due west of Ypres, and known colloquially to Brits as 'Pop'. It is now the site of a large war cemetery).

By now the Battle of Cambrai was in full swing.[2] This was a British offensive, followed by a German counter-offensive, in the Pas-de-Calais. The intent was to capture Cambrai which was an important supply area for the Germans, and to this end the new British Mark IV tank was brought into operation for the first time as a main component for cutting and clearing the deep barbed wire obstacles in front of German positions.

The usual pattern prior to this was to use heavy guns to pound German defensive positions, but that of course gave away the element of surprise. With the 400 tanks moving forward more quietly, the Germans were not ready (though the Germans had an idea of the plan through intelligence reports).

The first day was a huge success. It started at about 6am on 10 November with the Hindenburg Line severely broken with advances of up to 5 miles. The British lost about 4,000 men, and took 4,200 prisoners. By World War I rates, the numbers were not too bad—it was

Mark IV tank, now preserved at Ashford, Kent.

Peter Trimming, CC BY-SA 2.0.

only half that at Passchendaele—and the advance over 6 hours was greater than over three months in Flanders.

But the rate of advance was slowed on day two. The British took to consolidation rather than expanding further. Follow-up troops took over 15 hours to reach the front line. The final effort to push forward was on November 27 when the notorious General Haig tried to capture Bourlon Wood, but failed and suffered another 4,000 casualties.

The Germans launched a counter-offensive and the early British successes were reversed. On November 28 more than 16,000 shells were fired into the wood by the Germans, and the British machine gunners returned fire fiercely, with one group firing over 70,000 rounds. This was impressive, but the concentration of effort here inevitably allowed greater opportunities for the Germans to push back elsewhere.

Haig was forced to order a withdrawal from the north and by 7 December, all the British gains were given up, apart from a small portion of the Hindenburg Line to the north. Both sides lost a staggering 40,000 (including dead, wounded and prisoners taken). The battle turned into yet another bloody and pointless exercise on the Western Front. It is remembered principally for the successful use of tanks, which of course the Germans subsequently used to terrifying advantage in World War II.

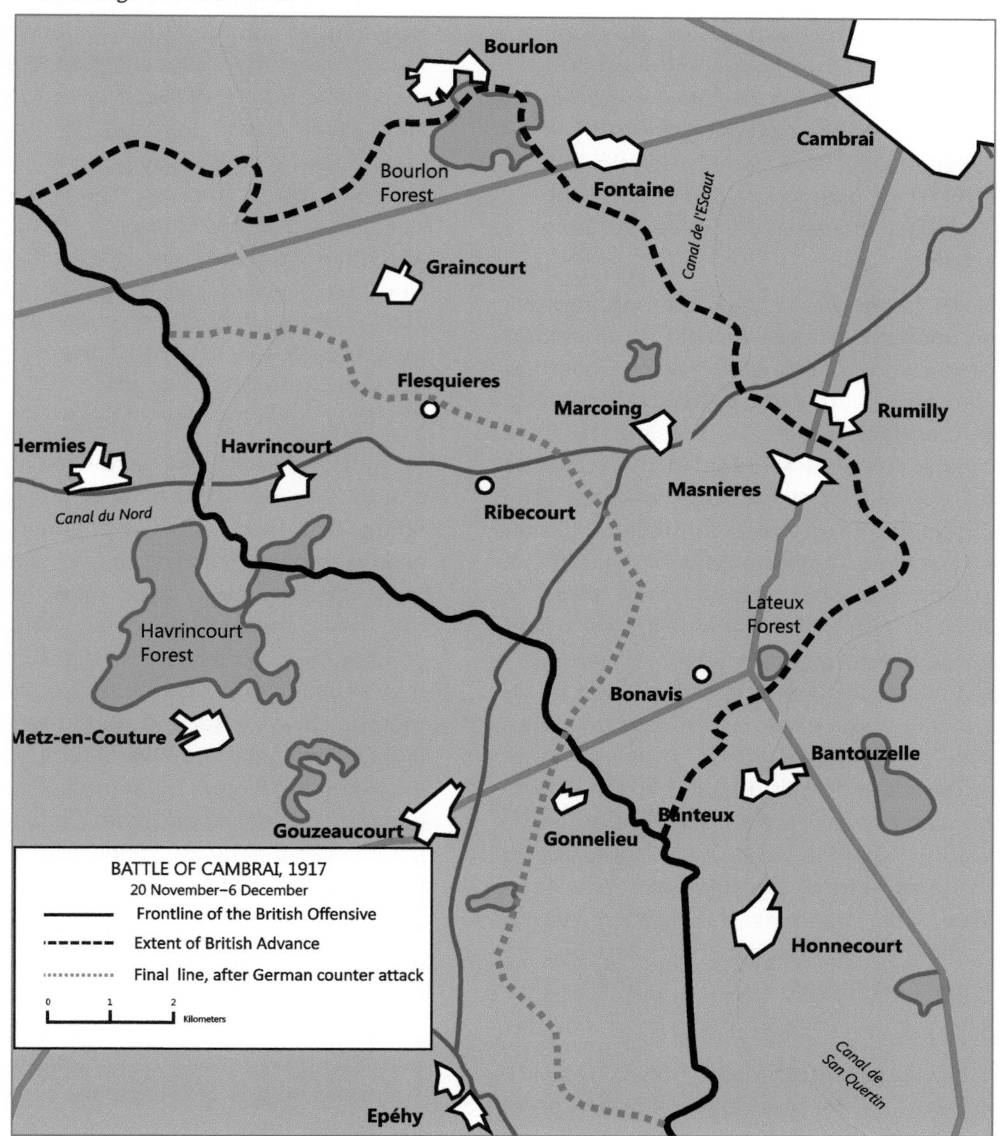

Battle of Cambrai, 1917.
redrawn from a map by W. Wolney, CC BY-SA 3.0.

Neville does not mention the battle by name and was not allowed to write home with details until the fighting was over. But he was quite excited by it all and wrote to his sister on November 15 from Winnizeele (on the northern border of France). 'We are still a great distance behind the line doing little or nothing. But we can easily hear the distant roar of the guns and at night the whole sky is lit up with their flashes. I have heard a few bombardments in my time and seen the effect at night but never have I heard or seen anything like this at so great a distance. It is something colossal.' And again, to his father on November 16:

> Please don't get the wind up on my account. We are miles behind the line and therefore out of it all. I am hastening to let you know that all is well. It looks as if they have forgotten us. We have moved again and the Regiment is now under canvas in the midst of oceans of mud though the officers are well off in comfortable billets.

His father wrote back offering support and encouragement—and asking what food the son would like sent out for the Christmas celebrations. 'You are a little vague about pork and sausages for the men's Xmas dinners. Angela has gone to the stores to find out what they can do. Pork is a little ambiguous. I suppose you mean carcasses of fresh pork. These would be rather difficult to send out owing to the time taken in transit. It seems to me the regiment would need a special permit to get sufficient pork for Xmas through, for it is not stuff that keeps very well and I have never heard of tinned pork, and should think it was rather dangerous stuff; salt pork in barrels used to be a staple food of the Navy in the eighteenth century. I shall be very glad to subscribe to the Xmas fund of the regiment. Who is at home who manages this branch of the regiment's commissariat? God bless you my dear son. With best love yr aff father.'

December

Neville obviously realised his family were very worried. He was right in the middle of the action, but he could not relate any details until he knew the action was over and it was safe to put it into a letter which might well have fallen into enemy hands. Finally, on December 11, he was able to put them out of their misery. 'You seem to be very anxious about me and I am sorry that I have been unable to put you out of the anxiety. I will now try to tell you what happened. The 5th Brigade was luckily for us in reserve when the enemy attacked the Division. We woke up to the tune of a barrage which we could see plastering our front line. I said to myself, "Now we are for it", and at noon the 52nd moved up to support the two brigades (6th & 99th) in the front line as help was required.

> We stayed at Lock 7 for some time and then orders were received for the Regiment to counter-attack the Sugar Factory on the Bapaume-Cambrai road; (as a matter of fact this factory had never been captured by the enemy though it was being pasted to hell). We moved forward again soon after into Hughes Support Trench which ran parallel to the Hindenburg Line. Here we remained from 5 pm till 2 am. The trench had been evacuated by some reserve troops of the 47th. Division, who had left their packs stacked high in the bays of the trench.
>
> We were packed like sardines, my platoon occupying half a traverse only. Some very heavy stuff was coming over at odd intervals and one 8" shell laid out twenty men. As you know, you can hear these very heavy birds coming from a considerable distance; they seem to take ages to arrive and there is always a second during their flight, when you know whether they are going to fall near or far from you. I heard this particular bird from afar and felt relieved that he was going to plant himself away from us.
>
> Then I began to doubt my supposition: a second later it was touch and go: then I realised that it was probably going to blot me out. I lived through one agonizing second of uncertainty. There was no way of escape; we could not dodge the brute as we were too

cramped for space. With a tearing, rushing mighty roar as of an express train screaming at top speed through an enclosed station, it crashed in the next bay from me, right in the middle of my platoon.

I darted round the corner and found a shambles. It had fallen in the centre of the trench, a magnificent shot from the enemy's point of view. Among the killed was Serjeant Archer, platoon Serjeant of No. 7 and a damned good chap. The only man who escaped untouched of all the men in that bay was sitting on the top of a pile of packs at the foot of which the shell had landed. The packs were utterly destroyed and he was lifted off his perch but unhurt. As soon as it got dark, we collected some bits of men, put them in a sandbag, carried out the recognisable bodies over the top and dumped them in a shell-hole; and Billy Barnard said the Lord's Prayer over their remains. I think it was probably the only prayer he knew for certain.

By 2 am we were pretty hungry as we had had nothing to eat since 7 am, but we moved forward again in the moonlight to Kangaroo Alley, a trench behind the Bapaume-Cambrai road. There was only desultory shelling at the time and we were extraordinarily lucky in that respect. We stayed in Kangaroo Alley till the evening of 1 December, when B Company went up to the front line for 48 hours. The trench was very shallow and broad, and the weather was excruciatingly cold, so much so that sentries could only watch on the fire-step for half an hour. We were in the front line from the evening of the 1st till the evening of the 3rd and had no casualties.

On the night of the 1st and 2nd there were bombing attacks on our left, made by the 6th Brigade to try and extricate a company of the 13th Essex Regiment, which had been cut off at Lock 5 and Moeuvres and surrounded when the Boche attacked on 30 November. This gallant handful of officers and men were still holding out in spite of their predicament and were annoying the enemy with great success by sniping over the parapet. I am afraid the bombing attacks failed in both cases and the Essex had to surrender when their ammunition was exhausted.

In the trenches (the officer is unnamed).
John d'Arcy / NRO Nev 7/33.

We watched these attacks from our front line. It was very thrilling. We could see the shells bursting over the enemy's trenches and the smaller flashes from the Mills bombs' (the first modern-type British fragmentation hand grenades, widely used in the Great War).[3] The darkness meanwhile was continually lit up by Verey lights which burst high in the frosty night and fell into the rolling clouds of smoke. They were rather grim firework displays.

We went back into support when the front line was evacuated, and we were left at the front line for 48 hours. A and B companies were in the front line, A holding Lock 6 where Dick Warren was in command, while we held about 400 yards of Kangaroo Alley on the right. This was a very long stretch and meant posting one man in every other bay for battle stations.

We had quite a quiet time until the morning of 5 December, when Fritz showed a lot of activity. We could see tin hats worming towards our line on the left where there was a trench along the canal bank. We sent back this information to headquarters and Seale came up to see if he could get at them with his trench mortars. This he did and discouraged the Boche a lot, by lobbing over a few really good shots. However, early in the afternoon they started to creep forward again and the bombing post was kept busy until at about 3 pm a whizz-bang barrage came over.[4]

I was sitting in Company HQ with Billy Barnard when it opened. I rushed upstairs and along the trench to the right to get to my platoon area. The shelling was pretty hot, the damned things bursting first in front of me and then behind me, so that I expected to catch one all to myself in each bay. However, I reached my platoon safely and found the men standing-to in battle order. Scarcely had I sat down on the fire-step for a breather when an orderly popped his head round the corner of the trench and told me I was wanted at Company HQ as the Captain was hit.

So back I had to go, running the gauntlet of the damned whizz-bangs. I found Billy B sitting on the top step of the dugout nursing his left knee. He had been hit by a shell splinter. The stretcher-bearers were just contemplating the removal of his great bulk when a man of the bombing post on the left reported that the enemy was in the trench. Billy B got up at once and hobbled down the trench towards the canal which was our only covered line of retreat and incidentally towards the post which had reported the entry of the enemy into our trench. As it happened, the lad who brought the message was not telling the truth, thank God. He was a bit windy, for the corporal (Tilbury) had only told him to tell Billy B that the enemy was massing in the trench immediately **opposite** his post.

Billy's departure left me in command of the company to carry out a rearguard action retirement later. I was taken by surprise and had the wind up badly lest I should make a mess of it. All afternoon rumours came round that the enemy was massing at different map references. One report stated that the Lock had been captured on our left. This came just after Billy was wounded and put the wind up me badly. Thank heaven it was also false but all the same it was most alarming.

We held this position until the evening of the 6th. A message from Regimental HQ reached me early in the afternoon stating the time at which we were to withdraw and I issued orders accordingly so that there should be no confusion or noise; but twenty minutes before the time, the Boche attacked Lock 6 and got into it so that A Company on my left, which was responsible for the Lock, was compelled to retire immediately. I had had no idea what was happening until a terrific explosion rent the air and bits of the Lock sailed through space. It had been mined by the sappers and was to have been blown up by a time fuse after A Company had evacuated it and when, it was hoped, there would be a big convoy of Boche making themselves comfortable inside the lockmaster's quarters. A few minutes after the explosion Dick Warren sauntered into my trench and told me that he had given the order to the sappers to blow the mine and that when it went up, there were about twenty of the enemy inside. So they were caught after all.

My original line of retreat down the Canal bed was now cut off, so I sent three platoons (one attached from D Company to help me man the line) down a road running towards the rear, led by Windross, the only other officer left in the Company. This road was completely exposed and liable to be swept by machine gun fire at any moment. I had visions of heavy casualties. The enemy, however, did not fire and the platoons got away safely. We got back without a single casualty which was extremely lucky considering how Fritz had plastered that road the night before.

The 2nd Division saved the whole of the ground won on 20 November in the Bourlon Wood—Moeuvres area by hanging on so long.[5] There were six enemy divisions against the 2nd and the front-line troops inflicted such severe casualties that all the six German divisions are now out of the line recuperating. The 52nd had none of the hard fighting or perhaps I should not be able to write this. The other two brigades, the 6th and 99th, did marvellously well.'

But there was one final injury for Neville. Unfortunately, Angela's Buzzard cake and a bottle of port and whisky were left behind in the dugout. I hadn't time to see to the packing up of the food so the Boches must have had a good feed off us, blast 'em.

We came out of the line on the night of the 6th and are now well back for a rest. We had the hell of a march back in pouring rain; the men were splendid and marched valiantly considering that they had full marching order with packs. The responsibility of that rearguard was the worst part of it and the knowledge that if I floated, one hundred men's lives would be on my head. I am now temporarily in command of B Company but Giles will be back soon to take over. Don't be anxious about me. I have done a year and there is no reason why I should not carry on for another.' Of course, his family could not help but be anxious, but they were also immensely proud of Neville for taking charge of so much during the battle, and his father wrote and told him so.

Reginald wrote:

I was delighted to get last night your letter written last Tuesday Dec. 11, giving us in some detail an account of your experiences in the line for the seven days ending Dec 5th. Horley has marked on my map where he left the regiment and I gather from today's map in the *Times*, that these trenches which when you entered them on Nov. 27th are now somewhere near, if not in fact, our present front line. I can well understand how deeply you felt your responsibility in being in command of the Company for a rearguard action, and I think you can take heart for the future from the very successful way in which you carried out the duties of commanding officer, without a single casualty, though your line of retreat was cut off by the loss of the lock and the absence of support consequently on your left. Thank God you are safely through that peril and that you did your job with conspicuous gallantry success and good fortune.

There is one more letter from father to son, written on Christmas Eve 1917, as the family prepared for their usual celebrations at Sloley Hall.

I think of you, dear lad, these cold and cheerless nights and pray that you may keep warm. You, like the shepherds of old, are keeping watch by night and I hope you will have the beatific vision like them—and have joy in your heart for your gallant duty done—your sacrifices patiently and cheerfully borne—and I hope you will have a festive time among your brothers in the mess. Be sure our thoughts and wishes and hopes and prayers will be with you.

I sent you off a little book containing Shakespeare's historical plays. I want you to love Falstaff, the Prince and Harry Hotspur and all the rest of them. I fear the little book got scarcely through the press of Xmas mails.' And touchingly Neville senior adds a little local gossip. 'I called and saw the Radcliffes yesterday and saw Willoughby who has ceased to be an Eton schoolboy. He joins the O.T.C. (Officers' Training Corps) at Bushey in February, so he gets a longer holiday than usual, clever boy. I heard no news of any sort from them. I also called on Mrs Blewitt who sent you her kindest remembrances. She is a jolly good woman, I think. Uncle Norman has sent us a Wensleydale cheese, jolly good of him, Ben Slocock left us yesterday to go to his people at Maidenhead. This is all my news, dear Jim. God bless you and give you joy and all the fortitude and comfort your heart desires from your father.

After Christmas Neville wrote and told the family how the festival had gone for him. He was no longer in the trenches, so was able to enjoy a proper dinner.

We all collected in our shack at 7.30. pm with a snow-storm going on outside. It was devilish cold and we were packed like sardines, and every time the servants came in to the entrance and parted the canvas curtain, a drift of snow blew in. At the other end there was a blazing fire, of huge logs. The fireplace made by us was a roaring success.

The Colonel carved the chicken or rather pulled it to pieces because, he said, he was not a married man. The

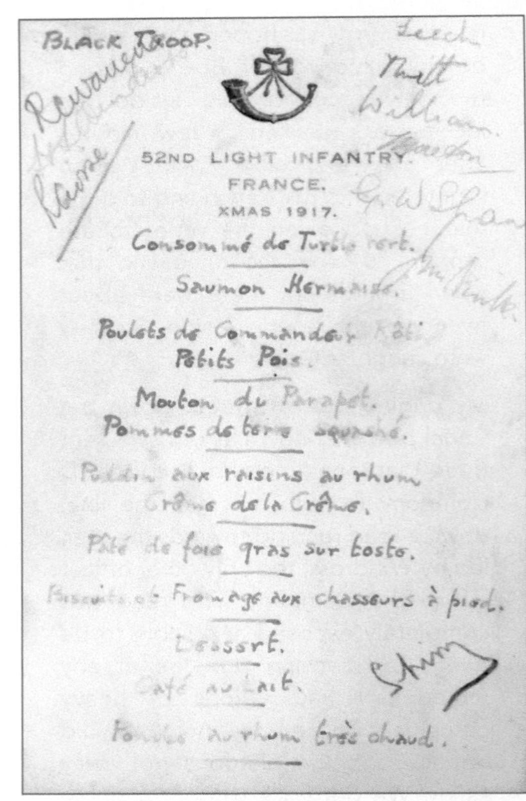
BLACK TROOP.

52ND LIGHT INFANTRY.
FRANCE.
XMAS 1917.

Consommé de Turtle vert.

Saumon Hermaise.

Poulets de Commandeur Rôti
Petits Pois.

Mouton du Parapet.
Pommes de terre squashé.

Puddin aux raisins au rhum
Crême de la Crême.

Pâté de foie gras sur tosto.

Biscuits et Fromage aux chasseurs à pied.

Dessert.

Café au Lait.

Ponche au rhum très chaud.

Christmas dinner menu 1917.
John d'Arcy / NRO Nev 7/33.

plum pudding was excellent and came in, in sheets of flame. Rum punch brought up the rear. A rather funny thing happened which had not been pre-arranged. The shack had been made when there was eighteen inches of frost on the ground, and when the snow thawed a great lump of mud fell down the Colonel's neck at which we all shouted and cried for a speech which was not forthcoming. After dinner we had the tables and trestles taken out and had a rough house in the dark as all our candles had been expended by that time. The Colonel and Twitt had a good scrap. We are now out of the line, thank heaven, but it has been almost impossible to sleep owing to the cold.

Just before New Year his Christmas present arrived from his father, a copy of Shakespeare's Henry V. 'Today I received my trench boots and also that Shakespeare which I am charmed with,' Neville wrote back to his father with thanks. 'I looked up Henry V Act IV Scene III and the famous passage before Agincourt. I love that passage. It is a priceless book to have out here.'[6]

> There was a snow-storm in the evening and the ground is now 6 inches under snow. It makes everything look so fine and sparkling and covers up the tortures of war indiscriminately. As you know we are now out of the line—maybe for some time. The Division has done very well this tour and has made another name for itself.

And so ended Neville's first full year of serving in the British Army. He was not only still alive, but had distinguished himself in battle, taking charge when his commanding officer had been called away. Not bad for a man who was only 20 years old.

January 1918

Neville was stationed at Warloy, near Amiens, at the start of January 1918, and while there were no grand offensives from the Germans, there were from time to time some 'good shots now and again'. His friend Dick Warren had returned to England for medical treatment on a badly injured thumb, and the Colonel and Shiny Horley were visiting Billy Barnard in hospital in Rouen.

By now the winter was biting and Neville complained in his letter to sister Jane that:

> The cold is intense and just as bad as last year. It is bad luck that we should have two such severe winters. The snow has been lying since 23 December. I am in a billet with a bed for the first time since 20 November, which is a great treat. All the same, I far prefer the floor of a Nissen hut with the Regiment, to a feather bed away from it. On the way here, we passed over the old No Man's Land of the Somme. I cannot compare it with Ypres as I have never been there, but there was no surface there at all. It is one huge shell hole knocked to pieces by other shell holes, if you follow me.

Neville does not say how he heard the news that he had been awarded the Military Cross for his actions in the Battle of Cambrai. Obviously, he was pleased to have gained that recognition, and wrote to his father on 13 January from the Musketry School at Warloy.

'Letters of congratulation have been pouring in lately, redirected from the Regiment,' he wrote. 'I shall be up to my eyes trying to answer them all. I am more glad than I can say that you should be so pleased about it. You must remember that it is only the MC. I might have got the VC by your letters. You may well ask what I got it for because I'm blowed if I know. Nowadays it signifies nothing considering that bakers at Rouen get it.' Not quite true!

Understandably his proud father was overjoyed and sent out four hundredweight of coal to the 30 cottagers in Sloley in commemoration of the award. On 19 January his father wrote to him to say he had

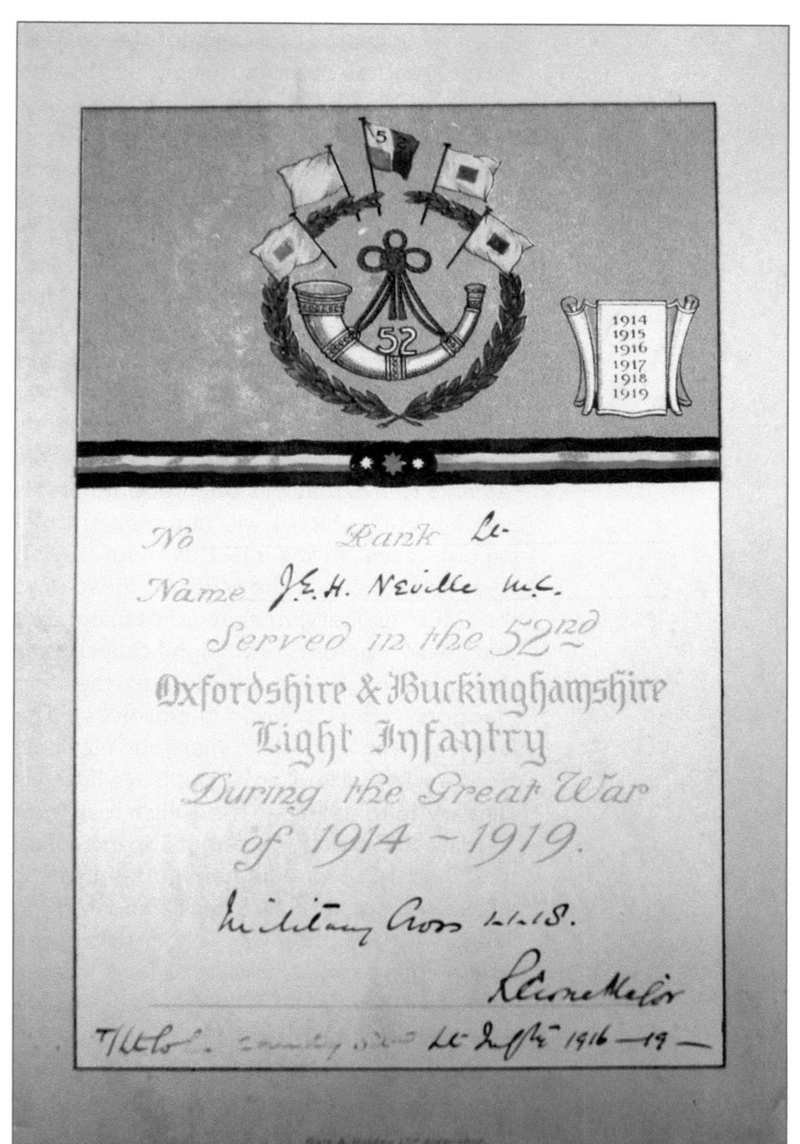
52

1914
1915
1916
1917
1918
1919

No Rank Lt.
Name J.E.H. Neville M.C.
Served in the 52nd
Oxfordshire & Buckinghamshire
Light Infantry
During the Great War
of 1914 – 1919.
Military Cross 1.1.18.

The certificate confirming the award of Military Cross to James Neville for gallantry.
John d'Arcy / NRO Nev 7/33.

received 'a chorus of thanks for the coal, all grateful and all speaking nicely of you and saying you have brought honour to Sloley. We will have the MC engraved upon your sword as you suggest. Just think how you would like it done and what said—merely 'awarded MC Jan 1918' or an engraving of the cross and the date or what. Have you received the ribbon yet?' His father added that after the war had finished, why did he not think about becoming an MP, taking over from him in Wigan? It was a career that the young Neville never gave a moment's thought to. (Neville has more acerbic remarks to make at this point about medals and honours which I will not report, but I cannot leave this subject without saying what he says about the MBE; 'In those days the MBE (military) meant something; but that was before its significance was degraded by being awarded to the pop maggots who called themselves The Beatles.' Not a modern man our Neville!!) Neville was 'bucked' as he put it in a letter of January 16 to get a pay rise, which rose from 7/- a day to 8/6 a day (ie. about 35p increased to 42 and 1/2p) for a lieutenant during 1917, and raised again to 11/6 (ie. 57 and 1/2p) in January 1918. But he was further depressed by the change in the weather—from intense cold to torrents of rain which turned everything 'into a quagmire'.

On his next leave he was granted two extra days to attend an investiture at Buckingham Palace to receive his award. The MC is given to any member of the armed forces for 'an act or acts of exemplary gallantry during active operations against the enemy on land'. On 23 February 1918 he and Dick Warren, who was drafted at the same time as Neville and was also to receive an MC, presented themselves at the Palace and were lined up by members of the household ready to meet His Majesty. The king, George V, had to stand on a stool with his back to the door in order to be able to reach up and pin medals on his loyal subjects. Neville was a tall man, well over six feet, and even on a stool King George had to reach up to hang the MC on the hook on his jacket.

As he came out of the Palace, there was a warning of an air raid. The warning to take cover was given by boy scouts riding bicycles blowing discordant notes on a bugle. Amazingly, Neville says that 'no-one took the slightest notice of either the warning or the bombs.'

February 1918

Neville also discovered while on leave that soldiers in uniform were irresistible to women. In February 1918, together with a friend called Ellam, Neville 'lorry-hopped' to Amiens, and they should have gone on from there to Boulogne by military supply train. But the pair decided to cheat and jumped unseen onto a French civilian train which only senior military personnel were supposed to use.

And what a leave this was when they got to London! Neville recalls:

> My diary contains a list of parties I went to after I had been persuaded to take up dancing by my sisters. I became an addict in a couple of days and met young women for whom I had hitherto had little or no use. (I think I have to forgive him his dated attitude that women have to be of some use, especially to him!). Angela was a VAD (Voluntary Aid Detachment) nurse, and whether by guile or intention, she introduced me to her extraordinarily pretty VAD nursing friends. Many of them joined us in dancing parties at the Empress Rooms (billed as *thés dansants)* in Kensington High Street, or at 25 Eccleston Square. I was introduced to one girl called Maureen Smith—an absolute charmer! I fell flat for her from the moment I met her and was only truly happy in her company. She turned out to be the little girl called PooBah with whom I had played as a child on the beach at Broadstairs.

Neville had to return to the war on 3 March 1918. But this time, he says:

> It was grim. I was leaving most of my heart in other hands than my family (I assume he means PooBah whom he now considered to be his girlfriend). The odds were against seeing my

February 1918 while on leave. Neville can be seen in the centre with 'PooBah' (Maureen Smith).

John d'Arcy / NRO Nev 7/33.

family or my sweetheart ever again.

Perhaps PooBah had given him a reason to live, and perhaps also he knew from experience what to expect.

March 1918

The next letter, again from Neville to his father, is dated 9 March. Neville had had a month's leave and on his return to France he remembered anew all the reasons he disliked his life as it stood at present. 'The journey back was pretty frightful, but I am thankful to be with Regiment again. I left Boulogne at 12 and reached Buire at 7.30pm. There I had to detrain. It was raining like hell and dark as pitch, and in stepping down from the high carriage, I missed the second step and fell flat into the mud at the siding.

> I waited for the next train for Ytres (not Ypres in Belgium). Luckily there was a roaring brazier and some food to be had and I was able to dry my clothes. The next ammunition train only took me as far as Plateau where I had to detrain again and seek shelter from the rain and cold. I eventually reached Ytres in a cattle truck at 3.30am and stayed the remainder of the night at a YMCA hut. I would have passed out from sheer misery and loneliness if it had not been for the chap in charge. In spite of the hour he found me some blankets and I slept till 7.30am. What a contrast from leave!

Neville found himself commanding B Company on Welsh Ridge, a new area to him, as his friend George Field was on special leave. He found the trenches knee-deep in mud and so shallow that he had to crawl everywhere. As he was well over six feet tall, his size was a great disadvantage in those conditions. 'It is like trying to walk or move in treacle,' he complained. 'I could get no leverage for my legs which were held in a gripping suction. I thought I would risk it and stand up straight, but hardly had I straightened my back when I heard the ominous 'pop pop' of a pineapple mortar. I had to decide whether to try and run for shelter through the mud, or lie face down in it.

> I struggled forward as best I could until I heard the swishing of the bombs in the air. Then I buried my person in the mud. It was an agonising minute that I live through. The first bomb burst in the trench fifteen yards ahead of me, showering mud over the back of my neck. The next burst behind me and thereafter all round me on the parapet and parados (a protective earth mound at the back of a trench). I expected at every moment to have one flash of realisation when one landed in the small of my back, and then extinction. I did not count the bombs but I reckon they fired fifteen

Ruins of Arras, photographed in April 1917.
US National Archives and Records Administration: 16579299, public domain.

at me. I lay doggo for about five minutes and then wormed my way along to the post.

A few days later he wrote again, this time to his sister Angela, to tell her his Regiment was now out of the front line, but that the past couple of days had seen an attack by his company against the enemy. This however was unsuccessful, largely because the wire cutting (shooting to remove the wire which defended the enemy's position), was left to the 6" Stokes Mortar Battery gunners which 'made a frightful hash of it'. 'They started the job just as the light trench mortars were making their emplacements in Ostrich Post. The latter were going to co-operate in the box barrage at zero. I watched the shoot and to my horror I saw the third bomb fall straight into Ostrich Post (i.e. into their own ranks). The result was a shambles and poor Seal (52nd attached to the light trench mortar battery) was among the killed.

I telephoned to Regimental HQ and asked the Colonel to stop the firing. The gunners refused to accept they were firing short—but that is the stock response of gunners when they are at fault. So after we had cleared up the mess in Ostrich Post, I got a message that the damned 6" Stokes were going to try again. I asked the Colonel if a gunner officer might be detailed to observe the shoot and at the same time, I withdrew the forward posts out of the way of harm. A gunner office duly arrived and we watched together. The first bomb sailed over into Bocheland and the officer turned to me and said "There you are, that is the range we were firing at before." The next one just cleared our front-line parapet and landed with a crash in our own wire. 'What about that one?" I asked. To which he replied "That is the bracket". (i.e. the margin of error). Then I heard the pop of discharge of the third and turned to watch it sailing through the air. It was not at all clear where the infernal thing was going to land, until the last second of its flight when I called the gunner officer to dive for the dugout. It landed approximately 150 yards behind our front line. After that, the officer hopped it back to his mortars and did not stop to argue. The standard answer of "the bracket" is supposed to mystify us poor ignorant infantrymen. It was clearly a futile exercise.

The Colonel asked that wire cutting should be left to the field gunners, but our men were so shaken that we concluded that it was better to risk uncut wire than have them further shattered by our own mortars. Pluckrose led the raiding party in the end as I was commanding the Company and he got slightly wounded in the leg. But it was the same old story. They never reached the Boche trench because of uncut wire which was a pity as the men in the Boche post were apparently completely unprepared.

Neville's father, as an MP, wanted to see the front line for himself, so he took a boat from Folkestone to the continent, along with a delegation of MPs invited to GHQ to tour the battlefields, arriving in France on March 12. He did not get down as far as Highland Trench at Villers Pluich where Neville junior was stationed and James was unable to leave his post to show him round. Neville senior visited St Pol in the end—though sadly did not manage to meet up with his son at all—where he saw 'gymnastics, wrestling, hand ball, bayonet drill, boar pigs, prize fighting cocks, and other interesting agricultural and military sights'. He then went on to Arras where he saw the 'poor ruined cathedral and the German barricades near the shattered Hotel de Ville' and from there on again to Bapaume and Albert where he spotted all the 'murderous ridges' his son had fought so bitterly over, and the big crater at La Boiselle.

But back to Neville junior. Over the next few days and nights the whole of James's Regiment was stood at arms all night in the expectation of an attack, sleeping in the mornings until 1pm. Neville reported that the Germans sent over gas all night long, not enough to force a man to reach for his gas mask but just enough to catch the throat and make the eyes stream, along with hurricane bombardments. He also found himself digging trenches in the dark, a 'foul business.' It was not dangerous in the sense that many lives could be lost, but the constant barrage wore down his nerves.

'I am not feeling fearfully fit,' he wrote to his sister on March 14. 'Rumours of earache in the left ear and also signs of a touch of gas which makes one feel rather rotten. It is the enemy's new kind, nothing dangerous, it just affects one's voice. I am losing mine and the whole of No 6 Platoon is dumb. It gives one a sore throat, cough and diarrhoea, but it passes off. The gas does not take effect until 48 hours after getting a whiff of it. That is the curse of it, one can't tell whether one has got a dose of it or not.'

Neville makes it quite clear in his letters that he had been told to anticipate the German Spring Offensive, and the much-vaunted assault finally began on March 21.

Ruins of the Hotel de Ville, Arras, May 1917.

US National Archives and Records Administration: 16579744, public domain.

The German Spring Offensive of 1918

The Russian Revolution of October 1917 had devastated the Russian Army. That released the German army and its thousands of soldiers from the Eastern Front, which could be brought in to concentrate effort on the Western Front—and the two sides geared up for a massive battle around Arras, not far from where Neville was stationed. The German Kaiser was, at this point in the war, so sure of victory that he prematurely declared March 24 would be a national holiday to celebrate the achievement.

This first part of the offensive was codenamed Operation Michael. (The second phase was designed to attack the French in Flanders.) The idea was to breach the British line at Arras and then go north to cut off supply lines from the coast. With the influx of troops from Russia, the Germans hoped they would be able to completely surround British forces and force them to surrender.

The failure at Cambrai (and at Arras, Messines and Passchendaele), had weakened morale among British soldiers. Also, they had recently taken over this part of the front from the French, who had left it poorly fortified. They had only just started to improve the defences there, when the Germans struck, on 21 March, 1918.

And thirdly, the Germans used new tactics, to great effect. They started with a four-hour massive bombardment, focusing on machine-gun posts and gun batteries instead of, as previously, on infantry positions. They created a substantial breach in the British front, literally annihilating several divisions, and through the gap poured small groups of German elite storm troopers.

These troopers travelled with only light weaponry (such as flame throwers), and they were skilled in fast and powerful attacks, then moving on to the next target. It was intended to cause absolute panic, and it did. Twenty-one thousand British soldiers were taken prisoner on the first day.
The British High Command completely lost control. They had been so used to trench warfare that they were taken utterly by surprise. The British Fifth Army, and then the Third Army, were ordered to withdraw and the Somme region, where so many soldiers on both sides had died in 1916, was given up to the Germans. Paris came under attack also, causing many civilians to flee. It was all so successful that the Kaiser declared 24 March a national holiday and the word 'Victory' was mouthed all over Germany.
But then the tide changed. The storm troopers deliberately carried nothing except weapons and their supply line could not keep up with them. The follow-up troops were so desperately hungry that they killed their own horses for meat. When they found shops full of food on the Allies' side of the line, they started looting. Discipline broke down and the attacks ceased. They had lost 230,000 men to death or injury. And finally, the Americans began to arrive. By the end of the month (March) 250,000 American troops were pouring in from Calais and Dunkirk.[7]

As the offensive started, at 4.45pm on 21 March Neville came under heavy fire. He wrote to his sister from Ytres describing the Germans' serious attempt to gain the upper hand and win the war.

Evidently the Boche offensive has come. The Regiment was ordered to stand-to at once. It was devilish dark and cold getting out of a warm fleabag. The strain of the last few weeks in this area has been greater than in any or all the other areas that I have been in. We have been waiting and expecting this to happen every day for weeks. We have got tons of wire put up all over the countryside and rows and rows of half-dug trenches. I have never seen such systems of wire before. Our brigade rests of 6 days have been spent on working parties digging vast trenches under the supervision of a Sapper corporal who has walked round with an A frame in his hand to see that the dimensions of the trench are absolutely correct. This has been going on for the last two months.

In the distance the barrage rolled like the beating of a mighty drum—I have never heard such a barrage. The chief bombardment seemed to be just on the flanks of the 5th Corps at Bullecourt and Gonnelieu. We stood to all day waiting for news which was scanty. We heard that the 4th Corps on the left was heavily engaged, but that the 51st Highland division was dealing successfully with the enemy. The 5th Corps front had also been attacked, but the 47th Division had lost only one post on Welsh Ridge. The whole division had been compelled to retire to Highland ridge to conform with the 7th corps of the 5th Army, which had been pushed back two and a half miles. The fog came down again at dusk and aeroplanes bombed us at night, too close to be pleasant.

Next day, 22 March, Neville continued:

The Regiment slept fully clothed in case a sudden move was ordered and orders came at 3am to be ready to move at 4.30. We formed up on the Ytres road in order, C D B A Companies, and we marched via Bus to Vimiers Camp at Barastre. The barrage was still very intense and 15" shells were falling in Bus and Barastre. It was bitterly cold and foggy and the march was tiring because of the continual checks and halts, bad roads and the flow of transport in all directions which blocked our passage. The fog lifted at midday and it became quite hot. We lay out in the sun near Bertincourt waiting for orders. At 1.30pm the Colonel went forward to report to the GHQ, 17th Division. Enemy aircraft buzzed round overhead apparently complete masters of the air. The 74th advanced on our left and came under shell fire as soon as they were spotted by the enemy planes.

The Colonel returned at 4pm and called a conference of all officers. The news seemed serious. The 17th had been able to hold the enemy but the junction between it and the 51st Division was very weak, and the reserve regiment of the left brigade of the 17th had been sent up to reinforce the line. The 52nd was likewise to support the weak spot.

I moved off with the 52nd at once with companies in artillery formation and platoons at 100 yards distance. The route took us across country and all possible use of dead ground was taken to avoid detection by hostile observation balloons which dotted the sky along the front for miles. 'At sunset the 52nd took up a position behind Hermies with the 74th on its left. The night was very cold and a bright moon made visibility very good.

Neville had been expecting some action, but there was by now little shelling, so for two days he and his company 'dug in and made ourselves comfortable!' Two days later on Saturday 23 March, he had orders to get ready to move back.

I was sent on ahead to meet the CO at the Green Line (an imaginary line which ran behind Martincourt) to get orders from him for the position to be held by B Company. I set off at once with my soldier-servant down the Hermies-Bertincourt road. The CO met us at 8am and gave us the following information and orders: "Bad break in 7th Corps on our right; enemy in Beaumetz and possibly Hermies. 5th Brigade to hold a switch of the Green Line from where it meets the railway about 0.2.b.3.1 on the right to 0.11.b.9.6 on the left, where it joins the 6th Brigade. The 63rd Royal Naval Division will be on our right holding from F.2.b.3.1. southwards towards main Green Line and facing east. The 52nd front is from F.2.b.3.1 to P.I.d. central about 800 yards. This will be held as follows: C company outside right, D, A and B on the left in touch with 24th Royal Fusiliers."

I returned to find the company digging in on the switch line. The weather was very warm and digging became thirsty work. By 2pm each man had dug himself a small hole with a thin parapet and work was started to connect these holes into one trench. All the companies except B had taken over partially dug trenches of the seven-foot-wide variety. They were to prove

In the trenches, 'Shiny' (Horley) and 'Twitt' (Tyrwhitt-Drake).
John d'Arcy / NRO Nev 7/33.

their uselessness this day. While we of B company had to dig like fury, yet we were better off in our little holes when once they had been dug deep and narrow. In front of this so-called 'prepared position' there were four rows of wire, both apron and '*chevaux de frise*'.[8]

At midday a battery of field artillery took up a position in front of this wire, but before it had been in action half an hour, it was subjected to indirect machine gun fire from Velu Wood. The battery limbered up at once and galloped away, the guns being drawn by only one pair of horses. It was a thrilling sight.

At 2pm, from the commanding position of our trench, we could see the enemy plainly streaming over the skyline in pursuit of our troops who were retiring in good order covered by machine guns in rear and Lewis guns on the flanks. We telephoned through to our guns to concentrate on the enemy but in vain. Not a shot was fired which indicated that they too were retiring. Through field glasses every movement and signal could be spotted and men could be seen to fall here and there. There was no shell fire or smoke to obscure the view. It was open warfare in very truth.

By 3pm the rear-guard troops had passed through our line and retired to another so-called line behind, which was non-existent except for rows of wire without a trench behind them. These troops were composed of men of different regiments, divisions and Corps, all retiring under unknown officers in many cases. None of them seemed to know where they were going next nor the line of retirement. It looked a rather sorry rabble and very nearly a rout.

One of the officers came to me for some water and food as he had been without rations and water for three days. I had to refuse his request for water because we were already short, and did not know for how long we might be compelled to subsist on our water bottles. I managed to find a tin of bully (beef) for him and some neat whisky for which he was very grateful. He was in a pitiful state. His face was black from powder, his hands bleeding, his jacket ripped from shoulder to wrist by shrapnel and his puttees and breeches torn to ribbons by wire. He said he had been blown up three times and had had three guns destroyed under his hand. He had lost his division which had retired early in the morning and he informed me that he intended to stay with us and see it through. He was rather bitter about certain troops who, he said, had retired without orders and left him and his guns in the lurch. It sounded bad enough that such a thing should happen but we were to experience the same shortly. Such was the disorganisation caused by the rapid advance of the enemy, that orders often did not reach the front-line troops simultaneously and indeed, some never received orders at all. At 3pm we became the front-line troops and all gaps in the wire were closed with moveable "*chevaux de frise*" (defensive barriers such as spikes used to obstruct enemy movements).

The enemy followed up very quickly and the trench was soon peppered with machine gun bullets. A company on our right had many casualties. The enemy mounted a light machine gun forward along the railway embankment which ran through our front and from a concealed position on top of it, he was able to enfilade the wide trench. As A Company's trench was on a slope towards the railway embankment, every movement in it could be spotted by the enemy. Also, as the trench was 7 feet wide and only 3 feet deep, there was no cover. In fact, it was a death trap and as bad as nothing at all. B company was more fortunate. We were just over the crest and the only casualties we suffered were caused by indirect enfilade fire from the embankment.

But Bunjie Littledale, commanding A company, was killed, hit through the heart and neck. Next Colville ran the gauntlet of a hail of bullets and managed to recover Littledale's body. The afternoon was quiet; only heavies were in action on both sides. Ours dropped some very heavy stuff into Velu Wood while the enemy plastered the Bertincourt-Velu road about 400 yards behind our front line.

Towards evening the frost came down and the shelling on both sides increased, the enemy registering his field guns on the Bertincourt-Velu road. Night came on and with it the awful suspense of waiting for the attack that was certain to be launched against us in the morning. We dug a little and tried to improve our narrow shallow trench. All round the enemy's Very lights twinkled in the sky, revealing the extent to which we were bottle-necked. And more surely than any map reference, the line which the enemy held. Our orders were to hold the Switch at all costs.

At dusk the shell dump at Ytres was fired. All night long we could hear the thud of exploding shells, while the sky was occasionally lit up with the red glare of burning dumps. The cold was intense, sleep almost impossible, and there was no mail, but rations came up. There was nothing to be done but wait and wait for the infernal daylight. However much we might be shelled, there was no chance of any retaliation from our guns. A rearguard is a nasty business.

Sunday March 24

At 2am I was woken by an orderly from a cramped sleep and told that George Field, commanding B Company, wanted to see me. He gave me a message to read, the purport of which was that we might have to retire before dawn to another position in rear. The hours slipped by but no orders came through. The suspense grew greater every minute. Dawn came, a glorious spring dawn. We stood to arms. No orders. No sign of an enemy attack. Just as it was getting light, two German officers came forward to reconnoitre our wire, and succeeded in finding two gaps made by heavy shells. They were allowed to wriggle through one row, and then No 8 Platoon stopped any further nonsense by shooting them neatly.

At 8.50am an orderly came to me with a message—the one word 'Corunna', the code word to retire. I went along to Field who gave me orders to retire with No 8 Platoon, from the extreme left. I was the only officer with a map of the area and I was given the job of leading the Company. I handed over to No 6 Platoon to Serjeant Stevens, and led out No 8. We started in single file through our wire behind the trench. There was a stretch of 400 yards before we could reach the Bertincourt-Velu road.

No sooner were we all in the open, than the enemy opened machine gun fire on us. We carried on steadily and, as it were, a thunderstorm seemed to bust over our heads in a deafening roar. The blazing sun was suddenly blotted out by acrid yellow smoke of shrapnel bursting overhead. The ground shot up all round in fountains of black smoke and earth. Everything on all sides was being heaved into the air. The Nissen huts bordering the road parallel to our line of retreat were flattened in one blast. I looked round and tried to collect the men together because there were inclined to straggle, and even as I did so a whizzbang caught the slanting roof of a Nissen hut a few feet away on my right, and cut away Private Grey's legs. Another man and I tried to lift him but he was too badly hit and we had to leave him to the enemy.

We crossed the road and halted

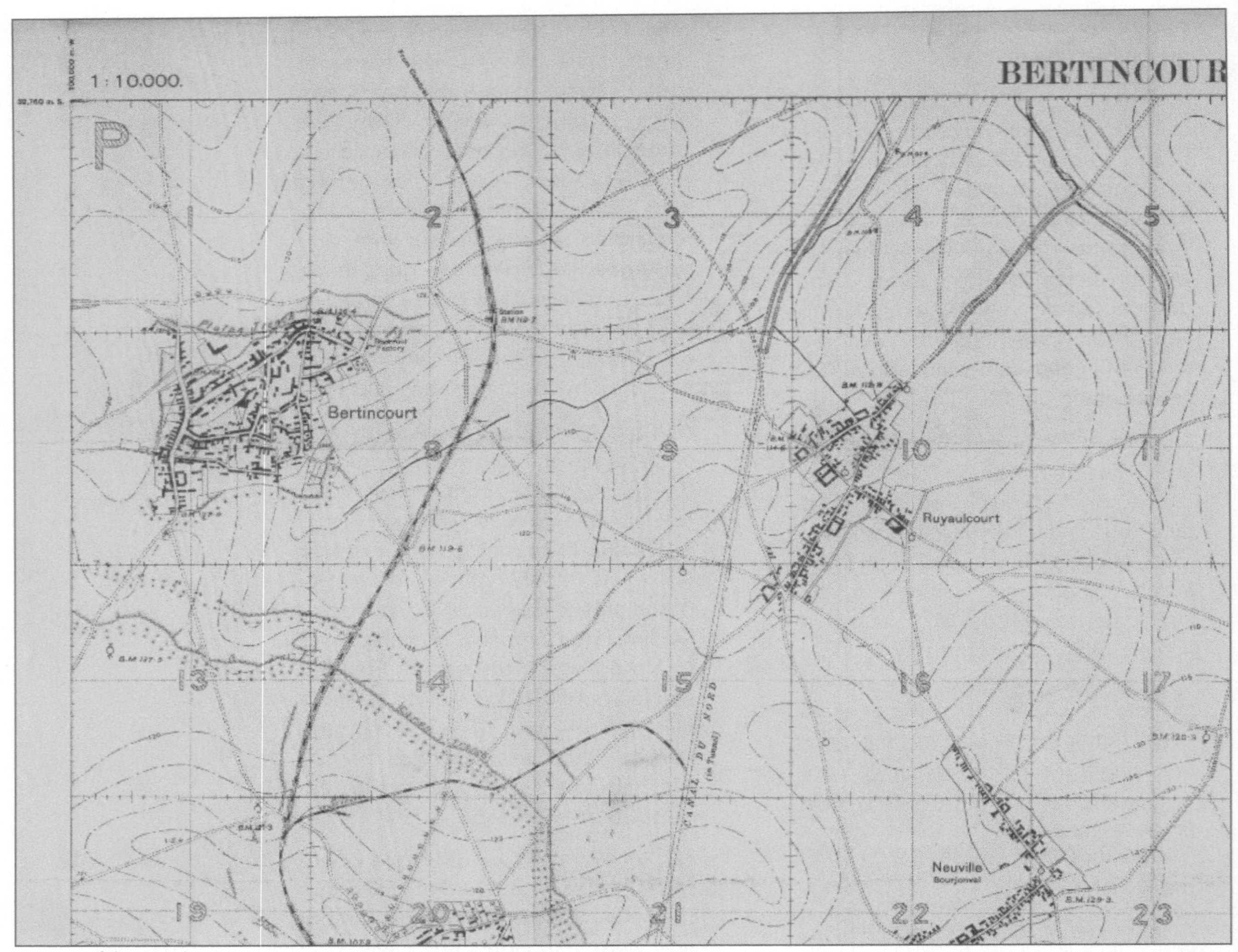

Section of the trench map Bertincourt, dated February, 1917. The red lines show the trenches. Bertincourt is shown top left, below the heavy entrenchment around Ytres.

behind a manure heap for a breather. Field and Wilson came up and Field tried to shout orders to me, but it was not wise to wait too long in any one place, for five whizzbangs burst beside us, showering manure all over us, and so we retired in small parties to the Bertincourt-Haplincourt road through some stables and out again into the open. Meanwhile Bertincourt was being plastered with every conceivable type of damnation and the noise was terrific. I never expected to see any of the HQ officers alive again.

It was a great relief to be free of the roads and buildings. The heat seemed to be very intense and the men were black and dripping with sweat. We marched on through the Green Line, up the slope and past some machine gunners who had dug in to cover our retreat. During this retirement it was possible to see to what extent the British were in fact bottle-necked. For miles I could see our troops filtering back across the rolling downs towards one spot, one narrow channel, while machine gun fire came from three sides.

On reaching the ridge in front of the Barastre-Bus road we met Brett, and there we sorted out the 52nd men, recognisable by the regimental ribbon on their steel helmets, from the rabble of troops of all divisions of the Fifth Corps, who were retiring through this narrow neck. We formed up into companies as the men came in and having re-formed reported to Brett. B company was ordered to go back to the original map reference given in the 'Corunna' message—0.22. central—and Field led the company back to an old German line running between Rocquigny and Barastre.

'We soon ran into the 19th Division on its way up to hold the ridge which we had just evacuated. Having settled into the new position, we came under machine gun fire from Rocquigny on our right, and our own 4.5 howitzers mistook us for the enemy and started shelling us. Here the company, about 40 strong, stayed until Field determined to join up with the 63rd Division which was digging in on the next ridge behind Barastre, since there was no sign of the 52nd.

In Barastre I gleaned the news that the 2nd Division was fighting a rearguard in conjunction with the 19th Division between Haplincourt and Villers-au-Flos. I gave this information to Field who decided to go back to Beaulencourt forthwith and await the 52nd there. It was not until 5pm when the enemy were in the outskirts of Le Transloy that we met the 52nd again. It was a pitiful sight, a small column of men led by the Colonel and Brett, about 80 men all told, marched wearily up the slope. D company had been cut off in Villers-au-Flos and only 12 men under Eagle had managed to escape. David Barnes and Bailey were wounded and missing, Vernon wounded and Ben Clocock killed.

Just before the 52nd came up with B company, what remained of the tanks waddled through our line of posts. The Boche field guns, supporting the front-line troops, had done them considerable damage and knocked out several. I noticed one tank crew through my glasses coming towards us. They all looked very strange and I could not distinguish their faces from their uniforms. As they approached, I could see the cause of this. The officer's face was completely raw. All the skin off his forehead and face hung like an icicle from the tip of his nose and the skin of his jaw and chin encircled his neck in a grey fold, like an Elizabethan ruff. His hands were raw too and he gave me the impression of having been lathered in blood. Actually, he and his crew had been flayed in a burning tank, and he was the most badly burnt of all as he was the last to leave. He asked for some water. I handed him my water bottle but he held up his hands and said he could not touch anything. So, I poured as much as I could spare down his open mouth; then he went on back towards Albert.

Wounded men came crawling up to our posts, beseeching us to carry them back to the main Albert road on our stretchers. These pitiful requests had to be refused because our stretcher bearers were already doing the work of four times their number. One man with a shattered ankle crawled up to me and asked me to get him taken back. When I told him that it was impossible, he started off again dragging his ankle and said he would get back to Albert as he was, rather than be taken prisoner. Some pluck! At 5.45 the whole of the 5th Brigade moved back as a brigade across the Somme battlefield from Beaulencourt, which was burning, to Ligny Thilloy. The 52nd formed the rearguard for the Brigade, and B company was detailed for the rear party and flank guards. My platoon provided the left flank guard. Away on our left about 2,000 yards away, marching in the same direction as ourselves, was a German column. We took no more notice of them than they did of us.

The shell-holed country over which we had to march made our progress exhausting. Grass and weeds in the course of time had matted over the old shell holes, obscuring the holes underneath. The troops were dog-tired after a hard day, and the last four miles as dusk came on were heart-breaking, stumbling into and climbing out of one shell hole after another endlessly, and down and round and round and never a solid step ahead, every minute of waning light making a path more difficult to find.

Eventually at about 7pm the 52nd halted at Ligny-Thilloy and we had an hour's rest by the side of the road, and never has a ditch seemed softer. Every man was fast asleep as he threw himself down. The night was bitterly cold after the spring warmth of the day and a frosty wind sprang up to make it chillier still. Rations came up in the night and we had lunch of tea mixed with tobacco and boiled in shell-hole water. The tobacco spoilt the tea by making it very bitter, but the shell-hole water was infinitely preferable to that which came up in petrol tins, as it proved to be composed of three parts water to one of petrol, and was almost worse than nothing. The hot drink did us good and made up for everything else. Thus ended a very long day.

Monday 25 March

At 2am orders came to move again and the 5th Brigade marched half asleep through Le Barque to the main Bapaume-Albert Road. This was a silent march as the enemy had been reported to be in our rear, in which case we were cut off. On reaching the main road there was a halt of 30 minutes to allow the 6th Brigade to catch us up. There was a faint grey streak in the eastern sky as we passed the famous Butte de Warlencourt. The road on which we were marching had been mended by the Regiment just a year ago after the Boche retreated early in 1917. Just as dawn was breaking, we wheeled off the road into the ruined village of Courcelette. The march along the road had been quite a pleasure compared to the Somme battlefield of yesterday but it was galling to pass all the well-known landmarks, to realise that all this hardly won tract of country was slipping back once more into the enemy's hands.

At Courcelette where the 52nd held the line for 3 months, we had a really long rest of 2 hours, and a hot breakfast. Before falling out, the CO formed the regiment in line and called it to attention. A and B companies became No1 Company under George Field, and C and D became No 2 company under Percy Bobby. Then he said "When you fall out, I want to see every man get some wood and drum up at once!"

Meanwhile the poor old brigadier was in a state of collapse. We had passed him on entering Courcelette sitting on a blasted tree stump holding his head in his hands. Each company had marched at attention, but he was far too weary to rise up and take the salute. Behind him stood the brigade major looking like death, and in this state I saw the brigade staff for the first and last time during these operations. At 8.45am we took up a position facing east along the ridge overlooking Dyke Valley and commanding Le Sars and the Bapaume-Albert Road. This was a very fine position indeed. The 6th Brigade continued the line to the left and behind us we had one battery of 18 Pounders. On the right there was not a sign of a soul. In front, the 99th Brigade was fighting a rear-guard action and was to retire through us to another ridge behind. We could have held this excellent position for a long time, for the enemy had not managed to move his guns forward over the shell-torn ground. Our only difficulties were scarcity of ammunition and exposed flanks. We had only 120 rounds per man and our flanks were in the air.

Here however was excellent scope for good and controlled fire, and through field glasses I could see every movement of the enemy. Although we only held here for half an hour, we had some good fun bringing down the

The Butte de Warlencourt photographed in 2017. This ancient burial mound is situated just off the Albert–Bapaume road. German troops constructed deep dugouts in the Butte and surrounded it by several belts of barbed wire, making it a formidable defensive position. It was subject to several attacks by the British in 1916, all costly failures. Occupied by the 2nd Australian Division when the Germans retreated in 1917, it was recaptured on 24 March 1918 during the German spring offensive.

enemy as they advanced across the open from Le Sars towards Courcelette. The Boche were no fools. They were well trained and made excellent use of ground and cover, and never exposed themselves unnecessarily. Their first consideration was to manoeuvre the light machine guns forward to cover the advance of the rest. Through my glasses I picked up a man carrying one of these guns and directed my Lewis gun on to him. He never carried that or any other gun again. It was almost impossible to miss the enemy from the commanding position, and our Lewis guns were doing good execution and holding up the enemy's advance when we received orders once again to retire because the enemy was crawling round our flanks.

For the rest of the day we retired continuously across the shell-scarred and desolate Somme Plateau, past the ruins of Pys where Eagle and I had spent an unpleasant evening in February 1917. Back we trekked from ridge to ridge with the enemy always close on our heels and our flanks continually exposed. The weather had changed and a bitter north wind was blowing… At last we halted on the left bank of the River Ancre, opposite Beaucourt-sur-Ancre, where we had tea, the second meal of the day at 6pm. I never saw a staff officer after leaving Courcelette. There seemed to be no one in command of the Brigade and likewise no one met us when we reached the river to pass on orders. Brett had gone back early in the afternoon to report the situation to 2nd Divisional HQ if he could find them.

While we were having tea, some

'Whitters' Ernest Whitfield.
John d'Arcy / NRO Nev 7/33.

machine gunners on the heights of Beaucourt must have mistaken us for the enemy for they opened fire on us. However, they were bad shots and we were too tired to take any notice of them. At dusk we crossed the Ancre at the ford and took up a position on the heights of Beaucourt on the right bank, with strong points forward to guard the ford across the river... So ended a tiring day to be followed by a bitterly cold night and little or no sleep. The wind whistled over the river from Thiepval, the long disused dugouts were damp and musty, the wind seemed to freeze the clothes to the body, and bitter as the wind, was the fact that we were occupying the trenches held by the Regiment in November 1916, some 18 months ago.

'Shoveller' CT Chevallier.
John d'Arcy / NRO Nev 7/33.

Back in Sloley Neville's family were beside themselves with anxiety. His father wrote 'We are longing to hear news of you. This horrible battle that has been raging since Thursday and the news of how it has been going, makes us horribly nervous. It looks as if there was a complete breakthrough at St Quentin which will or may nullify all the fighting of the Somme.

How are you, dear lad? I can think of nothing else but you, and curse my fortune to have to sit at home and do nothing. My son, I wish to God I was by your side to share your fortune with you, to be with you through all you have gone through, are going through and will go through. Everyone is confident that the army will hold and trounce the Boche—and proud of the magnificent resistance of our splendid troops against overwhelming odds. But I can't talk of the battle and barely dare think of it. Dear laddie, you know how I love you and long for your safe return. Best of luck to you Jim with warmest love, your aff father.

'Guillaume' MS Griffiths-Williams.
John d'Arcy / NRO Nev 7/33.

Tuesday 26 March

Neville wrote back:

At stand to orders came to pack up and retire again. B Company descended the steep slope to the Beaumont-Hamel road. The morning was very cold and foggy and I led my platoon to join Bobby. Our orders were to retire to Auchonvillers, but when we were half way there, Brett met us and told us that the retirement was cancelled. So we trekked back to the position we had just left, the march being enlivened by 8-inch shells from our guns, falling on the road at Beaucourt. We left the road and took a short cut to our old position as it is never wise to argue with an 8-inch shell, no matter whose.

The sun had just risen when we settled down to improve the position, and our aeroplanes were crowding the sky, a welcome sight after 4 days without the sight of one. One of these planes however, flew over us at 200 feet and its observer, in a fit of misplaced efficiency, fired on us deliberately which was a poor trick as we could not retaliate. Luckily, he too was a rotten shot.

We lit some flares and put them on the parados to show him our position and deter him from shooting us up. These seemed to tickle him so much that he turned and plugged us again. At this moment Brett came along the trench and cursed me into fits for giving our position away to the enemy by lighting flares. I told him the reason and his answer was to the effect that the .... aeroplane might shoot at us for a week and never hit us, but that I ought to know by now what the Boche gunners could do.

No sooner had we made fire-steps in this old trench than the order came to retire, so we filed out and took up another position but it was not nearly so good. Our field of fire was limited to 100 yards and we could not see the ford across the Ancre, the trench was very narrow and shallow and digging in the chalk subsoil was very difficult. No 1 Company was on the right and No 2 on the left; from the latter's position we could see the enemy's guns being brought into action, while away on our right across the river we could see the enemy wandering about on the crest of Thiepval ridge.

Ellan and I found an old dugout which had partially collapsed at the bottom. It was damp, cold, musty and smelt of decay and rats and putrescent vegetation and food. Here I found a half-opened tin of bully beef and picking out the biggest bits of chalk with my knife, I ate the remaining contents. How the tin had got there or how long it had been there, I never stopped to consider. We had been through strenuous days, marching far over shell torn country on underfed stomachs, never knowing if or when we should see food again, and here at least was something to eat.

But never shall I forget the taste in my mouth after it. For four days I had a dry stickiness in my mouth, incessant heart burn and a feeling of overwhelming depression which almost blotted out the instinct of life. Ellan would not touch it and he was far wiser than I. As a matter of fact, the regimental transport had achieved a well-nigh impossible task by getting rations up to the Regiment all through the retreat, when roads were blocked for miles and miles with all manner of guns and transport. We never starved like some less fortunate regiments.

We had not occupied this trench for more than one and a half hours before the enemy's patrols entered the trench opposite. For the rest of the day No 2 company was kept very busy sniping them. At midday we heard the grim tidings of the brigade major's ride—he had set off after we left Courcelette and had ridden for 6 miles and never seen a soldier. Divisions had seemed to disappear into thin air and behind us there was not a single rifle to support us. Bar the 8-inch shells which had nearly blown the few remnants of the Regiment to bits in the early morning, not a single gun had barked at the enemy for 24 hours. Incidentally Brett had told me that when we had received orders to march on Auchonvillers (this was known to the soldiers as 'Ocean Villas' and is now the location of a War Museum, with reconstructed trench, the only one in the Somme region) in the morning, the village was already in enemy hands, and luckily he had met someone on the road who had asked him where he was going and, on hearing his reply, had advised him to go elsewhere.

At 2pm it started. Shells screamed over and crashed behind in the unoccupied support trench. We could watch the blighters serving the guns and were powerless to hinder them. For two hours the bombardment continued but little damage was done as the trenches were so close together that a short was likely to do the enemy more harm than us. Then at 4pm the joyful news came round the line like wildfire that we were to be relieved at night and that the Australian and New Zealand corps was behind us. It seemed that the impossible and improbable was to happen and I had visions of being allowed to sleep the clock round. The troops were scarcely delighted; they probably didn't believe the news and most were past caring what happened. Many rumours had floated round when we were trekking like hell yesterday. One was that we had made a counter-stroke and captured Lille and that the Belgians were advancing on Ostend. As usual the yarns had emanated from Refilling point, that useful source of all lying rumours.

However late in the afternoon the news was confirmed for we could see the Australians advancing in artillery formation along the skyline way on our left. I don't think I have ever seen such a cheering sight... 'A bitterly cold night drew on and still no sign of the 12th Division which was supposed

'Shiny' Horley.
John d'Arcy / NRO Nev 7/33.

JD Grover.
John d'Arcy / NRO Nev 7/33.

'Pullthrough' LEWO Fulbrook-Leggatt
John d'Arcy / NRO Nev 7/33.

to relieve us. Hope waned, flickered and went out, and then suddenly at midnight an order came for us to pack up once more and evacuate the line since the 12th division was going to hold another position in rear.

Wed March 27

At 12.30 we filed out and marched through the cold moonlit night across the fields towards Mailly-Maillet. It was a long and wearisome tramp, for clods of ploughed earth stuck to our boots and still further weighted down our tired legs. The woods of the village, a black mass in the moonlight, never seemed to get any nearer and when at last we reached our destination there was no guide to meet us and we marched round the place before the blighter was found... It was a pathetic sight this village, which had only seen a year of freedom from war. The inhabitants had all fled except here and there an old man or woman who refused to move whatever happened. The only reassuring sight was the presence of ANZAC troops resting by the roadside in the village.

The guide led us back to the point where we had first entered the village and then down the road to Mailly Wood. At 3am we settled down for the remainder of the night, but the enemy started shelling the wood with heavy stuff and German aeroplanes must have spotted the fires, for a shower of bombs suddenly arrived and made the place very unhealthy. Once again, we packed up and moved out of the woods and lay down beside the road. A battalion of New Zealanders passed us here, marching in fours to rollicking tunes from a brass band. The fact that the village was under direct artillery fire did not seem to deter these enthusiasts. Had I any guts left in me, I could 'scarce have forborne to cheer.

At 5am the 52nd's cookers hove in sight and we had some hot tea which was very refreshing. Immediately afterwards we moved on again down the Warley road and halted in a small copse where we had breakfast and then lay down, but the wind was so bitterly cold that sleep was impossible, and we were almost too tired to sleep... Rumours flew around that the 2nd Division was going back to Abbeville, but these were discounted at 6pm when we had orders to park up again and return to a position in support of the 12th Division. Our hopes of a relief were dashed and it seemed that we were for it again.

At 7pm we marched off through Mailly-Maillet and Englebelmer to Martinsart where guides met us and led us to Aveluy Wood. We hardly seemed to march, for whenever we got into step there was a halt and one seemed always to be dragging a weary body out of a soft and comfortable ditch to advance a mere 100 yards. On one of these halts, Ellam came up to me holding a full bottle of champagne which an old civilian had given him as we passed through Mailly-Maillet and offered me a swig. I refused it as I knew the effects of fizz on my stomach, in its present condition only too well, never for one second was I free of heart burn.

On all these halts the men fell asleep where they stood and a minute's sleep seemed an age, but hardly had we sat down before the order came to advance. In such wise by short stages we found ourselves back again in support of the 12th Division with the 5th Brigade on the right, the 99th on the left and the 6th in reserve at Englebelmer. All ranks were allowed to rest until stand-to when we had a scratch breakfast. From that time on there was plenty of scrapping in front of us and the enemy started shelling heavily with shrapnel and high explosives which reverberated through the wood in intensified and re-echoing crashes.

George Field.
John d'Arcy / NRO Nev 7/33.

The patrols were very active, feeling their way to get in touch with the 12th Division. As usual the Boche pushed their light machine guns well forward and inflicted many casualties on the Royal Sussex Regiment just in front of us. At one time it seemed likely that they would break through, but George Field sent up 2 platoons to support the front line, who drove out the machine gunners and captured some prisoners, one of whom had on a British soldier's jacket under his own.

The shelling increased as the day wore on, until at midday it had become more than uncomfortable. It seemed obvious that the enemy was going to attack, the wood and back areas were being searched with all manner of damnation. Late in the afternoon the attack was launched in small numbers and was completely repulsed. By this time, I was a sick man. I could not hold any solid food and not always the chlorinated water and diarrhoea reduced me to weak listlessness. I could just stagger and no more, and whether a 5.9 inch hit me or not or any of the filth flying about, I cared not a tinker's cuss. So the colonel sent me down to Martinsart which was being shelled to glory by 5.9s, where I spent a most uncomfortable night in a cellar, that is to say as much of the night as a disordered stomach would allow.

George Field did marvellously well yesterday. I heard that he and Ellam had been wounded. At 7.30am I walked down with Rupert Brett to the transport lines at Englebelmer and we were lucky to get a lift in a limber. At the transport I was offered some food which, like a fool I ate but never digested and then I crawled into a fleabag and slept until sundown when the doctor came to see me. He said I was a filthy colour and pushed me off in an ambulance to Doullens. Wounded were streaming in. The hospital enclosure was covered with rows of stretchers, three deep and ever more coming in. My bladder was always full, my water the colour of stout but no one had time to give me a bottle. The nursing staff hardly had time to look at the labels and anyone who could move a muscle was at once evacuated to the Base. High pressure hardly described such superhuman efforts and yet the sisters and nurses remained cool and just worked on quietly, quickly and efficiently.

Sunday March 31

Neville was evacuated from Doullens to the Duchess of Westminster's hospital at Étaples with jaundice and gastritis. There he was fed on 'milk and water, nothing solid'. Beds were urgently needed for surgical cases so he was evacuated to England 'as yellow as a sovereign' and at midnight on 1 April was admitted to Sister Agnes's King Edward VII hospital for officers. Neville recuperated for well over a month, and had a pretty good time of it in London. His father took him to Edward Barnard, silversmiths in Hatton Garden, where they watched a Jacobean-style solid silver-lidded tankard being made with a blow lamp and hammer.

His father bought him the tankard to commemorate his Military Cross.

He also picked up the threads with PooBah which he had thought had been broken forever. They fell in love, dined, danced and went to the theatre. The only thing Neville says he cannot remember is how he paid for it all! But he was seriously depressed by jaundice. The worst thing, he says, is 'the malaise', by which I think he means the tiredness and listlessness, and the nausea. The reports in the British press of the course of the war did not help. 'The battles in France were still causing great concern,' he writes. 'The Boches on the Somme, for some reason unaccountable at the time, halted their advance and attacked further north on our old quiet front east of Poethune. At that time we had 5 million men in France, but only 1 million on the front line. Sir Douglas Haig issued his "backs to the wall" general order'.[9]

'In England,' Neville continues, 'little notice was taken of the gravity of the situation. There was rationing, and very little petrol for the few cars on the road, but that was about all. Father seemed to attend several secret sessions in Parliament. I can well remember my dismay at the colossal casualties of territory. It seemed utterly unlikely to stabilise the front, let alone to reconquer the lost ground. Father and I had several acrimonious arguments and I admit now that he was right and I was wrong, but neither of us for the reasons that eventually broke the Boches.'

The Second Battle of the Marne

In July the Germans launched one more desperate offensive, the Second Battle of the Marne, to try to win the war. Troops were ordered once more across the Allies' line. They advanced two miles, but were stopped by a French counter-attack. The offensive was a disaster with thousands more casualties. Between March and July 1918, the Germans lost just over 1,000,000 men.

Now the Allies were no longer on the back foot. They launched a series of attacks known as the Hundred Days Offensive, including the Battle of Amiens, the Second Battle of the Somme and several other battles along the Hindenburg Line. The Germans were pushed back and back, out of France, and were eventually forced to retreat into Germany.

Neville stayed in England for a variety of reasons—more leave, failure on the part of the army to ship him back to the front—until 5 July 1918 when he would celebrate his 21st birthday. He was expecting to return to France at any moment but suddenly contracted Spanish flu.[10] He was only 'laid out for three days' but was given leave to return home to 25 Ecclestone Square for his birthday party. With rationing the party was frugal, but his father produced a bottle of 1897 port and after a meal there was dancing in the drawing room.

The following day a telegram arrived telling him he was expected for draft on 11 July. His father and sisters saw him off on the train for Southampton with several friends—Dick Warren, Bob Fitzgerald, Ginger Smith and Brooke who had been wounded three times but never spent more than 36 hours in the front line. His journey back went well, and he shared the ferry not only with old friends but also with hundreds of American soldiers. They had been drafted into the war following the sinking by a German U-boat of the British passenger liner Lusitania on 1 May killing 1195 people including 123 Americans.[11]

Back in France, Neville records, 'Once again we had to while away the hours at the base dept at Rouen, going through the gas chamber and drawing kit etc. (By 'gas chamber' Neville means the training all soldiers received in what to do in a gas attack). On 20 July we left for the 52nd (his old regiment of the Oxford and Bucks Light Infantry). Our morale rose from the beginning of August due to our attack on the Boches at Montdidier when we took 17,000 prisoners and 300 enemy guns—and we realised that the enemy was not invulnerable after all.'

Neville was looking forward to being back with his friends, but at the same time he dreaded coming under fire again. It was not that he was frightened of taking a bullet

—more that he knew how it was going to feel to be part of an army under attack. He added that all the American soldiers he had met on the boat seemed to think the war would be over within a year. Neville arrived back with his regiment on 20 July. 'I was greeted by many old faces,' he writes. 'It was topping to see them again—Shiny, Twitt, Philip Booth, George Field and all the old gang of this time a year ago. I have been posted to C regiment, not B, my former regiment. Toby Sturges is due back today. Bingo Baines division is just behind and I have been over to see him.' His new friends in C Company were Percy Bobby, Wayte, Bartlett and Sailor Barnes. 'I wish I was back in B Company most awfully,' he wrote to his sister. 'The officers in C have always been oldish men and not like the young and skittish B. Never mind, one company is as good as another, though it's rather sickening after 16 months with one company to be posted to another.'

Neville was in the front line in Ayette, where it was 'quiet', but there were 'umpteen' Americans attached to the regiment. He was not altogether enthusiastic about their presence. 'They are fearfully keen and dangerous to their friends. They loose off at anything and never wait to see who it is, even when they are in the support line behind the front. They are apt to fire at anyone going along the top between posts. I'm afraid their discipline is not all that it should be, but they will soon knuckle down and lose that keenness which almost amounts to suicide.

> They had three men knocked out by their own men. One officer, their intelligence bird, was shot through the neck by their colour sergeant instructor in musketry, and two privates were killed by some of their mates while cleaning rifles. There have been no casualties from the enemy. But the intelligence office is not expected to live.

On the other hand, he met up with Maurice Buxton who was in command of a company of Coldstream Guards, with no fewer than 19 Old Etonians. Neville could not believe his luck. He felt he would meet a lot of old friends there. Then his father wrote to him from his chambers in London saying how anxious he was to hear news. 'I am wondering dear lad where your regiment is and what it is doing, and I hope you and it are safe and well, and in good heart and not engaged in the fighting. I am longing to hear from you. He continues, 'John Marcon (a cousin) is keen on butterflies and moths, and is eager to sugar the trees, but I can get no sugar.'[12]

And on 20 August his son replied saying he was 'all right (*sic*)'. In fact the front he was posted to was quite quiet and not only that, he was posted behind a bit of a ridge, so that he and everyone else was able to walk

'Bingo' Baines, Harry Vernon, 'Pullthough' LEWO Fulbrook-Leggatt.
John d'Arcy / NRO Nev 7/33.

about freely, and not scuttle along the trenches.

In the same letter Neville described a vicious air battle between a Boche Scout and one of our 'observing machines', and shortly after that he got a message to say the Guards were to relieve them that night, and then tank officers turned up for lunch. 'So, there is going to be an attack here after all', he wrote. 'I thought there was more in the air than mere aeroplanes, because dumps have been formed in the night all over the place.'

Another brief note from Neville to his father the following day reported that 'the attack has been successful so far ... not time for more ...can't promise to write for a little while, may be busy ... best love ... we're winning!!' And again on 22 August he wrote to say that he was a long way behind Adinfer Wood, beyond which was fierce fighting. 'Don't get the wind up,' he said. 'We've not been near the show, though we have had a dose of sneezing gas.[13] In haste; this goes by Shiny.' The fighting continued and it was touch and go whether Neville and his regiment would be involved. He spoke to a gunner officer who said the attack was going to be pressed the following day. In preparation Neville had a bath in a foot bath. 'Never done that before but accomplished it with some success and felt much fresher afterwards.'

On Friday 23 August he got orders to take up a position in front of Douchy behind the Ayette road. It was a very hot night and sure enough soon after midnight, a barrage started on his left and he realised he was going to see action again. He was terribly excited and dreading it at the same time. 'Too excited to sleep, horrible waiting to move, terrible needle. Moved at 10am in artillery formation past Courcelles. We came under artillery fire but got through that, though some heavy stuff was coming over. Ahead of us loomed the blasted railway cutting of the Bapaume-Arras line.

> Got through that safely though the fire was increasing and the railway cutting was being pounded. We ran like blazes across the cutting. The Boche was shelling like hell with gas and sneezer (sneezing gas). Once across the railway we made a right turn and had to halt in the open. Whizzbangs and 5.9s were dropping everywhere. My sections took cover in shell-holes. I got into one with my platoon serjeant and had a cigarette. The serjeant major Coulwell was hit two yards from me, very badly, by one of those 106 fuse shells. He was lifted several feet into the air, and both legs cut away from under him. (He died later of wounds). We moved on, crossing the Gomiecourt-Sapignies road. I got into some old gun pits and waited. I could see the Boche gunners serving the guns that were firing on us, lined up on the skyline to the left of Behagnies. We saw the flash of the guns through binoculars and we all crouched into the gun pits until the salvo burst. I actually saw the shells coming straight at us. We stayed there until dusk. I slept that night in a shelter with 5.9s falling all round. My Gawd, I could sleep for a week. I have never sweated so much in all my life. The smoke and gas as I write are perfectly bloody.

Poor Neville senior! At the very same time his son was writing from the battlefields in France, the father was sitting in his chambers in Fig Tree Court in London reading *The Times*, realising that this time his son was right in the middle of it. 'I am so anxious to hear news from you,' he wrote.

> I feel sure your regiment must have been in this push, for the map which Toby (Sturges) left me shows that it was holding the line opposite Moyenville as far as Ayette, and the reports show that our troops have captured Moyenville and Courcelles, and are up to or across the railway cutting ... Today the Guards are mentioned, who I gather from Toby were on your left ...so I believe your regiment must have been in the thick of it.
>
> I hope casualties are low. I am longing to hear news of you, my dear lad. I see several thousand prisoners were

> captured and some guns. Goodbye dearest son, and God bless and keep you safe and sound through that hellfire you are enduring. Send me a line as soon as you can.'

Neville senior was so proud of his son that he made 25 copies of the letters he had received and sent them round to various members of his family, where everyone was impressed both by the endurance of such terrible conditions, and the literary effort and ability.

On Saturday 24 August Neville junior started his day with bacon and bread mixed with sugar for breakfast which he proclaimed 'damned good stuff'. Then he wrote again to his father:

> Casualties to officers are pretty heavy. Heard that the Colonel has been hit, Fulbrook-Leggatt, Wilsdon, Pearson and Brown (who has since died of his wounds and it was his first time in the line). I cannot really sleep as I am always being woken by shells. I live in a kind of coma. Our company HQ are in the forward edge of Triangle Copse in a narrow trench and in full view of Jerry who holds the high ground, but we've not been shelled yet. That will come all in good time.
>
> Looking back on yesterday… the waiting was awful. Being the regiment in support, we came in for much of the Boche barrage. The railway was a nasty customer but the worst part came when we had to make a right wheel, thus exposing our flank. Then it was that we came in for the 5.9s, and the whizzbangs. 'The 52nd is to take over the front line from the 60th Rifles today, and that the whole THIRD ARMY is pushing forward tomorrow. That means we shall attack at dawn. The Boche seems to be retiring to his Hindenburg Line again and that means that we shall be living in desolated country for the winter. Oh hell!

Neville and his regiment took over the front line from the 60th around midday, taking the outpost line without casualties. C Company got established in a former German dugout on a slight ridge with a view into the village of Sapignies. They spent the whole afternoon trying to advance further, but Behagnies was well defended, so Neville and anther officer cooked up some tea sitting on the top of the dugout steps. A major from the Rifles came over to chat and turned out to be Frank Gull who was a contemporary of Neville's at Eton.

Still unable to advance further, the Company settled down to spend the night there.

> An excellent dinner was served up by my faithful servant, Private Midwinter, from some extra rations I had been able to scrounge from Bob Fitzgerald—soup followed by tinned salmon, rabbit and toasted cheese.

Once darkness fell the Germans started shelling sneezing gas which was so strong that the Company had to sleep with gas masks over their faces—not an easy task. I can only imagine the relief of Neville senior when he got these letters from his son. He must have been close to tears as he realised that despite the terrible dangers of the war, his only son was still alive. He wrote back:

> I received with great joy two letters from you today, one dated Thursday August 20th, and the second dated August 21th, in which you told us that the attack (by the Third Army over an eight-mile front) had begun. … I fear in addition to all the horrors of battle you will have suffered from heat and thirst for Thursday was a very hot day. I have pictured your regiment as engaged somewhere near Moyenville and Gomiecourt. This morning's news is that the Third Army is on the south attacking Thiepval and in some places is only two miles from Bapaume.
>
> It looks as if the Germans plan to retreat to the Hindenburg Line. The French have bitten into the German lines north of Soissons and with luck may outflank the Chemin des Dames. I hope the awful hard work has not brought back any of your jaundice troubles and hoping that you are

> strong and well in yourself. *The Times* announced yesterday that the DSO and MC were only to be awarded for service in action in the presence of the enemy. It enhances the value of your MC very greatly. Best of Luck to you dear lad. I wish to God I could be with you in body as I am with you in spirit. With best love, Your aff father.

Back in France Neville and his company were given orders to transfer to the HQ of 24th Royal Fusiliers around 3am on the morning of August 25. From there they were told to attack Sapignies. It was a foggy night, so in spite of a heavy sneezer attack by the enemy, they were unable to use gas masks as this would have made vision impossible. 'We started off in what we thought was the right direction for the village.' Neville writes.

> But the mist, and the gas, and the smoke from our own field guns made it impossible to be sure. We had not gone far when we encountered B company in the same plight. Bobby (Neville's CO) and John Blagrove (in charge of C company) had to shout at each other to make themselves heard over the crash of shells.
>
> Eventually we advanced in file towards the wood, picking our way over the many dead and wounded lying in the first trenches, including one man wounded through his carotid artery, spitting blood. On the outskirts of Sapignies we met a couple of Germans who legged it from us like hell. I had a shot at one with my automatic, and he fell forward with a crash. I was just congratulating myself on having at last killed a man with my pistol, when I realised that my platoon serjeant had dropped to his knees and fired at the same time! I knew what a good rifle shot he was, and there was no doubt whose bullet had done the damage—not mine. The back of the man's head was blown right out. The other Boche was neatly floored by Corporal Hollyoake. So far so good. It seemed too good to be true. Where were the other Boche?
>
> We crossed the Arras-Bapaume road and occupied some trenches on the other side. I had some food—an excellent breakfast consisting of cold bacon and a hunk of bread covered in sugar. We carried on trying to keep warm, but the mist made it hard to stay together and I lost sight of the men. I took out my whistle and blew it several times and bawled out 'C company' several times, but got no answer. But then I heard shouting. I had one man with me, Private James, so we moved towards the shouting and we found the others. I could see helmets floating along the top of the fog. Suddenly, too late, I realised that the helmets were Boche!
>
> There was a loud crack and my pistol dropped out of my right hand. I felt a numbing pain as if I had been hit on the funny bone with a sledge hammer. I ran back to some cover while the Boche streamed past me jabbering like monkeys in German. The rest of the patrol seemed to have disappeared and the chance of sailing into the retreating Boche with 5 rounds was lost. I called to Private James and received only a moan in answer. Also the fog had started to lift and I feared it would reveal us to the enemy, only 20 yards away. Why they took no notice of us I cannot conceive. Perhaps they were preoccupied with their own safety. Private James was swearing like a good infantryman and his left arm was hanging by a thread from his shoulder. As only one shot was fired, I suppose the bullet that had hit me had also ricocheted from my elbow and torn off his arm.
>
> Together we tried to retreat. This was no easy task as I was feeling terribly sick and was bleeding like a pig. I stopped and sat down while Corporal Hollyoake bound up my arm. The fog came down again and the Boche were shelling the road while our guns were dropping a few playful shots into Sapignies in case we had not captured it. The fog lifted once more and I saw

two of my men coming towards us. I told them what I knew and where the enemy were and then set off down the line, wasting no time getting through Sapignies, and on the other side, met Dick Warren of B company. I got to a First Aid post where a stretcher bearer had a look at my wound and said he did not think the artery was severed. Later on, a doctor confirmed that.

But Neville could clearly not continue fighting with a useless pistol arm. He was put into a horse-drawn ambulance and taken to Courcelles. Someone asked me where I had been hit, and when I said "In the elbow" he got angry and wanted to know what part of the line! The one word 'Sapignies!' seemed to have a magical effect for the brass-hatted person popped off and came back with a still more brazen hat in tow, who I believe was our revered Corps Commander. Their brass faces were wreathed in smiles when I told them that the 52nd had captured the village at 4.30am. It seemed that this infernal little village of ruins played a big part in their scheme of things. They purred over the information like a pair of cats, and I felt myself to be quite a hero, for I had never seen so many of the gilded staff before and wondered where they had all emerged from.

In the afternoon motor ambulances took the wounded to the rear. I was allowed to sit in front as a walking case. Back we went over familiar ground, over what had been No Man's Land, now a back area, through Douchy and Adinfer, crawling over the tracks deeply rutted by tractors and endless streams of ammunition lorries, and on to the Prevent Road. Every bump made the stretcher cases moan, but the driver kept on at a steady speed. The tents at the Casualty Clearing Station were provided with lovely beds and clean sheets, things that I had almost thought never to see again. Some angelic nurse gave me an injection of morphine and suddenly I was released from pain.

Back in hospital in Le Tréport, Neville waited for surgeons to operate on his arm.

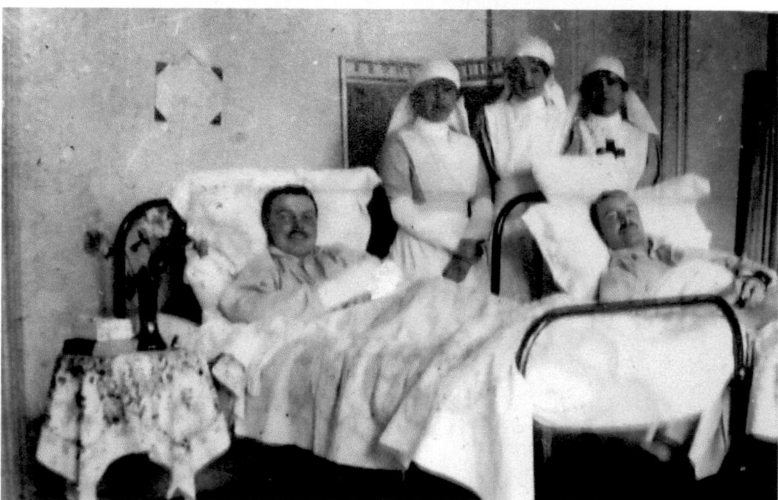

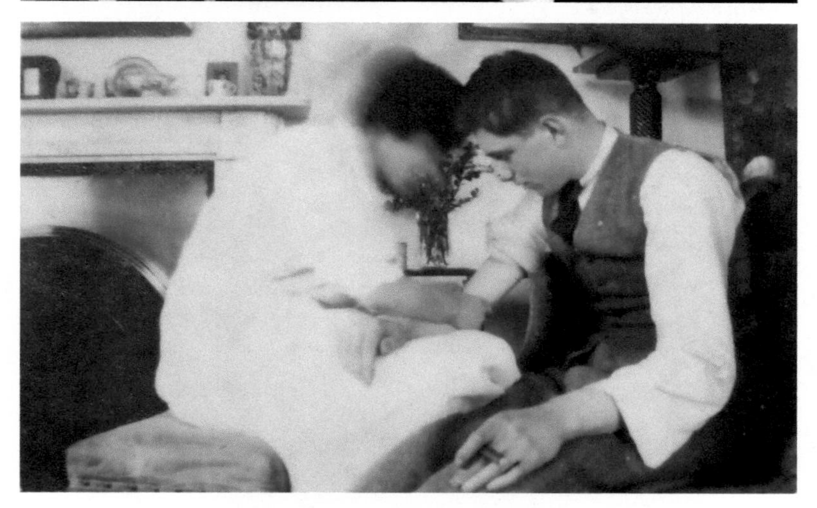

above: The hospital at Le Tréport where Neville was treated for a wounded right arm.

John d'Arcy / NRO Nev 7/32.

centre: In the hospital at Le Tréport. JVO McCarthy and Neville surrounded by nurses.

John d'Arcy / NRO Nev 7/32.

below: Neville receiving treatment at the hospital in Le Tréport

John d'Arcy / NRO Nev 7/32.

He could not write with his left hand, so another officer wrote home for him. Still in Le Tréport he wrote one last time to his sister on 2 September. 'The pain is now a dull ache, and the fingers are numb except for the thumb and first finger.'

His friend Dick Warren had also been hit, through the helmet which he kept hanging beside his bed with a hole through the back of it. It was, as he says, a wonder that neither of them were killed. So just a few weeks before the war finally ended, Neville was shipped home, in one piece, a bit of a hero, and with at least one friend still alive. One might say he had had a 'good war'.

Neville's shattered right arm was bandaged and splinted but it was stuck at right angles to his upper arm and thereafter he had very little movement in the wrist. At the hospital in London he received physiotherapy, but this did no good at all. Neville returned to Sloley where he and his sister Angela had 'a very pleasant time' through October and November, but Neville had his arm x-rayed at Whittlingham Hospital, and the resulting prints showed that the arm no longer had an elbow joint—it was just a lump of callous.

On the morning of 11 November Neville returned to the London Hospital hoping to persuade the surgeon there to operate. The surgeon agreed with the diagnosis but refused to do anything until the scourge of Spanish flu had abated. Neville was disappointed, but as he was walking back to Ecclestone Square past Hyde Park Corner, he heard the air-raid maroons sound at full blast. This was the signal that the Germans had, as hoped, signed the Armistice at Compiègne. It may have been hoped for, but there had been so many false ends to this war, so many stalemates, so many crushing casualties 'that hardly a soul expected or believed there could ever be an end to this war.'

> Suddenly thousands of people were dancing and ramping along thoroughfares, making their way to Buckingham Palace to call for the King and Queen. All traffic was halted while the crowds boarded buses and cabs, shouting and singing in almost hysterical abandon. It is no wonder that the people of London seemed to go made with joy and relief.' Neville finally managed to get his right arm sorted out in an operation at home performed by Mr Battle, and got some use back. But at least he was in England to join in the celebrations to mark the war's end.

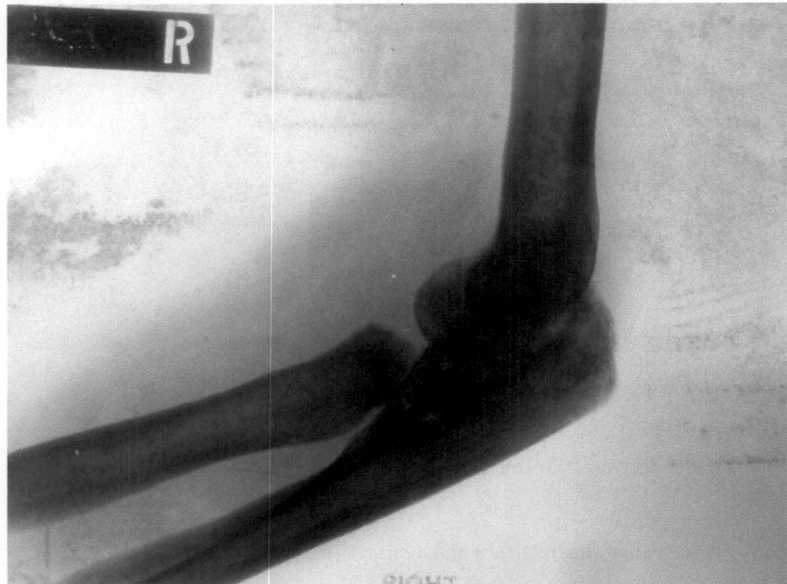

X-ray of Neville's injured elbow.
John d'Arcy / NRO Nev 7/32.

Exhausted and starving, Germany asked for an armistice (a truce while a peace treaty is drawn up). The Allies agreed and on November 11 at 11am, 1918 the war ended. The Paris Peace Conference saw four world leaders (from France, the USA, Great Britain and Italy) come together to decide how to plan Europe's future after the war.

US President Woodrow Wilson was reluctant to apportion too much blame to Germany, but the French Prime Minister, Georges Clemenceau, wanted Germany to take full responsibility for the war and be forced to pay huge sums of money in reparation. Clemenceau won the day. The Treaty of Versailles, signed on June 28 1919, which officially ended The Great War, was terribly harsh on Germany. The country was made to accept all the blame for the loss and damage of the war, to disband its armed forces, to give up land to France and to pay 132 billion marks (about $442 billion). Sadly, Adolf Hitler was later able to use all the resentment that the Treaty generated within Germany, to galvanise the nation into another terrible war just 20 years later. The origins of the Second World War lie firmly within the settlement of the First.

Notes

1 The Allies and the Italians made secret promises to each other in the Treaty of London, by which Italy hoped to gain part of Austria and Dalmatia, Trentino and South Tyrol at the end of the war. But the front soon got bogged down into trench warfare, similar to that in Central Europe, with the added disadvantage that it was all at high altitude and therefore even colder weather. Several thousand civilians, displaced by the fighting, died of malnutrition and disease in the refugee camps. The fighting came to an end with an Allied victory at Vittorio Veneto, and the Austro-Hungarian alliance. Wikipedia, November 2017.

2 The Battle of Cambrai, Wikipedia, November 2017

3 A Mills bomb is the popular name for a series of prominent British hand grenades. They were the first modern fragmentation grenades used by the British Army and saw widespread use in World War I.

4 Whizzbangs were German light shells, fired from one of the smaller calibre field guns. The name refers to the sound as the shell came to explode. A range of slang terms were used for different types of artillery shell, including 'woolly bear' for the burst and smoke of any big German high explosive shell. Imperial War Museum, December 2017.

5 Bourlon Wood is now a Canadian war memorial. It commemorates the actions of Canadian Troops during the final months of WW1, particularly when they flushed German Troops out of Bourlon Wood and their crossing of the Canal du Nord. It is located just beside the town of Bourlon about 6 miles west of Cambrai. Wikipedia, November 2017.

6 And here is a selection from that speech by the King.

What's he that wishes so?
My cousin, Westmorland? No, my fair cousin;
If we are mark'd to die, we are enow
To do our country loss; and if to live,
The fewer men, the greater share of honour.
God's will! I pray thee, wish not one man more.
....
But if it be a sin to covet honour,
I am the most offending soul alive.
No, faith, my coz, wish not a man from England.
God's peace! I would not lose so great an honour
As one man more methinks would share from me
For the best hope I have. O, do not wish one more!
Rather proclaim it, Westmorland, through my host,
That he which hath no stomach to this fight,
Let him depart; his passport shall be made,
And crowns for convoy put into his purse;
We would not die in that man's company
That fears his fellowship to die with us.

7 The German Spring Offensive, Wikipedia, November 2017 and Imperial War Museum November 2017.

8 Apron and *chevaux de frise*—during WW1, armies used chevaux de frise to temporarily plug gaps in barbed wire. These were portable wooden frames covered in barbed wire which could be moved easily. An apron was made by a wiring party—a highly unpopular duty! It involved carrying out six-foot steel pickets and rolls of wire. The pickets were knocked into place and the wire was fastened to the pickets to make what was called an apron. Spartacus Educational, November 2017.

9 11 April 1918, in which Haig talked about the victors in this war being the side who could tough it out for longest and there was 'no alternative' to his plan to hang in there. And I had always thought that TINA was a Thatcher original.

10 This pandemic between January 1918 and December 1920 killed between 50 and 100 million people worldwide (about 5% of the global population at the time), but seemed particularly virulent in Spain (hence the name Spanish flu). In fact the only reason it was thought to be more deadly in Spain was that the Spanish press did not suppress the mortality figures, because Spain was neutral in the Great War. Everywhere else the figures were manipulated to give the impression that the country had not been severely weakened by the outbreak of disease. history.com, December 2017.

11 Wikipedia, December 2017.

12 'Sugaring trees' with a solution of sugar and water was a popular pastime to attract butterflies which feed on nectar.butterfly-conservation.org, December 2017.

13 Sneezing gas is Diphenylchloroarsine (DA), a compound with the formula $(C_6H_5)_2AsCl$. It is highly toxic and was once used in chemical warfare. Wikipedia, December 2017.

NORTHERN RUSSIA'S WELCOME

Governor General Miller's Tribute to Britons.

In the reign of Queen Elizabeth daring sailors and traders from England arrived in Archangel, which was then part of the dominions of the Muscovite Tsar, John the Terrible. Here, on the banks of the Dvina, Englishmen and Russians met for the first time.

Archangel received the strangers with courtesy, and they were regarded by the Terrible Tsar with favour. He invited them to visit him in Ancient Moscow, where he received them cordially and granted them, before they left his presence, a Trading Charter which assisted the relations between the two countries.

Much time has passed since. England and Russia, guided by their statesmen, have pursued their own courses in history, more than once passing through historical crises which shook Europe—sometimes fighting shoulder to shoulder against a common enemy and sometimes meeting as opponents. And, as the political lives of our countries followed their own courses, so did the lives of our peoples.

In Ancient Moscow, the heart of Russia, in St. Petersburg, the young and splendid Russian Capital, and in other parts of the immense Russian State, British Colonies appeared and flourished. The British brought us their knowledge, and sent to Russia the merchandise she needed.

On the field of battle and in peaceful work among our people, Englishmen, from time immemorial, have been known to us as people of undaunted courage, of practical working ability, always unswerving in their aims and unwaveringly honest in their dealings. Russians came to value the word of an Englishman higher than any written bond. The English word "Gentleman" was adopted into the Russian language, and in every Englishman, before all else, we always expect to see a gentleman.

Three and a half centuries passed, and again the British landed on the banks of the Dvina, where their help was needed. Russia was under the heel of the Bolshevik—the Bolshevik who, in the middle of the great war, treacherously signed the Brest-Litovsk Treaty, committed the most unheard-of crimes in Russia (one of their victims was Captain Cromie of the British Navy,) threw hundreds of innocent sons of Britain into prison, and finally aroused the indignation of the British Government which, a year ago, sent troops to the distant North of Russia—to Murman and Archangel.

These troops formed the outpost, under the protection of which began the creation of the Russian Army for the struggle for the deliverance of Russia from the despotic power of the one-time German agents—the traitorous Bolsheviks.

These tyrants and outcasts—mostly aliens—stained with the guilt of every kind of crime, helped by Germans and supported by Lettish and Chinese mercenaries, have, by deception force and terror, enslaved a portion of the simple and ignorant Russian people.

Now we have witnessed the arrival of further British troops. These soldiers volunteered to strengthen the "outpost" in order to help Russia to free herself from the yoke of the Bolshevik.

Welcome! Gallant British Soldiers, hastening in disinterested and self-sacrificing aid in the struggle for the deliverance of Russia from the miscreants under whose yoke the majority of the Russian people groan.

Long live Great Britain, who helps us to re-build our Mother Country on a basis of Right and Justice.

WELCOME! BRITAIN's Outpost.

(Signed) E. MILLER

GOVERNOR GENERAL NORTH RUSSIA

Russia—Newcastle to Seltso

As Neville was a regular soldier he continued to serve in the army once the war was over (unlike the conscripted soldiers who had been called up as more manpower was needed on the front line). He was stationed at Aldershot when the news came in April 1919 that he was to be sent to Russia.

This venture, the North Russia Relief Force, was a bit of a footnote to the Great War, coming so soon after the war ended. It aroused little interest at the time—beyond the families of men serving in yet another campaign, this time fighting the Bolsheviks—but looking back it is of interest politically. Winston Churchill was then Secretary of State for War and known as 'The Great Interventionist' since he liked to intervene in the affairs of other countries without actually declaring war. This intervention came towards the end of the Russian Revolution which had forced that country out of the Great War in 1917. The intervention was a bid to reverse the outcome of the revolution and reinstate the Imperial family.

Churchill declared that 'Bolshevism must be strangled in its cradle' or Russia would be lost to the civilised world. However, in Britain Bolshevism had a lot of support among the working classes despite, or perhaps because of, the assassination of the Imperial Russian family, the Romanovs. The dockers and miners for example, regarded the Bolsheviks as their comrades in arms. The dockers even refused to load supplies and ammunition onto ships if they knew that those ships were going off to Russia.

Despite his assertions, Churchill's actual determination to do anything much in Russia was very limited. According to The Spotlights on History website (run by the National Archives at Kew in London), Churchill knew that the British public had no stomach for more war. The Prime Minister David Lloyd George and the US President Woodrow Wilson were 'extremely reluctant' to become engaged in a Russian conflict because of anti-Communist principles. Of the 30,000 men involved in this battle in Russia about half were British, and, according to Neville, they were mostly deemed 'unfit for battle'. Their primary job was to guard Allied stores and keep the Trans-Siberian Railway open. It seemed that the attempt to keep Russia as an imperial power was very half-hearted, despite the worldwide revulsion at the murder of the Imperial family at Ekaterinburg in October 1918. King George V in particular, who was a cousin of Czar Nicholas, was personally devastated by the assassination and his own inability to offer the family a safe haven.

Churchill appeared not to know that the White Russians (ie. those favouring the Allies, as opposed to the Reds who were Bolsheviks) had failed to sink their differences in order to keep an eye on the target. Neville claimed that when Admiral Kolchak (the senior officer in the Imperial Russian Navy) fell out with the Czechoslovakian Corps (a large and respected division within the Russian army), he defeated the whole anti-Bolshevik cause. As a Russian aristocrat, Kolchak treated the Czechs with disdain. They eventually deserted him and his cause was lost.

It was all very complicated. The White Russians were extremely divided, and no-one knew who they could trust and who they could not. The force sent by the Allies was a complex mixture from 14 different countries which made the line of command almost impossible.[1] Admiral Kolchak was then well west of the Ural Mountains. General Wrangel was in the Caucasus, Denikin was in the Don country, Yudenitch was in Poland and Korniloff was in the Baltic States. All these forces were attempting to squeeze the Bolsheviks back into the heart

Winston Churchill in 1919 as Secretary of State for War and Air.
Library of Congress, LC-USZ62-107479 public domain.

above: Yevgeny Miller the self-styled 'Governor-General of North Russia' who was in charge of the White Army in the region until July 1919.
US National Archives and Records Administration: 86729858, public domain.
opposite: Welcome to Russia from Yevgeny Miller
John d'Arcy / NRO Nev 7/31.

of old Russia. The North Russia Relief Force sent from Britain to help the White Russians consisted of no more than two brigades comprising four battalions of infantry and two machine-gun corps, nothing like enough to make a difference. The North Dvina and Vaga rivers and one railway to Moscow were the only means of communication in an area the size of France—and that area was 90 per cent forest.

The purpose of the Allied intervention in North Russia was three-fold; firstly, to try to reinstate the Tsarist family and prevent the Bolsheviks from taking over and running the whole of Russia; secondly, to rescue the Czechoslovak Legions on the Trans-Siberian railway; and thirdly, to secure substantial supplies of munitions, armaments and food in Russian ports, especially Murmansk and Archangel. These efforts were seriously hampered by a lack of proper strategy and public support, and war weariness. The intervention was a complete failure and the official attitude back in Britain, once the troops had been forced out, was to draw a line under the 'adventure' and forget that the expedition had ever happened. Once the Allied troops had withdrawn, the Red Army was able to inflict defeats on the remaining White Russian forces, leading to their eventual collapse. The Bolsheviks led by Lenin were victorious, established the Soviet Union and formed a Communist state.

By the time Neville was sent out in the spring of 1919, it was clear the intervention was going to fail. Neville's job was to relieve the troops who had been there for months and were tired, and to help in the evacuation. In this at least, he was successful.

Neville's letters back home to his father and sisters begin on April 3, 1919 from Salamanca Barracks at Aldershot. 'The situation is very vague at present,' he writes.

> I hope to get leave soon and come up and see you. No one knows much about this business. We are under 48 hours notice to go abroad, but as there are no men, that is impossible. I expect we shall sail at the end of the month.

He was however cheered by the good number of familiar faces—Dick Warren, Twitt Drake, Titherington and Bingo Baines.

'I am feeling awfully bucked,' he wrote,' because there is something afoot. All the regular officers are being recalled from the ends of the world. Roger Ames and George Field may turn up at any moment. So, we shall be a very happy family when we all foregather. We are going to be brought up to War Establishment, and naturally we are speculating on our ultimate destination. There are many possibilities; Archangel, Caucasia, Rumania, Egypt, Ukraine, Siberia or Danzig. Personally, I think it is a toss up between Archangel and Rumania. However, don't get the breeze up; we may go nowhere which is far more likely; and in any case we probably won't know till after we've sailed, if we sail at all. We are obviously a mystery Brigade of Regulars which rather points to Active Service somewhere.' It turned out a few days later that his destination was in fact to be Russia which he thought would not be very comfortable. 'I'm told that the mosquitos in summer are awful,' he wrote. 'And it is more than likely that, as we shall be a small force, we shall be entirely forgotten!'

He became very bored by the lack of action over the following weeks finding himself doing Orderly Officer duties most of the time. This changed his mind about wanting to go with the expedition, and he said in a letter to his sister Angela that the adventure would be great fun especially when surrounded by good friends. 'I might as well be fighting as doing anything else,' he adds. 'War-time soldiering is peculiarly fascinating...... but square pushing bores me. I love traipsing about the country ..... where there is an element of risk and the possibility of excitement. I have had no orders (except from Powell) to come here; but now that I'm here, I'm not going to quit.'

Finally, he got the news that they would sail on Monday, 12 May from Southampton. Men 'of all sorts and from a number of regiments' started arriving at the barracks ready to embark on ships which would take them north. To his disappointment, Neville was told he and his friend Twitt were to go via Newcastle and not with his old friends, but he quickly got over this. On 14 May he wrote to his father from HMT (His Majesty's Transport) *Czaritsa* which was by now

Embarkation of soldiers at Newcastle ready to leave for Northern Russia.
John d'Arcy / NRO Nev 7/31.

steaming north. He sounds elated! 'I am writing this on deck out of the wind and in the glorious spring sunshine,' he says. 'There is a haze over the horizon, the kind of haze you see at (Sea) Palling on a hot summer's day. There is no motion at all; it's as calm as a mill pond at present, but the breeze anywhere but on the leeward side is chilly.

> I will now try and describe to you our departure from Newcastle yesterday. For a long time before we pushed off, a crowd collected outside the gates and men and officers threw letters from the ship to the privileged few on the quayside to post after we had gone. Small boys fought for pennies thrown to them by the troops, scrambling for them like so many dogs after a bone. The gangway planks were raised at 12.30. and the tugs took us in tow. As the ship slid away from the quay, the crowd raised a cheer, the factory women showing great enthusiasm. The men struck up the well-known song "Good-bye-ee" Do you know it?
>
> Gradually we moved downstream, the crowd following as far as possible and waving farewell. And the whole way down to the sea little collections of people in their gaudy colours ran from houses, wharves and yards to wave to us. Each cheer was answered by the troops, and the cries of "Are we downhearted" from the banks were answered in ringing echoes of "No-o-o-o". Soon we came to the world of shipyards. They were a marvel to me. Every conceivable kind of ship was being born in them. Here merely a keel, here a skeleton, there plates being riveted, there a destroyer practically ready for the water. The whole aspect teemed with life.
>
> Cranes screeched and overhead rails roared on every side. In the river were ships of every country, and as we passed, they let off their sirens and whistles producing the effect as of fleets and fleets of ships feeling their way through an inky fog. The high-pitched yell of the little tugs, the guttural guffaw of the big colliers, the claxon horns whining up the scale to a heart-rending scream seemed to blast the very firmament! And so we came

> down to the sea, and a few people to bid us a last farewell ran to the lighthouse at the end of the mole and gave us a last cheer. We stood off at the mouth of the river and dropped anchor while a parade for boat stations was held, and the boats were lowered away clear of the deck. We sailed this morning at 3.30 a.m. by your time and 4.30 by our time as we have put our watches forward one hour.

He was accommodated in a small cabin six-feet square, with three others. As he was himself six feet tall, he found the bunks much too short but he was in such a good mood to be sailing off to a new adventure, he says he had no cause for complaint—apart from not being with his friends. On May 15 the troop ship was off the Shetland Islands and there was great excitement as a floating mine was sighted to port. Some of the soldiers fired at it but failed to hit the target.

> About midday, *HMT Czar* (the sister ship) was sighted and our captain dropped her a signal to come alongside. She altered her course and came within a mile or so and visual signals were exchanged. I believe she refused to be "matey"! She was too far away for us to be able to recognise anyone on board, but the 43rd is in her. She was making 17 knots to our 11 and so she will reach Archangel long before us. She is practically out of sight now and she will gain two days on us at our present speed. This morning we passed through a double minefield on each beam, and a Naval Officer pointed out Fair Island to me, an island north of the Orkneys, which was a famous lurking ground for Boche submarines. He said that any amount had been sunk hereabouts in their attempts to slip through to the Atlantic.

The sea was calm, the sun was shining and occasionally Neville spotted little steamers heading south which gave him a warm feeling of being still slightly connected with home. 'Ahead lies the deep blue of the North,' he wrote. 'Behind is the dazzling dancing of the sun on the waves, making a sheet of silver cloth just like the silver lamé which is the fashion for women's evening dresses nowadays. Most of the officers seem to play cards all day, from after breakfast to midnight and later. There are two rooms on the top deck which are perpetually filled with officers, cards and cigarette ends. Certain cliques monopolise the tables the whole time so that no one else has a chance to get near them. They are a very mixed lot. There are French Mortar officers of the 239th Brigade plus our details, as well as blue-and-green-tabbed gentlemen going out to continue their dangerous and arduous jobs of pen-pushing at the Base. There are also two Guards Officers on board who have not the foggiest idea what they are going to do when they reach Archangel.' Playing cards was a useful way of passing the time—Neville himself played many hands of bridge—especially at night. But by this time he was north of the Arctic Circle and at midnight, to his astonishment, he was still able to read a book and look at his watch to see the time without resorting to artificial light.

The estimated arrival date at Archangel was Tuesday 20 May, about a week after leaving Newcastle. As the ship rounded the north of Norway, Neville looked out towards the coast and gave his family this description.

> We are 1,366 miles out from Newcastle. The coast is very rocky; flat-topped mountains rise sheer out of the sea, capped with clouds like mantles. I suppose there are fiords running far into the mainland. The mountains are covered in snow, the air is chill, and a biting wind is blowing. The windows of this smoking room are glazed with ice flecks. It is freezing, and the sea has a black, fierce, icy cold look about it. We are truly in the Arctic Circle now. I wish the dear old sun would come out and cheer us up a bit.

Neville arrived in Murmansk on the north Russian coast on 20 May. Archangel was another 450 miles away to the east across the White Sea. He called Murmansk 'an unprepossessing place composed of just a few shacks.' But he added 'The air is very

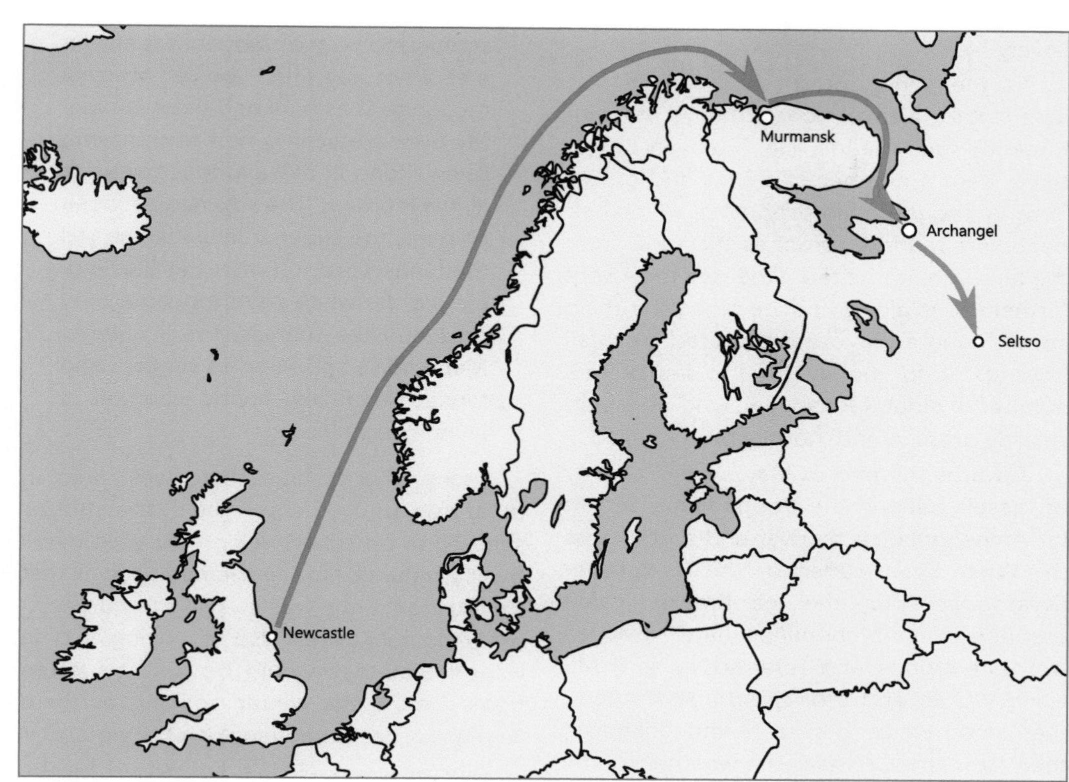

Map showing the journey from Newcastle to Seltso via Murmansk and Archangel.

keen but the sun is shining and we don't feel the cold though the country is clothed in snow. Someone told us it was an English summer!' Not warm enough however—Archangel was still frozen in after the bitter Russian winter, so Neville and his fellow soldiers had to stay in Murmansk for about a week. Another giveaway that they were in a seriously cold, northern latitude was the presence of whales and seals in the water. The sister ship HMT *Czar* had also arrived safely and Neville noted a number of men o'war anchored in what he called the fine natural harbour of Murmansk and another British ship, HMS *Glory* which was about to depart south taking with it mail for family back home. Neville hurriedly finished a letter and sent it off.

The following day, to his great joy, he saw a small dinghy full of men coming towards the *Czaritsa* and noticed the Regiment's badge among the occupants. The boat contained Bingo Baines, Toby Sturges, Giles, Booth, Guy Sturges and a number of friends, all waving and shouting! Neville grabbed his coat and a couple of other people from his ship and together they set off back to the *Czar* where they had a celebratory reunion dinner and a game of poker. As it was May when Neville and his regiment arrived, the weather was quite warm, even humid, and the air was full of mosquitos (these got much worse as they went south penetrating the forest).

Neville called Murmansk 'a small village composed of log huts each one of which is surrounded and enclosed by a filthy smell. I don't think I have ever experienced such a mephitis as emanated from these compounds, not even to be compared with the back streets of Rouen on a hot day.' The Russians he described as 'fearsome people to behold; dark, scowling, bearded scoundrels in fur caps, long boots and filthy jackets or coats. I thought Paris was a cosmopolitan place, yet in this weird cantonment there were British, American, Serbs, French, Russians, Chinese, Italians and Finns etc. The ground is black or grey sand and evil-smelling mud. It's really indescribable and while I am glad to have visited, I would never want to come back. During the winter months the inhabitants throw all their refuse and sewage out of window where it remains in the snow and preserved from putrefaction by the frost until the thaw comes. The thaw has come and the tracks are runnels of liquid sewage.

Lovely!'

As the spring progressed Neville was able to take a small boat out for a sail with three or four friends. He discovered that there were a number of creeks and gullies flowing into the main river, all of which had become a roaring torrent as the snow from the hills behind melted. One day they went further inland along what he called the 'main streets' where they were pestered by small boys asking for money. He also saw quite a number of older Russian men who were very smartly dressed and 'heavily be-medalled'.

Towards the end of May a small convoy of vessels bearing the troops finally set off for Archangel (first by river and then across the White Sea) headed by the ice breaker *Svyatogor.*[2] After the ice breaker came *Stephen*, then *Menominee* (later used to evacuate troops and referred to as 'HMS Hungry Guts' and 'a dirty old one-stacker'), then another ice breaker name unknown, then *Czar* and *Czaritsa*. The weather clearly changed very rapidly as Neville was told that the temperature at Archangel was now 90 degrees and that mosquitos already abounded. Even so, the river just to the south of Murmansk was still very cold. Neville says:

> I woke up this morning to the sound of ice scraping along the side of the ship, a very weird noise. I sat on deck after breakfast. It took some time for my eyes to get used to the terrific glare of the sun off the ice. As far as you could see there was ice sparkling and glinting in the sunlight. It was very thrilling to watch this old tub crunching her way through in the wake of the icebreaker ahead. I don't quite know what I expected to see up here; I certainly did not think that the ice would be so rough and jagged. I suppose it has been heaped up into bergs by tremendous pressure from all sides. Now and again we passed circular blocks of ice in the centre of which were pools of water of the most heavenly tint of blue, not quite opal, lighter and more limpid than ultramarine, a colour created by sunlight on water resting on the ice. It seemed to be the colour of the sky on a very hot day when you can scarcely recognise it as blue and yet it is blue. My eyes are aching now from having been sitting in that glorious brilliance all the morning. The ship has just been painted, the superstructure white and the funnels red. Yet after the dazzle of the ice the white paint looked a dirty grey and the funnels a dull orange. Men's faces appeared to be dark and tanned and my hands seemed a jaundiced yellow.

From time to time there was news of other troop movements—the Russian troops seemed to be 'doing well on the Vaga river'. By all accounts, Neville seemed to think that the Russian Army was swelling in numbers, with Admiral Kolchak also advancing, and he hoped that they would be able to return home before the winter, so long as there were no orders to advance on Petrograd.

Not only was Neville impressed by the colours of the countryside around him and the length of the days, but he also loved the sunsets. 'Never have I seen such glorious tints of colour,' he writes in a letter home. 'The sun set in a sheet of purple and saffron spread right across the Northern sky and this was reflected into the ice; the most delicate shades of pink mingling into deeper and yet deeper purple until they became azure and black. I can't describe it. I leant over the rail and wondered, absolutely amazed by the beauty of the sea and the colours reflected.'

About the end of May they arrived in Archangel which was 'more civilised' than Murmansk with white-painted churches built of brick, and roofs in either green, red, pink or vermilion and with minarets painted with stars and huge crosses on the top. The town stretched about four miles along the bank of the River Dvina and, according to Neville, it stank of dead men and putrefying fried fish, so not much better than Murmansk.

'There was a paragraph in the Russian Evening paper written in English welcoming us as saviours,' he writes. 'To them we seem to be little tin gods. We found our way to the quay where the *Czar* was berthed; all the world was there. Russians and in fact every

above: panorama of Archangel looking upstream showing ships at anchor and a part of the town, May 1919.
US National Archives and Records Administration: 86729808, public domain.
centre: Sabornia Cathedral, Archangel. May 1919.
US National Archives and Records Administration: 86729795, public domain.
bottom: British 'Volunteers' marching down Trotsky Street, Archangel, May 1919.
US National Archives and Records Administration: 86729822, public domain.

kind of ally were shouting and waving handkerchiefs to the troops on board, who, in their turn, threw to the crowd English pennies, their shoulder titles, cap badges and anything handy. There seemed to be a howling mob both on the boat and quay. The whole Brigade, consisting of the 43rd, 67th, 8th, Machine Gun Regiment, Sappers and Gunners are going to receive an official welcome from General Ironside and the Russian Government here. General Grogan, V.C. our Brigadier had to eat bread and salt which is the Russian proof of a hearty welcome.'

Neville and a friend walked round Archangel and found the locals a lot less friendly than the reception committee. 'There are many men in khaki but, on questioning them, they only purr and spit at you in Russian,' he wrote. 'So we strolled into the Cathedral. There was a service going on and the place was semi-dark and reeked of incense. On each side of the porch were many candles burning in front of eikons. The faces of the pictures struck me as good but, to prevent erosion from continual kissing by devotees, the design of these pictures was executed in silver or gilt, while the hands and faces alone were portrayed in the original paint. The result was that each one on examination looked tawdry, cheap, and gimcrack and yet there was a certain magnificence in the general effect. The congregation was standing up; indeed, there were no seats to be seen! A couple of priests were moaning a Litany while the people bowed and crossed themselves continually. To me it looked like a bobbing and crossing competition! When the congregation came out, they went up to the eikons, bowed and crossed themselves three times, kissed their particular saint's picture, knelt and kissed the stone floor, bobbed and crossed three times and then walked out bobbing as they went. Some idolatry, thought I!'

The weather suddenly turned and became very un-springlike—cold, windy and wet. Neville was very disappointed to discover that the rations they had been promised in England were well below expectations. The food was poor and not

Major-General Edmund Ironside commanding in Norther Russia c.1919/20.
Library of Congress, LC-USZ62-23352, public domain.

enough—he had been told it would be good and plentiful. Difficult for him to know who to complain to!

Then Major-General Edmund Ironside, the commander of the Allied forces, came to inspect the troops and Neville found him impressive. 'He is a huge man, as broad as I am long almost,' Neville wrote. 'He must be at least six feet six inches, can speak three languages fluently and gets on well in five others. (In fact, the highly-intelligent Ironside spoke all the languages of the different countries involved in the expedition, see footnote 1). He spoke to the men about prestige, saying that he had to deal with so many nationalities that if we did not behave well, he could not twist their tails; that they all look to us for an example. Then he spoke to the officers alone and told us that he had to send two Colonels home for being drunk and other officers for bartering rations and making money out of the Russian peasants. He hoped we would be back (home) by the end of the summer and gave us some details of the hardships which the men had suffered through the winter.' Ironside was extremely deprecating about the soldiers from other countries involved in the expedition and Neville comments 'Thank God I am British!'

In his book *The History of the 43rd Regiment*, Neville gives a further description of Ironside, who was clearly a mountain of a man and much respected by everyone. 'Standing with his legs wide apart,' Neville writes, 'wearing long, soft-leather Russian boots half-way up his thighs, his hands thrust deep into his jacket pockets, this giant of a general, a commander every inch of him and commanding in appearance, could not fail to inspire and enthrall his listeners. This man, who with his two great hands could have wrung the neck of the tallest officer, placed his trust—implicit trust—in the Regiment. The Regiment would prove worthy of it.'

The welcome from the Russian troops was warm. The officers were received by the local Mayor at an 'honourable tea' at the Duma and were described as the 'brave British Volunteers'. Neville was impressed by the older Russian soldiers in their ancient uniforms, covered in the orders of the Tzarist regime. An interpreter translated the Mayor's speech and the orchestra played God Save The King three times, even though no one seemed to know the words of the second and third verses. The tea was 'wonderful' with sugared cakes and all kinds of delicacies as well as real Russian tea—weak, slightly sugared without milk and flavoured with lemon.

'The Russian Officers, who were not wearing khaki, looked very fine,' Neville wrote. 'There was one old General, bald and bearded, who wore a drab jacket with the stars of orders plastered all over him, bright blue trousers with a thick red stripe, knee boots and jack spurs. I was told that he was General Savitch who was, at one time, Chief of Staff to General Brusiloff. He certainly was an imposing old man. The Mayor, in his speech, hoped that all the Russias would be united under one crown; in fact, they seem to want a limited Monarchy like ours.'

There was lots of marching and parades around Archangel, up to the cathedral and back again, lots more speeches, a service at the cathedral and an inspection by the commanding officers of all the different countries represented—Poland, France, the US, Britain to name just a few. It happened to be George V's birthday so everyone sang Happy Birthday to the king of Great Britain! Neville comments again that he was impressed by the Russians' clothing, especially their boots which were much better than his own and he resolved to buy a pair. This went on for a few days, but finally on June 2 Neville and his men set off again on the river Dvina deep into the forests of northern Russia. Neville had complained earlier that he felt very cut off as the only communication with the rest of the world was a primitive wireless on which the news was all about a new technological development—the internal combustion engine! He longed to know what was happening at the peace conference at Versailles where treaties were being agreed to end the Great War.

Sadly, just as he was moving out, the Quartermaster, Dancey, killed himself. Neville says that he had gone 'mad with overwork and loneliness and blew his brains out with a revolver.' Neville had some sympathy and comments 'I shall not be sorry to see a different place; this is unbearable. There seems to be no air nor space. The weather is exceedingly warm which is a great treat, but it becomes somewhat oppressive owing to the pungent smells of this place.' Neville added 'Dancey was worrying a great deal about the move. It certainly is no joke having to load, unload and load again without any form of organization or transport to call upon. He had spent days checking stores off boats and onto boats ...... I am not surprised that the responsibility turned his head. His death was an awful shock to us all. He was such a good fellow: a second Alf Barnes. Dick Warren has taken over the job pro tem. The tragedy gave us all a nasty shock. He was such a cheery, good-hearted fellow and an ideal man at his job.'

Leaving Archangel, Neville and his friend Toby took charge of an old paddle-boat along with the Company cooker, while the rest of the fleet was made up of 14 tugs. They stopped at Bakharitsa to pick up stores and their first meal—tea—was taken in the cabin which Neville proclaimed 'quite comfortable' though not all that clean. But he was less complimentary about the food—'some weird-looking pink stuff which we refused'—and even less impressed by the boat's skipper and crew who were 'filthy, greasy, unshaven Bolos'.[3] The skipper picked up Toby's hat and before either Toby or Neville could stop him, tried it on his head. Toby was worried the hat would be infected with some awful disease, while Neville 'shrieked with laughter at Toby's discomfiture.'

As ever Neville took great delight in the colours and variety of the countryside as he always had in his home county of Norfolk. He loved the intense green of the leaves and grass, the brown of the cliffs of the river, the many villages dotting the banks, the great width of the river itself and the forests abounding between the villages. 'The larches look very beautiful in their spring dress of crimson tufts,' he wrote. 'Each village has a square church painted in different colours and towered with minarets bespangled with stars and crosses; round it little plots of cultivated land and grazing cattle. Later on in the evening clouds began to gather and a thin drizzle fell. An icy wind, too, began to blow from the North. At 11.30p.m. we moored with the rest of the fleet, which had arrived 1½ hours before us. They were all bivouacked on the soft grass and we had to go ashore too, though we were all quite comfy on board. I heaved out my fleabag and blankets and crawled inside. The ground was as soft as a feather bed. Overhead sea gulls were calling and skirling, and that was the music by which I was lulled to sleep.'

He woke the following day with the rain wetting his face and since he was reluctant to move, the clothes in which he slept got soaked through. But his keen sense of humour kept him seeing the funny side of his situation—he could be at home living in relative comfort as he was a volunteer on the venture—so why was he putting himself through such a miserable time? He believed that it was 'only when one was living in the lap of luxury that one remembers how to grouse.' The sun came out as they set off again, only to run aground on a sandbank while the skipper was taking a break for a meal.

'The troops shrieked with mirth,' he wrote. 'The volley of Russian expletives and invective which ensued from the captain was almost more amusing than the actual display of seamanship. The men talk the most imitative Russian nonsense. It sounds like the genuine article to my ears. "Buzzoffsky, Trotsky" is a favourite expression, and, of course every Russian is called either Lenin, Trotsky or Bolo! Anyway, we managed to get off the sandbank all right after much bad language.' When they anchored for the night, Toby and he wandered off to the village where, with the aid of a few cigarettes and fewer Russian words, they managed to buy some butter and eggs from peasants dressed in very picturesque embroidered smocks. They had to enter a house in the village for this transaction which Neville described as 'a shack with the ceiling so low that neither Toby nor I could stand up straight. The windows were all shut tight and the room was permeated with the odour of unwashed sweating humanity combined with the stench of live-stock!'

On 5 June they arrived at Beresnik on the river Dvina. It was not easy getting their cookers, the stores, the Trench Mortar Bombs and all their other equipment off the boats onto carts to be dragged some miles—to the base at Mala Beresnik on the river Vaga. And it is not clear why the boats could not take them further, though perhaps the river became too shallow to allow the heavily laden boats to pass. 'The track was sandy and rough,' he wrote. 'We were dead beat from the exertions of unloading the ark and then reloading onto drosky carts; the mosquitos were damnable. At every halt they buzzed round us as thick as a swarm of ants. Precautions had to be taken since the forest on each side could well conceal a hostile patrol, a whole army, anything in fact. The atmosphere was stuffy, hemmed in as we were by the everlasting forest. The track ahead never altered—a rise- fall- another rise- and so on interminably. To pull the head net over your face so obstructed your view that it would have been impossible to spot anything untoward ahead, and also the asphyxiation underneath precluded its use. At the halts you could pull it down, but even then swarms of mosquitos found their way through the meshes where the net was tucked into the jacket collar. Through the seams of my breeches and the lacing holes they found room for the insertion of their proboscides. They settled like hairs on the back of my hands and crawled up my sleeves and inside my shirt. Added to this torture, there was the maddening wheezing hum of the little fiends, and the sudden intensified scream as one or more settled in my ears and buzzed out again. The very ether was plagued with a plethora of pestilential parasites.' Elsewhere Neville says that 'At the end of 48 hours in the line, many men could not see out of their eyes (because of mosquito bites) and their hands were as swollen as if they had been inflated by bicycle pumps. They suffered their trials with their usual good humour and cursed the " ....gnats unceasingly!"'

Finally, after four hours of purgatory, the column reached the front line at Mala Beresnik, after a march that Neville said he would 'remember to my dying day.' As they arrived, the 2/10th Royal Scots marched out for home, having made the in-coming troops completely aware of their 'unfeigned delight' of being relieved from such a pestilential place.

Neville was pleasantly surprised by the quality of the defences of the camp. It formed a semi-circle with the river as diameter, and on the other side of the river was a big expanse of burnt forest known as 'The Brown Patch', equivalent to No Man's Land in France during the Great War. He wrote:

> The centre and left "face" are composed of trenches with very strong machine gun nests and dugouts commanding all lines of approach. The right "face" is defended by a line of block houses connected with wire well concealed in the forest and

> commanding broad rides. We are covered by Russian Gunners who are a very stout lot.
>
> In the evening when it was cooler, we manhandled our kits over to a shack in the middle of the village where we have established our Company Headquarters. It occupies an exposed and unprotected position on rising ground. But there is nowhere else for us to go. By the time I had got my kit across I was absolutely dead beat so I rigged up my mosquito net and slept on the grass. Sawyer had omitted to bring a net and was eaten alive and had to find another pitch indoors! But I slept quite well immune from the attacks of mosquitos.

Fighting in a forest was very different from the trench warfare Neville had experienced in France. Northern Russia, Neville wrote, can be described in two words 'forest and swamp'. This gave the native army a huge advantage over any invading force, as the soldiers would be used to the land, having lived in it and on it for centuries. 'They knew all the tracks just as well as if each one had a signpost,' Neville wrote, 'and a sense of the forest just as some have an unerring sense of direction. They also had the advantage of well-defended interior lines of communication and supplies. (By contrast, the lines of the Allied forces were constantly being broken and supplies stolen). The forest consisted of pines and silver birches, growing very thickly together, giving a visibility of about fifteen to twenty yards in broad daylight. Added to that the undergrowth was impenetrable brambles, at least ten feet high. Once in the forest it was very difficult to keep direction without a vestige of a landmark to march on, and tracks radiated in all directions. It was essential to have a compass. The tracks were only passable by men in single file so it was difficult to protect a column on the march. The forest was always dank, sombre and sinister even at midday with bright sunlight. To stray from a track meant risking getting stuck in a swamp. The locals lived only on the banks of the river, growing rye and cutting wood for a living. Between the villages there was a track but this was inches deep in sand in fine weather, and inches deep in mud in wet. Bridges over streams were usually only fit to take very light traffic. The noise of shell-fire in the forest was horrendous. Adding to the explosion was the crash of trees and branches, and the reverberation was terrifying. I thought I was inured to the whole gamut of shell-fire from my experiences in France, but serving in Russia made me realise I was not. In France the only shell you could not hear coming was the one that hit you. In the forest, the trees added another hazard. We did not serve long enough to learn how to make the forest our friend as the Russians did. To me it never ceased to be sinister, a prison encompassed by inanimate warders by the million.'

But Neville quickly fell in love with the vegetation in the forest. 'The silver birches are just in leaf,' he wrote. 'Guelder roses and syringas are bursting into flower while sheets of golden anemones carpet the mossy banks and undergrowth. If it wasn't for the excessive heat and the mosquitos, we should have nothing to complain about.' Apart that is, from occasional attacks from the other side. The No 1 Platoon suffered machine gun fire from the other side of the river and a man was injured in the groin. 'Nothing serious,' writes Neville.

This was followed the next day by four whizzbangs within their perimeter, but this time there were no casualties. Neville at once decided to take out a patrol to try and 'snaffle' the Bolsheviks who had fired on them. Instead of using head nets against the mosquitos, they smeared their faces and necks with bad margarine from the rations mixed with rifle oil. 'It proved fairly efficacious in discouraging the mosquitos but the smell was revolting!' he recorded. They went out late in the evening wading first through the streams and swamps of spongey moss to an area of higher ground in front of the enemy position. They lay in wait but could see no-one moving about, and the buzzing of the insects inhibited hearing so the attempt was abandoned. Neville's camp was shelled and sniped at on and off over the next few days but no-one was hurt.

To his great joy Neville received two

letters from his family on 14 June and was able to return the favour by sending them his diary. He had feared that there would be no communication at all with the outside world. As during the Great War, there were long periods of time when nothing happened. The weather changed from hot and sultry to cold and wet. Various shooting parties went out to try to 'snaffle' ie, kill, sentries on the other side. Neville got slightly better living quarters. There was great excitement one day when a Bolshevik gave himself up, having waved a white handkerchief. The man said he had been forced into the army under the conscription scheme and had been in uniform for only three days before surrendering. Rumours came and went that the Allies were going to do a raid on the Bolshevik front-line, or an order would come down one day, and get cancelled the next. Otherwise, it was very boring.

Neville had with him summer clothing which he said was 'ideal' for the conditions, except that he got bitten half to death by the mosquitos.

> My knees are so bitten and sunburnt that I have been compelled to wear breeches,' he recorded. 'The rainstorms are short and very heavy and it is possible to get soaked to the skin and yet dry oneself in the sun in 10 minutes. The mosquitos create the greatest problem of life in these parts. They seem to invade even the sanctity of a mosquito net. The best plan is to take it in turns to beat them off while crawling underneath the net. And then, woe betide you if you fail to tuck the net under your fleabag, or sleep with any part of your anatomy touching the meshes of the net. I suppose they are long sick of Russian fare for they never seem to worry the Russian Gunners, whereas we are fresh and succulent and a change of diet to the little brutes. There is also another, venomous pest in a giant type of horse fly which has just hatched out. It is somewhat like a hornet but has brown instead of yellow stripes on its body; its head consists of great big iridescent green eyes. This brute can and does bite through practically anything.

Neville's platoon moved to Seltso on the other side of the river Vaga (though he does not say why), and he found it very pleasant. (Confusingly, there is another village called Seltso some miles to the east on the river Dvina). 'The village is quite close to the river,' he wrote:

> In the early morning we don Burberrys and plunge into the tepid water and come back for breakfast. The day from 11.a.m. onwards is too hot for work, so we loll in the mess, bathe again before tea and after dinner go out in gum boots shooting across the swamps. The other day we got a brace of oyster catchers which provided the first fresh meat since we disembarked at Archangel. We shoot anything we see because bully (beef) and maconochie[4] become so monotonous after a bit and any change is a delicacy. That is the order of the day here, and I can tell you that we are thoroughly enjoying ourselves.

The plan for the Allies to link up with the White Russian generals to force the Bolsheviks back into central Russia (and then presumably surround and take them prisoner, or otherwise defeat them) had been abandoned. Ironside therefore had to content himself with raids on the Bolshevik positions to break up their lines of communication prior to ordering the retreat. The first of these came on June 24 with an attack on the enemy front line at Mala Beresnik followed by a procession down the Moscow road to the village of Ignatovskaya.

'A and C Companies on the left bank and B on the right,' Neville wrote. 'It is going to be a pretty big affair. The first position is going to be assaulted by Nos 1 and 2 Platoons ably led by "yours truly" and Toby. On capturing the line, we disarm prisoners and demolish everything. Meanwhile Nos 3 and 4 Platoons pass through us and demonstrate in front of Ignatovskaya (some miles away to the south on the River Vaga) hoping to take the whole village prisoner as part of the aim). C Company in turn passes through them and captures the village.

> We hope to have no casualties, and, as we are going to attack the Bolo in flank, it ought to be a howling success. The guns are going to fire rapid, machine guns are to traverse along his front line and trench mortars are going to keep his right flank busy from the other bank. Toby and I rush in from the right and take his on his left flank. This is the scheme. It's going to be damned good fun, I think. Anyway, I'll let you know in 48 hours' time what happened.

That was the plan. But the assault fell far short of what had been expected, leaving Neville feeling very depressed. It was, he says:

> the same old story, late on the forming up point and shelled by our own guns. Our casualties were two killed and 16 wounded from A Company, nine killed and 12 wounded from C Company. I do not know what casualties B Company sustained.

The assault was due to start at 11 pm at which point Neville and his platoon should have been lined up in the forest ready to crawl forwards towards the Bolshevik front line during a bombardment from behind. But Neville realised too late that he had to lead his men over a mile through thick forest and he did not have enough time to achieve this. They floundered through the forest and got to within 200 yards of the enemy position from where Neville was supposed to advance still further to the right and get well on the enemy's left flank.

He describes the bombardment in this way:

> The noise was simply terrific when the guns and machine guns got going. The echo and reverberations of bursting shells and flying bullets were deafening and though there were only nine guns firing it seemed as if there might be nine hundred, as the noise of each shot ricocheted from tree to tree. However, it seemed that our guns were firing short. I quickened my pace and reached the clearing in front of the Bolo line and turned slightly right. Then it was that I found that there were only six men behind me. I shouted to them to lie down and went back to try and collect the rest of my platoon. I found Toby with both legs shattered, but no sign of Naylor who was commanding the right half company. I collected a few men, and advanced after sending back my servant to warn Bingo of the shambles.
>
> I found my six men of the Lewis Gun team just as the bombardment stopped at 23.05 hrs, and we all lay down at the edge of the forest facing the front of the Bolo line. As soon as the guns stopped, the Bolos let fly into the forest with two machine guns. Bullets were cutting young fir trees in half and cracking and crashing through the forest like a tornado. At 23.10.hrs our guns started again and my party crawled forward again to the high fence in front of the Bolo line. ... But once over the 7-foot fence (protecting the enemy front-line) we found his front line deserted except for 17 very frightened individuals and 2 machine guns.
>
> The majority of the men had never been in action before. I escaped being killed by a stroke of luck for as I was scaling the fence, I saw a man behind me letting off his rifle from sheer wind up and regardless of who was in front of him. I am sorry to think that the noises drowned the curses that I

Seltso, 1919.

John d'Arcy / NRO Nev 7/31.

hurled at him! However, there was an excuse because the men are mostly boys of 18 who have had very little training and less experience. We found the 17 Bolos cringing in funk holes. While mopping up, one young soldier came rushing up to me with fire flashing in his eyes and lusting for blood. "I've found a Bolo, Sir. May I kill him? Do let me, Sir." I had some difficulty in preventing him but was pleased to see that he had a better spirit than some! Then we re-organised, mustered the prisoners to fill in the trenches and make a road for the rest of the troops, evacuated the wounded, destroyed equipment and dugouts, and sent back the machine guns.

As soon as the protective barrage lifted, Nos 3. and 4 Platoons went forward as advance guard followed by C Company, transport horses, gun teams to take away captured guns, and lastly my platoon as rear guard. No 2 Platoon was left behind to carry on the systematic destruction of the Bolo front line. I did not see much more of the fight from my position as reserve. Contact with the enemy at Ignatovskaya was indicated by wild and indiscriminate firing, the bullets presumably aimed at the advance guard kicking up the dust in the road where I was, 300 to 400 yards behind our front-line troops! We had to wait for two hours for the barrage on the village because the signal arrangements had broken down with the first shell that was fired, the shell so frightening the pony of the signal cart that he turned and bolted to be no more seen. And for two hours the Bolos kept up a terrific fusillade with machine guns and rifles. As reserve platoon I was called up to within view of the Bolo position in case I was wanted. Meanwhile, Nos 3 and 4 Platoons had worked forward by rushes to the enemy's wire, only to be withdrawn a little later to allow the barrage to be put down. The latter was weak and so ineffective that when C Company and our platoons went forward, they were still held up by machine guns, and strong wire. Early on in this fight Bingo B was wounded in the groin. I saw him while he was being dressed and I'm afraid he suffered a lot though the doctor said it was not serious or dangerous.

Bolshevik prisoners, captured by the French fighting along the railroad between Archangel and Vologda
United States Army Signal Corps photograph collection, 1918-1919 [Folder 4, Item 7].

Source: Bentley Historical Library University of Michigan, public domain.

At 3.30 the Regt retired according to plan and I found the rear guard with my platoon and we reached Canadian Village[5] at 5.30.a.m. where we found the wounded lying on stretchers. Bingo was in frightful pain because his wound was swelling and he could hardly bear the sway of the stretcher. Yet never did a word of complaint pass his lips. He bore it very bravely. He set a wonderful example to us all in calmness under fire and patience in extreme pain. Try and imagine a journey of 5 miles over a rough road in an old drosky cart! The colonel was splendid, very cool and calm. It was not his fault that the show was not a howling success. The Bolos fought much better than we have been led to expect; we suspect that the machine gun teams were manned by Boche.

The prisoners were a miserable looking lot. They seemed to be younger than our boys. Their uniform was anything but uni-form. They were in fact indistinguishable from such of the civilian population as I have seen. A few had our pattern of Box Respirators which they had captured from the Americans at Shenkursk (further to the south). Their great coats were of varying colours, grey, drab, lavender, etc and their rations simply awful consisting of black bread, that's all. I expect that those that we did capture had every intention of being taken prisoner while the others did a bunk after the first bombardment. The enemy had had every indication of an attack. Our aeroplanes were flying over their lines all day yesterday dropping bombs and spotting guns, and in the evening, just before we attacked, they came over again and dropped eighteen 112lb bombs on their forward position and gun emplacements. Such unusual activity on our part must have told them as much as a written message from the Staff telling them that we were going to attack.

The raid failed because it developed into an attack. We were never close enough on his heels and felt the want of cavalry. Doubtless we could have captured Ignatovskaya if we had had more men, or if we had surprised the enemy or prevented the front-line troops rejoining the main line of defence. But all hope of surprise disappeared with our heavy preparatory bombardments. We suffered a good bit, too, from the inexperience of the men and especially section leaders. I found that I was always doing their job as well as my own and that they had no idea of leadership through lack of training. I think also that if the two leading platoons, Nos 1 and 2, had had time to form up and attack according to the plan, we would have taken many more prisoners. The Bolo put down a pretty heavy barrage on Nos 3 and 4 advancing behind us but luckily only one man was hit slightly. Anyway, it was quite a pretty little battle and gave us some experience in forest fighting from which I hope we shall be able to profit ... though I don't think our captures justified the casualties and the toll in officers was heavy.

Meanwhile there were rumours of other attacks. Neville and his men might move to the Dvina front for an offensive there. Or, in a month's time, 17,000 Siberians from Kolchak's Army might join up with the Allies on their front and so unite the two armies, though considering what separated them—forests, lakes, rivers—it was unclear how this would happen.

Notes

1. Britain, the US, France, Italy, Russia, Serbia, Poland, Czecholslovakia, Finland, Canada, Australia (volunteers only), Estonia, Austria and Spain. This was complicated further by the fact that some Finns and some Russians were Red and some were White. *The Day They Almost Bombed Moscow*, p. 39, Dobson and Miller, Athenaeum, 1986.
2. This ship was built 1917 in Newcastle for the Imperial Russian Navy. She had a long and distinguished career as the most powerful ice-breaker in the world, was later re-built and continued in service until 1989. She is now a museum ship berthed in St Petersburg. saint-petersburg.com/museums/icebreaker
3. Bolo, short for Bolshevik, is a derogatory term.
4. Bully beef was a tin of British Army issue corned beef. Maconochie was a tin of mixed meat and vegetables, and some wags claimed it was packed in soapy water! Wikipaedia, December 20213. Maconochie was the name of the company that produced tinned stew. It was widely applied as a slang term within the British Army of WW1. The Military Medal and the Military Cross became known as the Maconochie Medal and the Maconochie Cross, respectively. "Maconochie" was also slang for stomach. A telephone receiver, due to the resemblance of the can to the devices in use at the time, also became a Maconochie. www.imperialwarmuseums.org.uk, February 2018
5. Canadian Village—so-called because it was part of the camp where teepee-style tents were used.

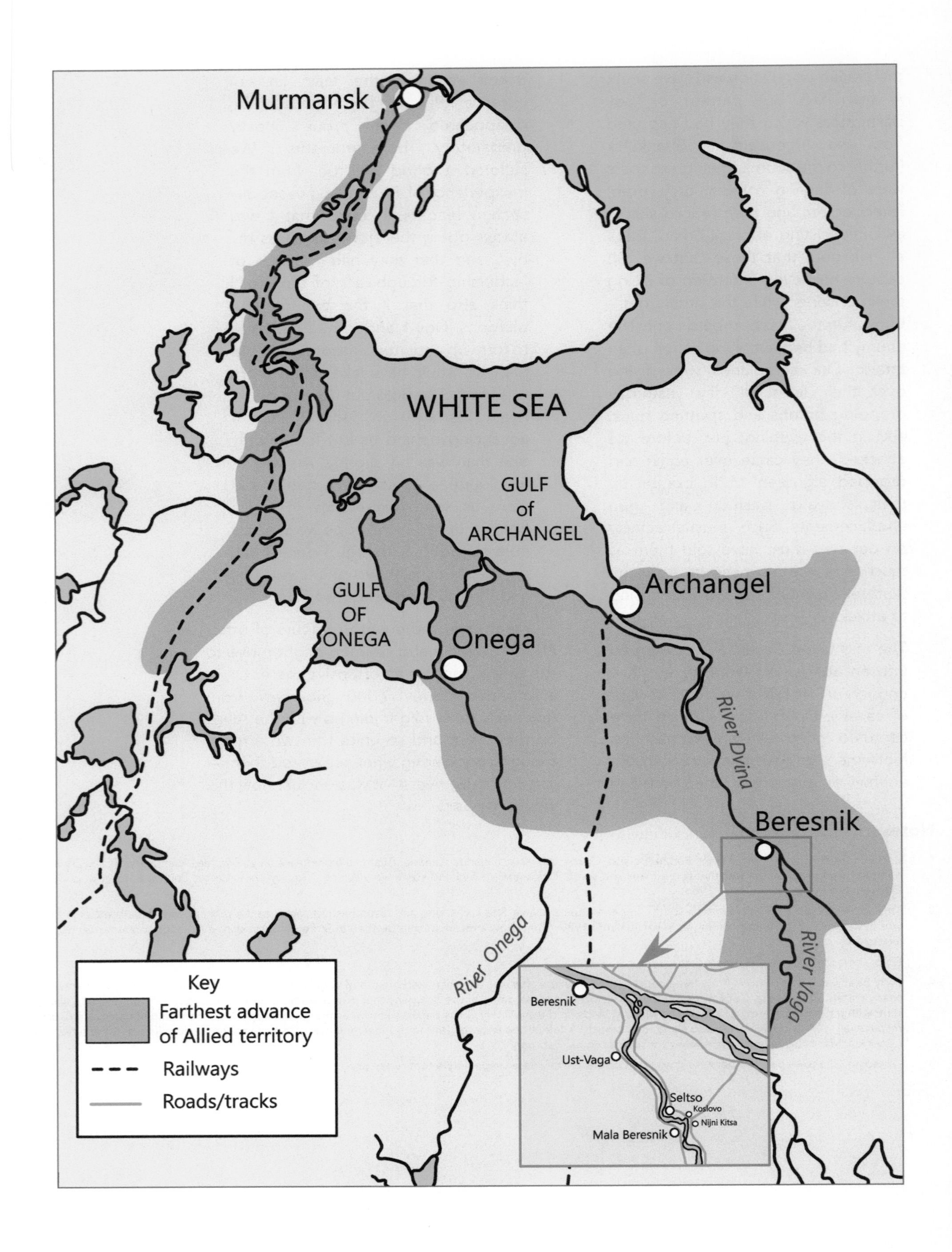
Murmansk
WHITE SEA
GULF
of
ARCHANGEL
Archangel
GULF
OF
ONEGA
Onega
River Dvina
Beresnik
River Vaga
River Onega
Key
Farthest advance of Allied territory
Railways
Roads/tracks
Beresnik
Ust-Vaga
Seltso
Koslovo
Nijni Kitsa
Mala Beresnik

A Birthday and Withdrawal

This section begins with Neville's 22nd birthday. He does not mention presents or letters from his family so this birthday may have been memorable to him for the wrong reasons. He describes a number of skirmishes fighting the Bolsheviks in the forest, a very different form of warfare from World War I during which he was wounded again, this time in his left arm. He and his men start to break out in boils from a lack of fresh food and Neville is infuriated by support for the Bolshevik cause by the dockers back in England. Press reporting back in England of the whole expedition was inaccurate for political reasons. Withdrawal from Russia occurred over a matter of a few weeks in August and September.

On 2 July 1919 it was Neville's birthday—he was 22—and as a gift, he got news in a letter from home that Churchill, speaking in the House of Commons, had described the British Expeditionary Force in Northern Russia as 'policemen'. Neville was, understandably, outraged. Another birthday gift came in the form of orders to make another assault on the same position as before—ie. Mala Beresnik followed by an attempt down the Moscow road. Neville was actually frightened this time in case he was badly hit and left to be taken prisoner by the Bolsheviks. (He survived the assault, but got a not-too-serious wound in his left arm, meaning that both arms were now compromised.)

By now the river was so low that crossing was only possible on foot or in waterlogged boats. They arrived at Mala Beresnik, from where the assault was to begin, three hours early. 'Of all the damnable things on earth,' he wrote back to his family, 'waiting to attack is the most damnable. You know the sensation of suppressed excitement, when your imagination runs riot and you can see yourself a mangled corpse or wounded or a prisoner obnoxious to frightful atrocities, and a hundred and one other empty visions. A chap without an imagination is the man I envy. As the time passes the needle in the pit of the stomach pricks more poignantly until you pray for action, movement, anything in fact rather than this infernal waiting.'

His platoon, No 1, was to form up on the enemy's extreme left flank and give the signal for attack by moving forward in *enfilade* on the Bolshevik's trench. Sawyer's platoon, No 2, was then to carry on the advance, sweep across the front of the section of trench that Neville was attacking and take the enemy's right section of trench in enfilade from the left. No 15 platoon was to pass through and mop up the enemy's trench overlooking the river bank. There was to be no bombardment so their movement in the forest had to be very quiet so as to give the enemy no advance warning. That was the plan, and so long as they could establish their presence on one flank without being seen, the prospect of success seemed favourable.

'There is something uncanny about the great silent forest,' he added:

> The slightest noise starts your heart thumping; and it is easy to approach within a few yards of a Bolo without seeing him, even with your eyes skinned as the Americans say. We started from "Canadian Village" at midnight and wound our weary way up the trench ... and entered the forest. ... When within 200 yards of the clearing immediately in front of his road position (ie. the enemy position), five shots rang out indicating the presence of an enemy patrol. This was awkward because it was important

opposite: map showing the extent of the allied interventions in North Russia.

redrawn from an original map by Hoodinski CC BY-SA 3.0.

above: 'The rolling character of the ground, the twisting of the road, the clearing through the forests on each side of the road are typical of miles and miles of roads in northern Russia.' centre: 'A convoy winding its way along a forest road. This was taken early in the afternoon at the start of a journey of nineteen versts. In a distance forty four versts only one log cabin was seen, and that was the rest house, where the convoy rested five hours before proceeding.' Jillena, Russia. (Rest stop between Archangel and Beresnik), 18 January 1919.

United States Army Signal Corps photograph collection, 1918-1919 [Folder 6, Item 12].

below: 'American soldiers on patrol wearing white capes to reduce the chance of discovery while operating in the snow-blanketed forests.'

United States Army Signal Corps photograph collection, 1918-1919 [Folder 8, Item 4].

Source: Bentley Historical Library University of Michigan, public domain.

that the Bolo should know nothing of our numbers or intentions. As my platoon had furthest to go, Naylor ordered me to strike off to the right and try to reconnoitre my position. There was no landmark to march on, so out came my compass and I checked the direction after every 100 yards to make certain that we were moving S.S.E. We toiled on very slowly and cautiously, keeping to the ravines in the forest and relying on the flankers on the left to report the presence of any enemy.

Suddenly the flankers reported seeing a Bolo about 50 yards ahead. I halted the column and went forward and scanned the forest through my glasses. Not a sign of a soul! After this scare we pushed on very slowly, and yet our rate of progress seemed to make no difference to the amount of noise from the troops behind me. I could not imagine how it was that we were not heard in Archangel; the troops sounded to me like a herd of elephants crashing through the forest. The nearer we got to the Bolo position, the more the point and flankers saw "men like trees walking". At each alarm of "hist, Bolo" I went forward. Each reconnaissance of mine produced the same sight—trees, trees everlasting trees and not one being on two legs. Naylor behind me waxed a trifle impatient; "Can't you move a bit quicker. Are you sure you are going in the right direction?" On the latter point I was not at all sure, but it shook my confidence to have our direction called in question.

I don't think I have ever enjoyed a job less than that compass march through the forest. Tracks and paths were always being encountered to distract me from my bearing. They afforded easy and silent going but I eschewed them as "a snare and delusion". Shorn of all steel trappings, I stood with my eye glued to the prism of my compass while the gnats swarmed over my face. I knew that there must be Bolos

prowling about and the possibility of an ambush was very apparent. I was responsible, practically speaking, for the safety of the troops behind me and I had to turn a deaf ear to the entreaties from behind to "get a move on, for the love of Mike". At about 2.a.m. Naylor came up and asked me if I thought I was well behind the Bolo position. I had not the foggiest idea really, but it seemed probable. I suggested that we should go a bit further and make certain of being well in the enemy's rear. Naylor overruled this in consideration of the time we had taken; I was not sorry for I was very bored with the pace of progress and the incessant alarms of "Hist, Bolo". In fact, my temper had risen and I felt like braining any soldier who said these words. So I turned left, intending to try and find the edge of the forest and get my bearings. Gradually the forest got thinner until at last I saw daylight between the trees and I knew that the clearing wherein was the enemy's position, must be quite close.

I halted the platoon, and took my platoon Sergt, servant, and two scouts forward with me. We came to a thinning in the forest across which was a path leading to the Bolo Position. "This," thought I, "may be their advanced gun position". I assumed that we were well in the rear of their trench position and that my chief care must be a reconnaissance with my right shoulder forward. Very cautiously I led the patrol forward. But when I was plumb in the middle of this thinning, I realised instinctively that my men were not following. I had a cold and lonely feeling. I looked round to see them all lying down on their bellies. "What the bloody hell is the matter with you all" I asked in a stage whisper. "Bolos," whispered Sergt Botley, pointing to my right rear. "You've seen nothing but Bolos the whole godamned night," I replied. "Come on, for God's sake". I had hardly uttered these words when there was a cracking of whiplashes all round me. I was facing the men when the machine gun opened fire. One of the first shots hit me in the arm but the rest ... went wide.

We made for cover pretty quickly, and I reported to Naylor. By this time blood was trickling down my arm and my breeches felt extremely wet! I wasn't certain whether I had been hit in the bottom as well or been childish from fright! But when my servant took off my equipment, he showed me ... that a bullet had removed the cork of my water-bottle. That was a near one for my kidneys! ... How the Bolos

'Canadian Villages' were established by the Allies to provide accommodation in front line positions, 1919.
United States Army Signal Corps photograph collection, 1918-1919 [above: Folder 7, Item 15, below: Folder 7, Item 16].

Source: Bentley Historical Library University of Michigan, public domain.

Allied soldiers preparing a meal.

United States Army Signal Corps photograph collection, 1918-1919 [Folder 11, Item 22].

Source: Bentley Historical Library University of Michigan, public domain.

missed me at less than fifty yards range is a mystery to me. A donkey with his eyes shut could have laid me out for keeps.

While I (ie. the wound) was being dressed a terrific fusillade broke out on both sides, during which Naylor somehow managed to deploy the three platoons. Then they advanced in line, scaled the 7- foot fence while L/ Cpl Martin swept the Bolo trenches with his Lewis Gun. The result of the raid was 8 Bolos killed and one machine gun captured, while our casualties were 2 men slightly wounded. It transpired that we were in front of his position, so that all my care was wasted. Perhaps if we had taken more risks and moved faster, we should have attacked him in rear. This mistake only goes to prove how deceptive distances are in this infernal forest and how difficult it is to gauge ground covered. I hope you will drink to the health of the 43rd and the success of the new North Russian Force of Constabulary! You might ask the Government to send us out some truncheons with which to deal more effectively with these turbulent Bolos. We don't want whistles!

Neville talks in a letter home about the sort of food they have to eat. 'To the delight of everyone a ration of fresh meat arrived,' he wrote. 'But the Quartermaster buried it as soon as the volunteers had carried it ashore.' (This was a form of preservative). More intriguingly, an order was circulated showing how to germinate tinned peas which, apparently, could help to prevent scurvy. Neville says:

> It is called "Organised Germination," it has to be carried out under the supervision of Captains of Companies who are to obey the instructions to the letter. Mason, the Quartermaster, gave a demonstration to the assembled captains, reading from the book of the words. He read out:
>
> 1. A blanket is to be saturated thoroughly in the river.
> 2. Lay the blanket out in the sun.
> 3. The peas are now emptied out onto half the blanket. (This was done).
> 4. The peas are to be placed in fours on half the blanket as in column of route.
>
> At that, Private Sadler on his hands and knees placed each pea in its proper position in the column. One wit asked "Won't the peas germinate unless they are in fours? I should have thought they would have felt more "matey" and natural in pairs but, doubtless, the Army knows best." The Quartermaster carried on manfully.
>
> 5. The unused half of the blanket is now folded over the peas and left for at least 24 hours. Only germinated peas are to be used for subsequent cooking.'

Neville's final comment was that 'We have tried to entice life out of their stubborn anatomies but so obdurate are the peas that their hearts have never once so much as fluttered! Also, Mason has been deputed to bake bread without yeast. The result is only fit to be fired out of a gun and probably then it would spoil the rifling!' Neville's family continued to send him parcels of food—home-made jam was a favourite—and he was also able to fish the river so he was not utterly dependent on germinated peas!

Neville's most recent wound was healing but still resembled 'a piece of half-cooked bacon.' And he was not able to swim in the river where the water was like a 'warm bath' because of the dressing on his arm. There were rumours that the British element was shortly to be sent home as it seemed they were surplus to requirement, but by now Neville had developed an attitude of 'wait and see'. There was another rumour that 5000 Bolsheviks were marching on Beresnik to cut the British communication lines. Neville dismissed this as 'hot air, I think.' He had been disappointed so many times by rumours.

Neville's father sent him a report from *The Times* of London of the Southport Conference in the middle of July, where the North Russia Expedition was being discussed. Throughout the whole of this period, press reporting of the campaign gave a completely false impression of its success, i.e. that the Bolsheviks were in retreat and their defeat was imminent! Neville was infuriated. He wrote back to Neville senior:

> These bloody men are at it again, the same unmentionables as were pacifists in the last war. After all, what the hell does it matter to them what happens in this wretched country.... Anyone with the brain ... of a louse could see that our intervention in this country was essential. The Bolsheviks, not the Russians, let us down in the war, so why should we betray our allies to this scourge of Bolshevism.... ? The time is approaching when we shall be able to evacuate with dignity and leave the loyal Russians to carry on and administer the doses periodically. Bolshevism is like rabies and if the suspects are muzzled, it will die out naturally.[1] Can anyone suppose that nationalisation of women can last? Again, if they try to eradicate religion, something worse will spring up to take its place. I wish you would write a letter the "*Times*". It is bad for the morale of the troops. They will begin to think that they ought to be at home. I also hear that the dockers in England are refusing to load goods for us here. The canteen at Archangel has been forced to close down because they declined to load the stuff as soon as they knew it was bound for Archangel. Pretty!!!

Neville got back on duty on 27 July even though his wounded arm was still an issue. The hole made by the bullet had closed up but the skin had not formed properly because of sepsis, which meant he had to undergo more 'hot fermentations.' He complained that it was taking much longer than he had expected to heal, that it was already a month since the injury and the last wound (during the Great War) had healed in a week. Even so, he was better off than some. Neville had heard from his friend Toby that Bingo B, injured in the groin during a raid, was in a 'dangerous condition.' Bingo eventually had to have the leg amputated because of gangrene.

Troop morale had sunk very low because of inactivity, made worse by an outbreak of boils and diarrhoea probably because of a lack of fresh food. Even more depressing was reports in the press back home which seemed to criticise the troops rather than support them. 'We are very sick at the articles in the "*Times*",' Neville writes:

> One says that the new troops are not so good as the old category men. That is not doing us justice, though no end of harm was done by telling the troops that they would be back before winter, and by stuffing them with "summer picnic" balderdash. We haven't really had a chance to do anything very wonderful, and the Bolo has had a year in which to organise his forces. .... Our men are all young and partially trained. Only about half my platoon had been in action before! I can't bear these aspersions being cast on the name of the 43rd, though we are only that in name. There has been friction between a captain of another company and the Colonel, as is almost inevitable where regiments are mixed and forced into one.

Already the short Russian summer was coming to a close and the nights were drawing in. They ate around 10pm, then sat talking and reliving their battles until just past midnight. Then they had hot milky coffee at 1pm before bed at 2am as the sun was rising, and breakfast around 11.30am. That was their daily routine and it was not often that there was a change. However, one of the men caught a 20lb pike by exploding a 10 lb Mortar bomb in the river. 'My Gawd,' wrote Neville, awed by the size of the fish, 'that pike was a brute! It took us ¾ hour to get him onto the boat which was rapidly filling with water owing to our great activities and the shouts of laughter from the four of us. Every time we touched him, he gaped at us, flicked his tail and disappeared. He took a bit of killing when once aboard in spite of his shell shock. I beat him twice and again over the head with an oar and still he gaped at me! And what teeth! The men had pike steaks for breakfast the next day.'

The skirmishes continued with gains and losses on both sides with so many instances of luck, heroism and pluck that Neville felt he could not mention them all.

> The greatness of the achievement … lay in the fact that the village is long and straggling and required much "mopping up". A party of very determined Bolsheviks held the blockhouses at the South end. In the end they had to be systematically attacked and the occupants killed as they never showed any signs of surrender. Again, in the afternoon, Bolsheviks were spotted moving about in the rye fields. A gunner officer shinned up a tree, turned his guns on to them and 'shot them up properly.

From then onwards all was quiet. A patrol went out and picked up a badly wounded platoon commander; Neville assumed there were also many dead in the forest but they were abandoned.

> On my return to Koslovo I found another platoon of the 46th but they left today as soon as our platoon of C Company had arrived from Ust Vaga and taken over. Anyway, this show has done one good thing; it has woken Sadlier-Jackson[2] up to the fact that this column does exist and has some importance. If we had all been scuppered here, he at any rate would have been in the cart. The Bolo prisoners, taken at Mala Beresnik, have stated that it was known to them that we were holding this front very lightly but it was also thought that we had Russian troops as well. They had been told that the latter, on hearing the shout and bugle, would mutiny and shoot up B Company from within. Unluckily for them but fortunately for B Company, there were no Russians in Mala Beresnik!

At the start of August, the supplies were down to 2 slices of bread and 2 biscuits, 2 dates in lieu of jam, and lard in lieu of margarine, per man per day. It seems as though a great deal of the food was being stolen en route by the A.S.C.[3] and sundry Russians. Two A.S.C. Serjeants were put under arrest for "skulkering" (bartering) the troops' rum with the civilians of Ust Vaga. There were many complaints from the men, which were forwarded to Brigade level but they got no satisfactory response or compensation for the shortage. Neville felt his men did not have a chance. As he said 'It is boring enough to sit in a godforsaken little village, week in week out, with nothing to do and nothing to look forward to, but it is infinitely worse to have to put up with it on an empty stomach. The men take the shortage very philosophically and pull my leg about full rations. What annoys me is that I cannot give them a reason for it, neither can anyone else.' Even harder was the idea that they did not seem to be doing much good.

And there were now signs on August 10 that they genuinely were about to return to England as their heavy kit had been packed and sent down to Archangel. Neville thought that they would make an offensive under cover of which they would hand over to the Russians and then retire gracefully to England. To begin with there was a grand push on the Dvina in pouring rain, and then 2,500 men were to cross from the Dvina to the Vaga and take the Bolsheviks from behind. A Russian regiment and the 43rd were to bump them in front at the same time. Neville thought that most of the 'sticky work' would be done by the Russians with support from the British. He was upbeat about the coming conflict, but admitted that his nerves were not what they were at the beginning of the Great War. He found he had a:

> childish dread of the forest. I find it harder every day to force myself forward. I imagine another ambush in every thicket like the fool I am. I wish I had not got this ribbon.[4] I know within me that I am not worth it and its presence on my jacket lessens the value of the cross.

But the attack was cancelled due to such poor weather that the forest tracks had become impassable. By this time the river had risen seventeen inches since the wet weather started.

The troops were now in the process of leaving and Neville found, by 20 August, that half the men had gone. Three platoons of C Company had departed for Semetskoe which is half way between Beresnik and Ust Pinega, leaving A and B Companies to do the front-line work. The wound on his arm was dressed every other day but it was not doing well. He reported that all the new skin that had formed with such difficulty, had now softened and gone septic. Apparently, the doctor had applied raw iodine which had softened the skin and turned it septic again, and also caused other septic sores to break out all round the original wound. 'The doctor has only just qualified,' Neville wrote. 'And has had no experience of wounds. However, it does not matter much except that it's uncomfortable.' On August 21 he wrote that he did not need any more oil of citronella because the mosquitos had all been drowned in the terrible rainy weather so that they could now sleep quite comfortably without a net.

Neville now began to realise the true nature of the expedition he was engaged with—political rather than military. 'The government (in Britain) knows that all security ceases on our departure,' he wrote. 'And, therefore, it is better to propitiate by desertion and treachery before, rather than by capture after, our evacuation in order to preserve their necks intact. It is very bad luck on many who are loyal. We are not at war with the Bolos, yet we are fighting them; and as Germany has signed peace, our only excuse for fighting the Bolos has ceased to exist. As with Turkey in the 19th century we have backed the wrong horse! I am very sorry that all of you at home should have been so anxious on our behalf. "Wind" is always far more vertical the further you get from the front line. In March 1918 the only people who were thoroughly optimistic or philosophically indifferent were the front-line troops, while the "wind" in rear was strong enough to be called a "gale".'

Neville was not considered fit to command his platoon plus a platoon of Russians with a wounded arm, so a captain from B Company was sent over from the other bank, and Neville became his subordinate. The wound, so far from healing, was getting worse and this gave him time to both read and resent press reports in *The Times*. He was seriously disappointed and wrote on 21 August:

> From reading your letter of July 28th, it seems that you, poor souls, have been sadly gulled by The Times in its pessimistic article on the situation on the Dvina. I have read all *The Times* between the 24th and 30th, and have come to the conclusion that much has been written for political purposes. The things the papers say about the new troops are not very flattering. There seems little doubt that we have been put into a false position by the politicians and not the military. Had we been in the hands of Ironside solely, we should either not be here, or we would stay on through the winter and see the campaign through in a proper fashion. The civilians whom we leave behind won't think much of us when we withdraw, will they? ...The Government does not seem to know its own mind, and fears the loss of votes and salaries far more than the enemy. The mistake was made in the

beginning. Ironside has had an awful time trying to keep things going. He has only four battalions of British infantry and two machine gun regiments wherewith to offend or defend. Had he been given two Divisions instead of two Brigades, he would never have had the trouble he has had. Ample supplies are being sent to Denikin in the south; yet we only have the old pattern field gun up here. If our guns could outrange the Bolo every time, he'd soon hock it; and above all, a couple of whippet tanks would have sent him flying up the Vaga to Shenkursk. The Moscow Road was quite good enough for tanks. The policy seems to have been 'let them carry on with what they've got: it doesn't matter much whether they do well or not.

Neville realised his family had been worried about him during a mutiny[5] among the Russian troops where 100 Russian regulars had gone over to the Bolshevik side. There had been many casualties—Neville himself was not involved, but he reported this small piece about one of the battles.

> The serjeant major was foully done to death. One of the murderers cut his throat, and when the poor man put his hand up to close the wound another murderer chopped off his arm with a felling axe. He was then dragged down to the river where they proceeded to disembowel him while still alive. Having castrated him, they left him to die a slow death. Pretty!

By the end of August, the weather was very wet with incessant rain for 10 days. Neville was ordered to take a patrol deep into the forest as a covering party for a gunner observation officer, but he found himself nervous.

> There was a continuous drip of water from the trees which sounded like distant machine gun fire,' he wrote. 'I am very glad we did not meet any Bolos; I was feeling far from hearty. The observation officer sat up in a tree but only saw a few shots burst owing to the very bad visibility.

Neville had a very poor opinion of the Russians, both the officers and the regular soldiers. One Russian subaltern, he wrote, was ordered into the forest with a patrol to a particular spot where several tracks converged, to see if there were any signs of a recent Bolshevik occupation. 'The subaltern duly handed in a very detailed report the following morning stating that the junction was unoccupied and that there were no traces of the Bolo ever having been there,' he writes:

> The Russian subaltern was confronted with his report and asked to give an explanation. He admitted, quite frankly, that he had never been to the place himself for the simple reason that he did not consider it an officer's job to take 10 men on patrol: that as soon as he had found the track he had handed over the job to a Corporal. The latter never found the place, and, fearing to return empty-handed, had

Prisoners taken in the raid of 26/27 June, 1919. The two men in uniform are British Intelligence Officers—Tamplin and Watson.
John d'Arcy / NRO Nev 7/31.

concocted the story from a fertile imagination. The officer was not at all ashamed at his dereliction of duty. We have yet to find out what a Russian officer can or will do!

The Russian 'men' ie. the regular soldiers, got a slightly better review.

Neville writes:

> Watson and Tamplin are the two Intelligence Officers attached to this column.
>
> They have both lived most of their lives in Russia. Practically every week one of them takes a mounted party to find out what is happening behind the Bolo lines. They start off with 7 days' rations and ride down the wide rides out North and South through the forest. They make a rendez-vous and then a couple of the gang trek off in the evening and drift into a village and get into conversation with the Bolos. In all the villages behind the lines they know of sympathisers who are ready to hand on information, and report the presence or otherwise of important commissars.
>
> On one occasion the whole party of eight came to the outskirts of a village at about midnight when it was still dusk. They formed into line and cantered down the village street, firing their revolvers as they went. This, naturally, awakened the inhabitants who rushed out of their shacks to see what the fuss was about. The party then wheeled about at the end of the street and galloped back shooting down the particular commissars whom they knew to be somewhere in the village. As a result of these incursions, big prices have been put on the heads of the Intelligence party; and these increase in value after each successful raid. By such ruses they have caught some useful specimens of the genus "commissar" and carried them off into the forest. But as their prisoners have never been brought to our lines, one can only guess that they met their fate in the forest as soon as all useful information had been extracted from them. This party gives no quarter as they expect none themselves if they are captured by the Bolos. I don't think these stories of their adventures are flights of fancy, for the information they glean precludes that.

Neville lived from one mail delivery to the next and he writes with gratitude when he receives parcels and letters.

> A mail of terrific proportions came up on the 26th (August) bringing me four letters and eight parcels from you. I write with the fragrant aroma of an "Anoo" cigar filling the room. Your prunes, almonds, raisins, and chocolate I keep as an emergency ration until the next parcel arrives when I eat up the old ones. My Gawd! How lovely it is—Honey!—and a huge cake. Last night we had Plum Pudd'n and excellent it was too! To-day Apple Pudd'n, no less excellent. .... It is sickening to find, day after day, that the men's rations are 50% short. In France one felt that one was doing something to help England; here in this howling silence, one hasn't even got that satisfaction. It looks very much as if we are the dupes of this shifty Government. The mutinies, thank God, have not affected us on this column. However, they are nasty things to hear of, let alone experience.

The countryman in Neville greatly enjoyed watching the seasons.

> The topmost branches of the birches are beginning to fade. The undergrowth is a mass of moss, whortleberries, cranberries, and bilberries and aren't they good eating? I went for a stroll in the forest the other day in the hope of seeing a capercailzie, blackcock or rabshikkie.[6] It was a very wet but wonderful walk. I tramped across swamps carpeted with this blood red moss which gave the impression of treading on sponges. Then I came to a piece of very thick forest where trails went off in every direction. I had hoped to find some

> spoor of bigger stuff than birds but was unsuccessful. The birches are lovely, standing like silver sentinels among the dreary pines. They are tall and graceful and I love the way in which the breeze sighs through their leaves. The forest is awe-inspiring. I feel how puny a man is compared to nature in the wild, to this forest stretching for miles and miles, to almost incomprehensible distances; and to whose vastness a man is no bigger than a louse. There was in some places a kind of lichen on the ground. To see a clearing at a distance covered with this makes me think there was a lake beaten up into foam by a high wind.

There were reports almost every day now that Neville and his troops were to be withdrawn to Archangel. Tiger Wyld came over on August 26 to say that A and B Companies, now holding the line, were going to form the rear guard of the whole Dvina and Vaga Forces. Owing to the rains and the rise in the river, the fleet would be able to move without difficulty though until that point they had been out of action, anchored in deep pools in the Dvina.

> Tiger told me that the Bolos will have to cover 15 versts (a verst is a Russian measure equivalent to 3500 ft or two-thirds of a mile), before they find out that our troops have gone which will mean a lapse of twelve hours and sufficient time for us to evacuate. Not so, this river. On the left bank, the Bolo is only 2000 yards away and he has a pretty shrewd idea that we are going soon from Russian deserters. The other day 2 Serjeants and 8 men of the Russian Gun Battery deserted. This is the policy of many of the Russians now serving on our side. They know that the Bolo will catch them in the end and that a timely desertion now may in some way atone for the crime of having fought against him. The same applies to many civilians behind our lines who are now showing Bolshevik tendencies to cover themselves. Rumour has it that the people in Archangel are distinctly Bolo and we may have trouble.
>
> Having acted as rear guard we shall embark at Beresnik, and go straight through to Archangel, picking up the 67th and our companies on the way. On our arrival we shall reform as a Brigade and hold the right flank of the line which the Russians intend to defend when we've gone. The withdrawal has been greatly delayed by the state of the river and shortage of tugs to remove the stores and dumps. Also, the Russian higher command is very undecided on the line to be held.

But he was still there on 29 August when he and a platoon marched in a circle to give the Bolsheviks the impression that an attack was coming at the same time as an attack from elsewhere. Neville wrote:

> Sawyer's platoon went out as a mock advance guard to the 'Brown Patch'. Booth and I did the stage work. We marched round in circles in the hope that the Bolos would see us and think that a terrific force was advancing against them. We all laughed very heartily, including the Colonel who was watching. Meanwhile the guns were plastering his (ie. the Bolshevik) front line with all manner of frightfulness, and a platoon went out from Mala Beresnik and gave the Bolos a dose of .303 from a Lewis Gun, to complete the illusion. As a piece of bluff, I hope it was successful. If not, we were amused; and that is worth a lot in these days.

On 30 August there was an attack on the Railway Front, in which 350 Bolsheviks and all their guns were captured. The Bolshevik fleet was caught anchored in pools unable to move forward or back, and, according to Neville

> ... quite ready to surrender. But when the latter saw we had no guns to pound them, they fought hard and did a good deal of damage. Just a piece of bad luck prevented the show being a decisive victory. The Bolo sailors

opposite: map of Mala Beresnik.
redrawn from Neville's original sketch map.

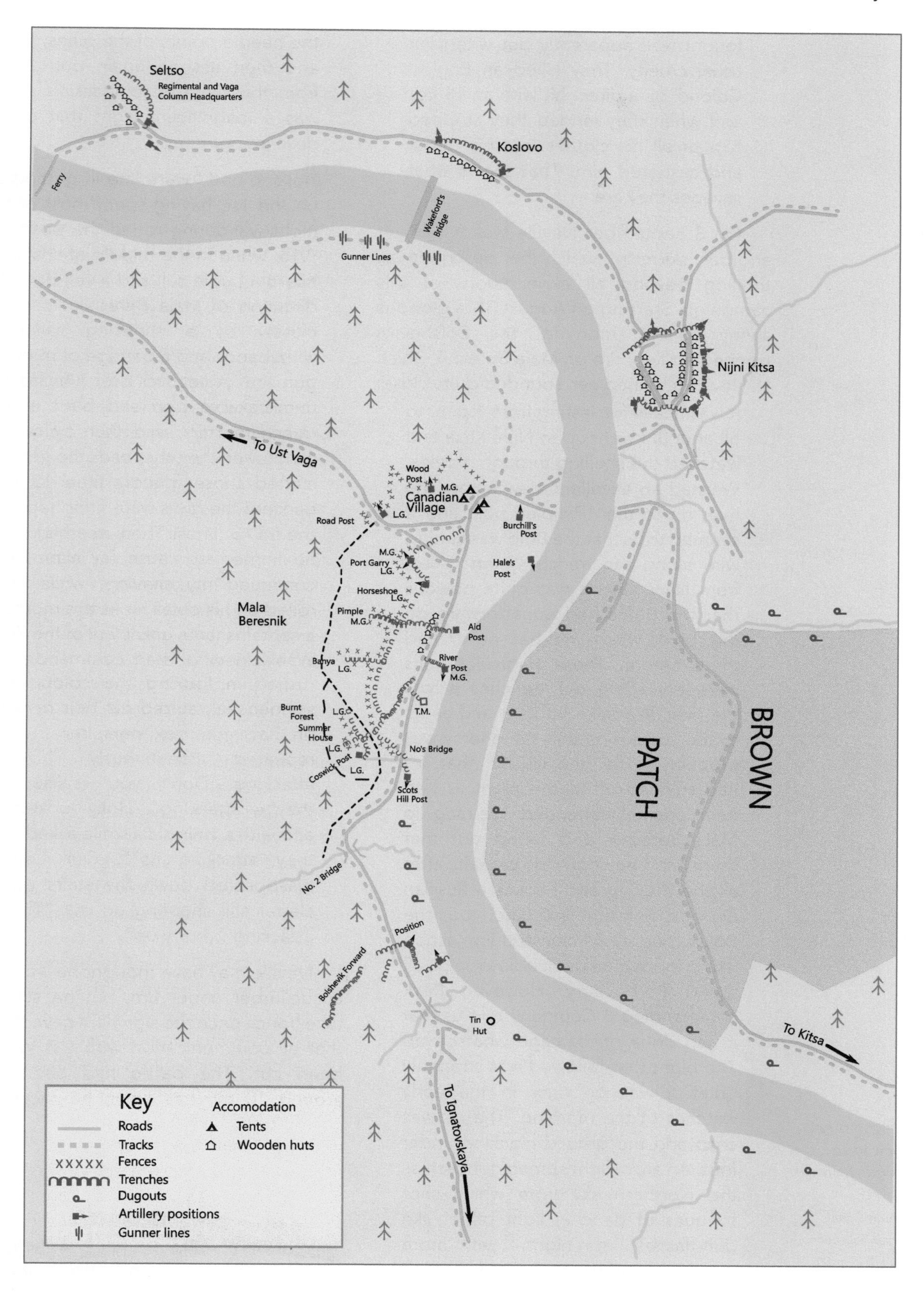

Seltso
Regimental and Vaga Column Headquarters
Koslovo
Ferry
Wakeford's Bridge
Gunner Lines
Nijni Kitsa
To Ust Vaga
Wood Post
M.G.
Canadian Village
Road Post
L.G.
Burchill's Post
M.G.
Port Garry
L.G.
Hale's Post
Horseshoe
L.G.
Mala Beresnik
Pimple
M.G.
Aid Post
Banya
L.G.
River Post
M.G.
T.M.
Burnt Forest
Summer House
L.G.
L.G.
Coswick Post
L.G.
No's Bridge
Scots Hill Post
PATCH
BROWN
No. 2 Bridge
Position
Bolshevik Forward
Tin Hut
To Kitsa
To Ignatovskaya
Key
Roads
Tracks
XXXXX Fences
Trenches
Dugouts
Artillery positions
Gunner lines
Accomodation
Tents
Wooden huts

fought well apparently but with their usual cruelty. They killed an English Colonel by a direct hit with an 18 Pdr and when they landed they stripped him of all his clothes, cut his throat and castrated him. That shows what savages they are.

On 3 September Neville was full of yet another skirmish, which he describes as thrilling beyond all expectations of this campaign. Starting on August 31, a glorious sunny Sunday morning, the Bolsheviks opened artillery fire on Mala Beresnik which to Neville's trained ear, sounded quite close:

> It was heavy fire lasting from 1.p.m. to till after 8. I went up to Nijni Kitsa and watched the shelling through glasses. We had an excellent view across the river on to the "Pimple" post and it seemed to us that the Bolo was cutting wire along the trench system. Also, from Nijni Kitsa it was quite obvious that the Bolos had guns forward on this bank where he has never had them before. These particular guns were enfilading our trenches across the river. We talked it over and came to the conclusion that the enemy was probably under the illusion that we had shinned off in the night as had been originally arranged. We rang up Mala Beresnik and found out that there had been only one casualty after all the shelling and he was a Russian Gunner! For the first time, too, the Bolo brought a 6" Howitzer into action which lobbed its damnable crumps all round Port Garry. However, Peck commanding B Company told us that it had done no damage whatsoever! The night that followed was strangely quiet. I was on duty in the early watches of the morning. The air was crisp and the ground crackled under foot. An arc of light spread right across the Northern sky from which shot tongues of dancing light rather like gun-flashes at night, yet more piercingly bright, more sparkling. It was as if the world was crowned with a tiara of fine diamonds. The fiery facets flickered and flashed, darted among the needle points of the pines, faded and then flashed again but always from the same encompassing arc. It was a magnificent sight that defies description.
>
> Holland and I were late in getting up on the 1st, having spent most of the night wandering round the posts. At 9.15. when in the middle of shaving I heard a bugle call and a yell from the direction of Mala Beresnik, followed closely by a shrieking salvo of whizzbangs and a barrage of machine gun fire. A second later I heard the unmistakable pop and blast of our trench mortars, and then below my window on the other bank the gunners started those friendly little 18 Pdrs barking: the guns were firing rapid on the S.O.S. lines! There seemed to be no immediate cause for alarm, so I continued my shaving, while Holly rolled on his puttees. At this moment, a captain (name unknown) of the Royal Warwicks who is in command here, rushed in looking the colour of a skinned eel, seized his belt revolver, tin hat, and box perspirer .... and repeated continuously "They're attacking. Don't you realise that they're attacking". Holly looked up and with a whimsical smile asked "Are they attacking us?". Our Captain disappeared down the stairs with a clatter still shouting up out "They're attacking ...hurry up".

Neville may have thought he was cool as a cucumber under fire, but he started to take notice once the signalers gave the news that all communication with Ust Vaga had been cut. The battle had been raging around 10 minutes when he received an

Trench leading through the deep snow to an outpost Vologda Railway Front, April, 1919.
United States Army Signal Corps photograph collection, 1918-1919 [Folder 7, Item 17].

Source: Bentley Historical Library University of Michigan, public domain.

Group of officers at Nijni Kitsa. Left to right: Lt. Booth, Lt. Lowndes, 2nd Lt. Sawyer, Lt Neville, Lt. Giles, Lt. Hamilton, Lt. Bernett. Machine Gun Corps. Capt. Naylor, Lt. Trewheler. Kings' Own Royal Regiment, interpreter.
John d'Arcy / NRO Nev 7/31.

order from Regimental HQ to lead his platoon across the river and stay at the Gunner Lines to act as a reserve in case of need. 'I handed over the defences of Koslovo to the Sappers and Russians,' he wrote. 'And was ready to move at 9.45. Having crossed the bridge to the Gunner Lines, I reported to the officer in command for instructions. But he could give me none as the lines to Mala Beresnik were still "dis". However, the line was mended by 11.a.m. and we heard that the Bolos had come over through the rye fields and been mown down by our machine guns and trench mortars.'

Around 11am a message came through that about 200 Bolsheviks had been spotted in the forest and Neville was called upon to go and disperse them. Neville was a little hesitant about yet another forest battle, but information then came in that the Bolsheviks had been chased out by another patrol. At the edge of the forest another 200 Bolos were discovered forming up for a second attack. The officer in charge of the patrol returned to the trench mortars, gave them the exact position of the enemy and then let the bombs to do the rest. 'Fifteen rounds rapid fired straight into the jabbering mob of Bolos produced the desired effect,' Neville wrote. 'They dispersed to healthier climes for the time being. I was therefore not required for the moment to do anything except remain as a reserve.'

The temperature fell sharply in September and the days shortened, much as they would in an English December. Neville got the stove going in the platoon headquarters, and found that it was certainly efficient. When the heat was great enough that there was no smoke, he shut the draught and opened the vent above the firebox, and colossal heat filled the room. This roused the bugs in the wooden ceiling! 'They dropped in their hundreds onto our valises,' he wrote. 'And fed off us and the Keatings powder[7] with which we had armed ourselves. All night long, we could hear the plop, plop of falling bugs.'

Neville was still in Koslovo on 5 September, but a message had come through to say that two blankets per man, plus tin hats and entrenching tools should be sent over to Seltso the next day, along with officers' kits. It looked as though the British troops would withdraw on 8 or 9 September. Was this finally the moment when they could be certain of getting home?

Neville was told that the troops would withdraw on 10 September but that he would be required to hold Koslovo alone while the rearguard action was carried out. He went out into the forest laying bomb traps across the traps leading to the village which he described as 'rather good fun! If anyone touches the trip-wire he will find a bomb fizzing on each side of him. The only trouble was to work the pin sufficiently loose to ensure that the slightest touch will extract it and allow the lever to fly off.'

But as usual the plans were cancelled at the last minute. A convoy of 70 carts was waiting to evacuate the men and their equipment on the night of 9 September, but a telephone message came through saying they should wait for further orders. 'A terrible gloom spread over the mess,' Neville wrote:

> No one spoke until I swore like a division of good infantrymen! It was bitterly cold and the stove in our bedroom had 15lbs of gun cotton concealed in the chimney as a trap for the Bolos. We heaved this out and lay down on the hard floor while bugs dropped off the ceiling, roused by the warmth of the stove to seek their food in due season. Outside an icy North wind whistled round the eaves. We had rations for just one day and the minimum reserve ammunition which consisted of 1000 rounds per platoon and 4000 per machine gun. In the evening rations came up for five days; there were no more at Beresnik except sufficient to take us down to Archangel. I walked down to Seltso with friends; it was a clear autumn day with bright sunshine and fleecy clouds. Seltso was like a city of the dead; no one stirred in the street and we failed to glean any information.

There was more fighting, another message to say evacuation would be the following day which was cancelled a few hours later. Finally, on 15 September at 5.30am carts came up from Seltso to take down Lewis Gun boxes and cooking utensils. Neville and his platoon got busy burning or otherwise disposing of everything they had—every scrap of English literature, every tool, every bomb, all their ammunition, and they replaced the gun cotton in the stove of the bedroom, covering it carefully with cold ashes. Then (a bomb specialist called) Wakeford arrived to set the bombs which were to explode 75 slabs of gun cotton if anyone trod on the bridge at the South end of the village. By 8am A Company was ready, marching through Koslovo, down the cliff and over the bridge to the Gunner Lines. Neville's platoon was now a rear guard and as soon as A Company was clear they crossed over the bridge. Neville was the last man to leave Koslovo, and behind him the sappers started to hack away the anchor ropes to let the bridge collapse. This was finally the moment when the troops could be sure they were on their way home.

A snow covered dugout, at a point on the high ground overlooking, in this case, the Padenga river. It is equipped with one Vikers and one Lewis machine gun. A non-commissioned officer and two Vikers, men, two Lewis men, and six privates are on duty in the dugout.
United States Army Signal Corps photograph collection, 1918-1919 [Folder 6, Item 3].

Source: Bentley Historical Library University of Michigan, public domain.

> A Company moved off into the forest towards the Moscow road,' Neville wrote. 'It was a different road from the one we had marched along in June! The air was chill, the birches yellow and the track an inch deep in mud. As for mosquitos, I had almost forgotten their existence! Some old women came out and watched the column, howling and beating their breasts, in paroxysms of grief. I hardly felt sorry for them; they or their families have played a double game too long to deserve any pity. On reaching Ust Vaga at 12.30pm. A Company took over the defences. The village is a long straggling settlement, in the centre of which stands the characteristic white Church of Russia. It does not lend itself to defence and I could see how easy it was for the Bolos to enter on the 1st. Our orders were to allow no civilian out of the village during our stay. The bridge on the Mala Beresnik road had been blown up by the sappers.

They took with them some men and women who were known Bolshevik sympathisers as hostages for good behaviour. The route north back towards

Archangel lay along the river bank since the short cut through the forest had been reported impassable to artillery and transport because of the heavy rain. Only a short while after leaving Koslovo shots rang out in Ust Vaga which Neville thought must be Russians practising on the range. But at the next stop—caused by great difficulty in getting the column over a large morass—a local Russian ran up shouting 'Bolo, Ust Vaga!' There was a minor battle with a few casualties on both sides, but they reached Beresnik at noon—where boats were waiting for them—and B Company embarked at once followed by H. Qrs, A Company and Trench Mortar Battery.

Neville wrote:

> We were ready to move at 1.30 but it was not to be so. Aeroplanes reported that the Bolos were within two versts of Beresnik advancing in two columns. Then a most unfortunate thing occurred: a barge containing some Royal Fusiliers came down with 14 casualties on board, the result of Bolo's fire from the mouth of the Vaga. Later, Sadleir-Jackson came alongside in his coastal motor boat. He, too, had been shot up from the same place, but unfortunately his person was still intact. Resplendent with gold knobbed cane and yellow-wash leather gloves, he climbed on board and insulted the Colonel in front of many men and swore as badly as I do when I'm really annoyed. This exhibition was not necessary to prove that he is a hairy-heeled mountebank; we all knew that already.
>
> A platoon of marines was sent up in a motor boat to make a landing and drive off the Bolo. The wretched Sawyer and his platoon clicked for this job and set off in the pouring rain for a destination unknown. An hour later, Sadleir-Jackson, still waving his arms like an infuriated gorilla at the Zoo, ordered a platoon of the Fusiliers to relieve our men. The latter returned at 5.30 and ¼ hour later our barge was taken in tow and anchored in midstream. We went to bed in our flea bags, warm and comfortable; and what a relief to get a change of washing! We left Beresnik to be held by the Fusiliers and some Russians. The latter were very windy; indeed, five of them tried to slink on board our barge and desert. That just shows how much heart they've got in the show.

Neville felt very sorry for his men whom he described as 'a sorry sight to look at. Their uniform is torn and dirty, boots in holes, puttees frayed, in fact thoroughly dishevelled but wonderfully cheery withal.' But it was a great luxury to wake up the following morning to find their boat gliding down the river taking them further all the time from the 'monotonous villages of Mala Beresnik, Nijni Kitsa, Koslovo and Seltso.... Sitting in the sun on the leeward side, we preened ourselves and damned those villages to everlasting purgatory!'

On 18 September Neville and his men spent the day trying to refloat stranded barges—two had to be abandoned—and that night they anchored off Sisskoe. As the journey back to Archangel continued—not uneventfully—Neville was treated again to a vision of the Northern Lights. 'Away in the North like a fountain of fire,' he wrote, 'the waves of iridescent light burst up behind the jet needles of the tree tops, silhouetting each branch against the sky: Like veils of rainbow silk dancing, changing, flitting: now spreading right across the sky in a fairy curtain, now vanishing to spring to life again in yet more vivid brilliance straight overhead. And that is a poor description of their magnificence.' I think Neville is at his best when talking about the splendours of the natural world.

By lunch time on 19 September, he could see the red and black funnels of a Cunader anchored on the quay at Archangel. By tea time, they were passing the *Czar* and *Czaritsa* and many Naval craft. On September 21, they disembarked very early in pouring rain and marched to their billets which he described as 'quite comfortable for all ranks. When I arrived, what do you think I found? 25 letters and 8 parcels from you all at home. It took me practically the rest of the day to read them!'

On the 27th everyone had boarded the *Czar*. For breakfast they dined on bacon and eggs, a treat after the monotonous diet in the villages. They sailed at noon for Britain, watching the towers and minarets of Archangel fade into the distance, and wondered how long it would take the Bolsheviks to arrive there.

'Naylor, Bill Smyth, Philip and I share a cabin,' he wrote. 'There is a Russian next door who stinks like a badger.' Out at sea the weather turned stormy. The troops were seasick 'paralytic in the bowels of the ship,' and a good many of them were absent from both lunch and dinner. One of the men, Sergt Thomas, was so sick that he lost his dentures overboard and another, Serjt Thorne, was so ill he could not speak. It did not last long. By 3 October there was a heavy mist, the sea was calm and the ship was off the Hebridean Islands heading rapidly for Liverpool which was just 267 miles away. Neville wrote:

> 'On landing from the *Czar*,' 'we were all given tea and … chocolate by the Navy and Army Canteen Board and Red Cross, God bless 'em. Then we formed up with A Company leading, and marched to the Town Hall. There were a few people at the gates of the quay who clapped as we marched out. The public seem more enthusiastic over departing than returning troops! We formed up in front of the Town Hall and were addressed by the Mayor. There was a … cheer for the Russian Expeditionary Force, but otherwise, the spectators were very few and far between. On the march up to this camp, there were a good many hoots and jeers from the strikers[8] though some people seemed pleased to see us. The animosity of the corner boys was always aimed at the officers, a sure sign of Bolshevik tendencies. We had bottles thrown at us, but I think on the whole that we were lucky to get off so free. We have spent our time gazing at the shop windows and wondering at the hum of the town after months of complete silence. We have eaten abnormally, making up for the bully and machonochie. The next thing is leave, aye LEAVE!'[9]

Notes

1 This was a totally different perspective from that of the famous author of sailing books for children, Arthur Ransome, who was there as a Guardian correspondent. Ransome was broadly sympathetic to the Bolshevik cause as he wrote in his little book, *Russia in 1919*, published at the time.

The Bolsheviks were the driving force behind the revolution in Russia, which occurred between 1917–1922, and which forced Russia's withdrawal from the Great War. The Bolsheviks ultimately became the first communist government of Russia, and on the way were responsible for the murder of the Russian Imperial Family, Tsar Nicholas II and his wife and children, known as the Romanovs. 'Bolo' was used as a derogatory expression for Bolsheviks used by British service personnel in the North Russian Expeditionary Force, which intervened against the Red Army. Neville was part of that force, but the Bolsheviks were no more bloody than other parts of Europe at the time. www.historylearningsite.co.uk, February 2018

2 Brigadier-General Sadlier-Jackson launched an attack with his brigade on the Dvina front on 10th August 1919. This was a resounding success. Over 3,000 prisoners were taken and heavy losses inflicted. The objective of enveloping and destroying the enemy was to open the way for the peaceful evacuation of British and Allied forces.

Brigadier General Lionel Warren de Vere Sadleir-Jackson CB, CMG, DSO & Bar (1876 –1932), to give him his full name and title, was an officer of the British Army, serving in the Second Boer War and the First World War with distinction before taking command of the evacuation of the North Russia Relief Force. Wikipedia, December 2021

3 The Army Service Corps.

4 I think he means the Military Cross awarded to him in WW1.

5 Many of the British and foreign troops often refused to fight. Bolshevik attacks were therefore launched in the belief that British troops might even defect to their side once their commanders had been killed. The numerous White mutinies among the Russians demoralised Allied soldiers and affected morale. The Allied forces were affected by their own mutinies among British, American and Canadian forces. Wikipedia, November 2021, North Russian Relief Force.

6 Capercailzie—woodgrouse; blackcock—blackgrouse; rabshikkie—despite widespread research, I have been unable to identify this bird/animal/plant. If anyone can help, I would be very glad to know what it is.

7 Thomas Keating was a chemist with a shop in London in the mid 19th century. He sold a powder which would kill 'fleas, bugs, emmets, flies, cockroaches, beetles, gnats, mosquitos, moths in furs, and every other species of insect in all stages of metamorphosis.' Wellcome Collection Online, November 2021. However other online sites claim that the powder was not available until WWI, when it was widely used by soldiers in the trenches to kill head and body lice. The powder contained pyrethrum, a natural insecticide found the aromatic flower heads of the aster family.

8 Many trade unionists were sympathetic to the Boshevik cause, especially the railwaymen who went on national strike on 25 September against the government's proposed reduction in their wages. The government backed down and they returned to work on 5 October. Wikipedia, December 2021.

9 Those soldiers who had not seen service in the Great War were to be given a Victory Medal in recognition of their efforts in Russia. But there was a protest—the Russian expedition had been unsuccessful and therefore a Victory Medal seemed inappropriate. Eventually the first timers were awarded the Great War General Service Medal with the Allied Victory on the reverse. Neville's memorial.

A few family changes!

James Neville was stationed in Ireland when he got a letter from his father saying he was engaged to be married again. He returned to England for the ceremony to discover that the new wife was a former girlfriend of his own – not only that, but a former mistress was threatening to derail everything by turning up at the church to denounce Neville senior's deceptions. Soon afterwards both young Neville's sisters got married leaving Neville himself feeling very alone.

Neville had a period of leave from November to January (1919–20) when he picked up the threads of his social life and received many invitations to balls and parties. One invitation came from the Phillips's of Unsted Park, near Godalming in Surrey. They were cousins of Bingo Baines, a fellow officer, who had had a leg amputated after wounds in the war, but his party-going and life-loving spirit was unchanged. Neville met Bingo's oldest sister, Violet, for the first time at Unsted. Violet was a widow with two children, whose father, Jock Hunter, a captain in the London Rifle Brigade, had been killed in action in 1918 on his first day in the front line. Neville felt rather sorry for her being left to bring up two children on her own, and as she was very friendly and good company, he introduced her to his father, Reginald.

In March 1920 Neville, now back in Ireland, received a letter from his father to say he and Violet were engaged to be married, and would he, JEH, be the best man at their forthcoming wedding at the end of April. Neville writes, 'This was good news to me, for not only would Father's loneliness be ended, but my sister Jane would be let off his carping temper and sharp hook. But it would also mean the end of her home which she had managed so tastefully and efficiently for seven years, except for the years she had been a land-girl during the war.'

Neville got leave from his regiment, which was currently stationed in Ireland as a peacekeeping force, for the wedding on 29 April. On his arrival at Ecclestone Square he found his sisters Jane and Angela looking 'as if they were going to a funeral'. The wedding was due to take place at Sloley Church in Norfolk, and before leaving with his father and his friend Toby Sturges, Neville's sister Jane told him a 'somewhat sordid story'.

Unsted Park.

Stephen Richards CC BY-SA 2.0.

Jane had met their father with another woman recently, not Violet Hunter, but a Mrs Hayward. This Mrs Hayward came to the house in Ecclestone Square claiming that she had been their father's mistress since 1914, about 6 years. Neville says he was not at all surprised by this revelation, but his sisters were shocked.

Neville writes:

> Apparently Mrs Hayward had threatened to denounce Father by making a scene during the wedding, that was the reason for all the secrecy and getting a special licence for the

ceremony in Norfolk. There was more. Mrs Hayward was being kept by my father in a love nest in Eaton Place, which he could not really afford as he was already keeping the house at Ecclestone Square, and Sloley Hall. As a result, poor Jane was trying to manage on a tiny amount of money, and father would behave dreadfully towards her, insulting and unpardonable, every time she brought the housekeeping books to him for payment. So Jane was persecuted in order to keep Mrs Hayward in luxury.

Violet Hunter only agreed to marry my father on condition that he bought off and discarded Mrs Hayward completely. Before and after the marriage, Mrs Hayward bombarded father with unstamped letters, telephone calls and trenchant telegrams. I received a letter from her in Ireland, which was illiterate and unintelligible. The irony is that father met her when mother was still alive. Mother had belonged to some society which helped fallen women. Mrs Hayward came to her just before or after she had given birth to a daughter, Iris.

There was doubt about Iris's paternity. Neville suspected that she was actually the daughter of a Royal Navy commander. There was some blackmailing and some murky payments.

But back to the wedding. The sisters, Jane and Angela, refused to attend, and Jane warned her brother she would never speak to him again if he agreed to be best man. However, their father issued an order that they must all go to the wedding, and they were eventually persuaded to do so by an uncle, Dr Michael Foster, who saw them off on a train at Liverpool Street. All three siblings were clearly very unhappy at the situation.

Neville then starts to refer to Mrs Hunter in his memoir as 'The Grasper'. (His grandson Simon, the current owner of Sloley Hall, says that she was also known as 'the violent woman'). I am assuming from this that it was, in his view, not so much a love match but a business arrangement from which she would benefit financially, and he would not be lonely any more. I am also sure that he was very worried about the nature of his new step-mother seeing her as a threat to his and his sisters' inheritance, and family life in general.

Violet Hunter.
Richard Barton-Wood, April 2023.

He writes:

The Grasper and her mother stayed the night before the wedding at the Hall (ie. Sloley Hall). In the morning Bingo and his father, Colonel Baines, and I got Howling Herbert (the car) going to meet Jane and Angela at Worstead (train station), and drove them straight to the church where we sat together in a back pew. They were tight-lipped, white and rebellious. Our family pew was occupied by the Baines family. Father was obviously nervous, anxious and jumpy as a frog, for fear that Mrs Hayward would discover where and when he was to be married. There had also been a row between him and his bride-to-be that morning. She had wanted a marriage settlement, and he had refused.

Interior of Sloley Church—Neville used to sit just in front of the pulpit.
Simon Knott.

Conrad Bankes, the rector, was splendid. He married them calmly, and father's face on signing the register, was as relaxed and relieved as a criminal on being found not guilty. Jane and Angela went straight back to the station after the mournful proceedings, and I set off for London in Howling Herbert with Toby Sturges soon after lunch. The happy pair departed for a long honeymoon in Italy at such expense as staggered all of us. In a letter he told me that he had gone to Stresa on Lake Maggiore, Venice and Florence, and he was going to buy a small car, and a horse for the Raleigh cart.

So it remained all through his life with The Grasper. She saw to it that he fulfilled all the conditions of her acquiescence. Indeed, she confessed to me soon after the marriage that she had accepted him at the age of 33 because of his wealth and his London and country houses—homes for her Hunter brood, Rosemary and Michael. Father was 57.

At the end of May 1920 both Neville's sisters became engaged to be married. Angela was to marry John Macartney-Filgate, MC, and Jane was to marry Reginald Vick, OBE, a surgeon at St Bartholomew's hospital. James was pleased for them, but realised this meant his sisters' first loyalty was now no longer to the family they had grown up with, and he no longer had a family to call his own.

Neville's sister Jane was to be married in London on 30 June. As soon as he started to make plans for the journey from Ireland, a railway strike was threatened. He writes, 'Travelling by train was hazardous. Officers in uniform and even in plain clothes had been abducted by the IRA on several occasions from trains at stopping places, never to be seen again.' But he arrived back in London in time for the wedding and confided in his diary that 'Jane looked very beautiful and Angela, her only bridesmaid, looked sweet in a Georgian frock.' Finally, Neville says he tied an old boot to a long piece of string which he flung under the newly-marrieds' little two-seater car.

Angela married in December the same year at St Martin-in-the-Fields Church. Her husband was to be John Macartney-Filgate, whom she had nursed when she was a VAD during the war. 'She looked very sweet,' Neville writes. 'She carried a bouquet of holly and mistletoe and was followed by Anne Slack (a first cousin), Eileen Cotton and Janet McCorquodale as bridesmaids. There

Jane's wedding. Angela and her father are behind her.

John d'Arcy / NRO Nev 7/31.

was a mass of relations at the wedding breakfast in the drawing room at Ecclestone Square. I got properly whistled and played a very neat trick on Angela.

She and Jack (the new husband) were going to St Moritz for the honeymoon. In a valise was a rug roll which I filled with about 1lb of rice. Angela and Jack went on deck (on the boat) with the rug roll, unwrapped the rug and shook the rice out on the deck for all the passengers to see that they were

Angela's bridesmaids: left to right—Eleen Cotton, Anne Slack and Janet McCorquodale.
John d'Arcy / NRO Nev 7/31.

newly-weds. Angela waited 12 years for her revenge. When I married and was leaving for my honeymoon, Angela sprang at me with a bag of rice. I just managed to turn my jacket collar up in time to avoid most of it.

The days following the wedding were 'very gay'. Neville went to the theatre nearly every night, and on Saturday to a matinee as well. Thereafter Neville visited one of his girlfriends, Ruth Farmer, where he also met another girlfriend, Helen Payne-Gallway. The latter walked back with him to Ecclestone Square and on the way told him that she also was engaged to be married to Wilfred Lloyd. Neville's first reaction to this was that she must be joking. He thought Lloyd was a 'damp sponge or a tap without a washer.' But she was serious.

'I was simply dumbfounded,' Neville writes. 'We had written to each other for months and she had never mentioned it. I knew that I was in no position to get married —I was 23 and a subaltern's pay, plus the £300 per year from my father, was not enough (to support a wife). I also knew that my two sisters disliked her intensely. But there goes another romance and I am in my little square box again.'

Neville and his father saw each other quite seldom, but James found he had to stay at Ecclestone Square from time to time. His father was very critical of him and the way he lived his life. 'He had little sympathy with my carefree junketings and seemed disinclined to realise that I had been on active service for 5 years and wanted to make the most of freedom from danger and boring duties in aid of civil powers in Limerick. Luckily for me, Philip Booth, (who had served with Neville in Russia), was also on leave from the 52nd and we used to meet practically every day to enjoy inexpensive meals and amusements together in Soho.'

Another year in Ireland passed and Neville stayed with the regiment for Christmas this time. He describes it as 'a very rowdy affair'. 'We had to officiate at the Company's dinners, and drink far too much whisky too often. It was great fun and better by far than being at Sloley where I was not wanted. I never spent another Christmas in the parish until 1948.' He went on leave in January (1922) hoping that he would not have to return to Limerick. Apparently, his Colonel had been told that the 43rd would be the first to leave when Southern Ireland was abandoned to its own devices.

He went first to London where he relaxed in a Turkish bath in Jermyn Street, then went to see his sister Angela who had had her first baby the previous October, and Neville was godfather. Then he went on to Gloucestershire to stay with friends and to hunt with them. As usual it was also a highly social occasion—hunt balls, dinners, theatre—and Neville found himself 'quite smitten' by Heath Harrison, the daughter, but was 'scared' by the obvious wealth of her home and her family. They lived at Coates Manor built of wonderful soft Gloucestershire stone, which was 'vast and richly appointed.'

The outbuildings with staff quarters, garages and stables covered as much ground as the house,' he writes. 'The gardens were beautifully kept. I believe the wealth came from the Harrison shipping line, but her father was very ill and died of cancer soon after my visit.

Neville returned to London 'a little glum', but continued the round of parties, visits to the country to see friends, go to dinner parties, visits to the theatre and, of course, a long string of dates with girlfriends. One, Bettina Maryon-Wilson, frightened him badly. 'She was a beauty and a good dancer,' Neville says. 'We went to the Oakley Hunt Ball and she and Margaret Forbes spent the whole evening talking about their various "society goings-on". It gave me a good experience in what to avoid in young women! And when Bettina deliberately cut two of my dances, I wrote her off.'

Fortunately, Neville received another invitation to Coates Manor. He was a bit surprised, but also delighted, to be asked to escort Heath to the Crickland Hunt Ball. 'Just as before, I was stupefied with fright,' he writes:

> But this was soon dispelled when I met Heath's sister and her husband, a jovial Irishman called Bertie. The ball was a howling success and I slipped a little deeper in my admiration for the quiet and unaffected Heath, such a relief after the spoilt Bettina. We danced and dined together many times, and I was in a world of fun and wonder. The night before I left, Bertie came to my room and told me that I ought to marry Heath who, he told me, thought of me as more than a dancing partner. I had to tell him that I had only my subaltern's pay of 10/- per day, and this was not enough to support a wife. However, I did buy from him a great big Irish chestnut gelding, not quite sound in the wind and therefore quite cheap. I borrowed the money to pay for the horse from the bank and called him Bankruptcy.

He admits being 'quite saturated' with glamour when he left Coates Manor. Both visits stuck vividly in his memory, but he did not keep up with Heath. Inevitably she married another man and together they went to live in Cairo.

Neville got leave again in July to go to Lords and met yet more of his girlfriends, in those days known as 'lady-friends'. From there he went to Sloley and recorded that he slept in his old room, now called the Holly Room. He writes:

> The house is filthy. I felt like going round with a feather duster to remove some of the cobwebs festooning it. Although we sailed at Barton Broad and bathed at Irstead, it was not a bit like our days before father remarried. I always feel nowadays that I want to be alone with father. I suppose I still feel that Bobbie (another name for his new step-mother) is an interloper.

Ireland 1920–22

At the start of the twentieth century the whole of Ireland was part of Great Britain. At the outbreak of the Great War, most Irish, like most people in the rest of Britain, supported the British war effort. Over 200,000 Irishmen served in British armies throughout the world and nearly 50,000 died.

The Nationalists, a political party in Ireland, had been campaigning for Home Rule (i.e. independence) throughout the 19th century but were persuaded by their leader John Redmond to put aside their differences while the war was going on. The Unionists, the other main political party, were mostly located in the northern province of Ulster and needed a lot less persuasion to join up. They were opposed to Home Rule and were more naturally inclined to support decisions made in London.

But in 1916 a small number of republican radicals broke away from the Nationalists to form the Irish Volunteers. Led by James Connolly they seized the General Post Office and various other major buildings in Dublin, proclaimed an Irish Republic and held out for over a week before British forces overwhelmed them.

James Connolly.
The Irish Labour Party,

The British administration was enraged by what it perceived as disloyalty during a bitter war, believing also that Germany had assisted the rebels. Britain therefore ordered the execution of fifteen of the rebels, causing widespread revulsion in Dublin. This in turn fuelled support for the Republican movement, Sinn Fein, which romped home to an outstanding victory in the general election called at the end of the war in December 1918.[1]

The British Army, having fought its way through the killing fields of France and Belgium and attempted to halt Bolshevism in northern Russia, was now required to try to hold Ireland together while the politicians decided how to proceed. Huge numbers of Irish people had voted for Sinn Fein, but their elected MPs refused to go to Westminster to take their seats. Instead, on 21 January 1919 they set up a new parliament called Dail Eireann. This new parliament declared that Ireland was now independent and chose Eamon de Valeera as their first president.

This meant that Ireland now had two governments—the new Dail in Dublin and the British Government at Westminster in London. Both claimed the authority to hold courts and collect taxes which resulted in violent disorder. A war began, later known as the War of Irish Independence (1919-21).

The Irish Republican Army (IRA) wanted to force the British out of Ireland completely. It attacked buildings used by the British government, attacked British Army compounds and used guerrilla tactics to attack British soldiers by surprise, and then escape quickly without being caught or identified. Initially the British government responded by sending reinforcements to Ireland and James Neville was one of those soldiers.

Statue to Tomas MacCurtain, Cork.
K. Glavin, CC BY-SA 3.0.

It was certainly no place for wimps. Neville was stationed in Cork with the 52nd and he writes, 'It was an awful place, swimming in mud, the huts leaked and the latrines were wicked[2]. There was very little furniture and it was quite inadequate for my needs. Dick Warren was there, and Algy Sawyer, but otherwise no friends.'

It was also violent. On 20 March 1920 the Sinn Fein Lord Mayor of Cork, Tomas MacCurtain was murdered by armed and disguised RIC (Royal Irish Constabulary) men who broke into his home. Winston Churchill, then Secretary of State for War, responded by sending in veterans of the British Army, who become known from their improvised uniforms as the Black and Tans. The Black and Tans were notorious for their unorthodox methods of 'peacekeeping'. The regular army, in which Neville served, had to stick to the rules—ask questions, don't provoke the locals, keep it low key. The Black and Tans were a law unto themselves and would shoot whoever they liked or disliked, and Churchill could disown responsibility.[3]

'Soldiering was a very pleasant occupation,' James writes however. 'Early parade was at 0700 hours and dinner (i.e. the midday meal) at 12.50, after which there were no more parades except for special duties. We had entertainment from local people, and bicycled miles to play mixed hockey, followed by vast teas, dancing and games. Bachelors were at a premium and Claude Crawford (a fellow officer) often took me to meet people no-one else in the mess knew, and Claude seemed to attract girls to follow him wherever he went. Another officer, 'Daddy' Holt (so-called because he was 5 years older than the other subalterns) had a car in which he often took me to meet the Purcell family, where there were two girls, Maisie and Lulu. Maisie was "a bore", but Lulu was a "good dancer".'

However, even Churchill recognised, after the December election, that Britain could no longer expect to rule over the whole of Ireland and the House of Commons began the work of setting up new separate administrations in Dublin and Belfast. On 27 February the text of the Home Rule Bill was introduced in the House of Commons. It provided for the establishment of a 128-member parliament in Dublin and a 52-member parliament in Belfast.[4]

In June Neville's regiment moved to Limerick, about 80 miles to the north. The signallers went first on their bicycles as the advance guard, and Dick Warren's platoon was rearguard. It was a very hot and slow march until they got to Limerick at 1900 hours, when the heavens opened. Neville writes:

> We had to unload and picket the horses in a pelting tempest. The day after our arrival, torrential rain swamped the mess and ante-room marquees and flooded out the lines. Even for Ireland that June was exceptionally wet. The transport horses had no cover for weeks, and stood hock deep in mud on a picket rope, with their rumps facing the weather. The drivers had the very heck of a time to groom and clean their horses, while harness and saddlery became an agglomeration of mud and rust. I spent much of my own money in trying to cover the horses and protect them from the fiendish torrential downpours. They nearly

broke my heart.

There was a curfew so the streets had to be patrolled by bicycle between 0300 and 0600 hours every night. Anyone found on the streets had to be searched and asked his business. If he ran away, they had to chase him, generally in vain, because Limerick Old Town was a warren of unlit narrow alleys. Neville's turn came round every third day as there were very few subalterns. It was not the Great War and it was not Northern Russia, but still it was dangerous. On Sundays the whole regiment would march down to St Mary's Protestant Cathedral at the north end of the town (not to be confused with St John's RC Cathedral), accompanied by the Royal Fusiliers who would sound the trumpet for the start of the parade, and then bang the big bass drum for the marching beat. Even on Sundays, they carried rifles and ammunition.

Sinn Fein, the Irish political party whose main objective was, and still is, to end British rule in Ireland, had, in Neville's words 'declared war on us'. But the British army had somehow to deal with 'ambushes and murders with tied hands.' 'We were not allowed to open fire until we had been shot at,' Neville writes, adding rather sarcastically that 'this had the great benefit for the politicians in that a dead man cannot retaliate. Two young soldiers disappeared from the regiment's detachment at Tulla (a town in County Clare, twenty miles north of Limerick). Their bodies were eventually found but they had been shot through the backs of their heads.'

His first experience of the Black and Tans occurred in August on a Sunday, when there was a shooting match in Limerick at lunch time. He was stopped by one of them on his way to the mess in Strand Ally, which overlooked the Shannon and the County Clare side of Sanfield Bridge. Officially the Black and Tans were auxiliaries to the RIC.[5]

Neville writes:

> The RIC did not understand the hostility of the rebels, nor were they trained to deal with it, armed with rifles and buckshot, they were no match for the rebels armed with rifles bought and supplied by Irish Americans and smuggled into Ireland. Reports came in regularly of police barracks set on fire by Sinn Fein and the constables murdered as they tried to escape. The arrival of the Black and Tans soon put paid to that.

To us, what was remarkable about the

A Black and Tan on duty in Dublin... smoking and posing with a Lewis gun. National Library of Ireland, HOGW 121.

new arrivals, commanded by General Tudor, was that it appeared to be free of the Police and Arms Acts, which meant that it could do what, where and how it liked so long as its actions were not disclosed. It was immune from the frustrations imposed on the Army as laid down in the Army Act when in aid of civil power. We had to try to control the rebels by gentlemanly and peaceful persuasion, so as not to provoke them. The Black and Tans gave no quarter, and expected none. The rebels gave no quarter, yet expected and always got quarter, when caught. If we caught a murderer, then he would be imprisoned and thus be safe, and he was never shot for rebellion or treason. The Black and Tans did not bother with court martial or sentences in prison; they had neither the time nor the inclination to go through the rigmarole of a trial. They dealt with murderers then and there. Of course, they made some mistakes. That is a tragedy of war. But the Black and Tans harassed and arrested several well-known villains, and generally had a regular RIC constable to identify suspects.

As orderly officer I had to turn out four guards after 2300 hours, which meant bicycling through the lightless streets during the curfew from Ordnance Barracks down John Street, the cobbled hill through Irish Town where safe houses were provided for murderers on the run, to Castle Barracks to turn out B company's guard, then on to Strand Barracks for the quarter guard provided by D company, and on down the Ennis Road to C company's guard in the workhouse. This duty took not less than an hour. The local inhabitants knew well enough that it was done every day and the subaltern who did it was easy meat for an ambush. It was always an anxious duty, and an army bicycle was not built for comfort or speed. It was so heavy that I was never able to peddle up William Street from Strand to Ordnance. Yet not one subaltern was ever hurt.

Sunday 21 November came with dreadful news:

> Sebastian Jagger and I drove over to some great friends the Megaws, at Ballywilliam. When we returned to Limerick after midnight, we were told by John Eastwood of the Grenadier Guards that fourteen officers had been murdered in their beds early in the morning. This came to be known as "Bloody Sunday". The soldiers had all been on the Intelligence Staff at GHQ and were living out of barracks in Dublin. The incident woke the government up at last to the realities of the situation in Ireland. The odd officer kidnapped and murdered, and the odd party of soldiers gunned down in an ambush created little or no impression on the politicians. But they could not evade Bloody Sunday with their normal platitudes, and three weeks later martial law was proclaimed in Limerick. This freed us to treat the IRA as the enemy they surely were.[6]

The Bloody Sunday murders caused an enormous upheaval. No trains ran from Dublin at all, and newspapers failed to appear. Only the *Cork Examiner* reached Limerick with a few details of the savagery:

> The officers were either shot in their pyjamas or dragged out of bed and shot like rats.

Neville records:

> As a result, officers were only allowed into Limerick town in pairs and armed as well. Recreation of any sort became minimal. We were allowed to exercise the horses on King's Island, but we had to have automatic revolvers in our pockets. The colonel would not allow us to play games with the men. We had to watch armed. All the married officers living in the town were concentrated in Cruiser's Hotel and guarded day and night. When the men were not on patrol, they were on guard duty.

R.I.C. military and armoured car leaving Limerick on a scouting expedition.
National Library of Ireland, HOGW 147.

As time went on conditions seemed to deteriorate further rather than improve, and he writes:

> The officers and men were accommodated so far apart in the town that they were seldom off-duty and, when they were, their movements were confined to the areas that were under patrol. There was little opportunity for organised games or exercise apart from pedalling a bicycle or meandering up and down the main roads of the town, watching all the time the doors and windows and the behaviour of other pedestrians. I felt that I was learning little of my profession by acting as an untrained police officer, and the boredom was no stimulus to morale. What we did learn was to be prepared at all times for the unexpected bullets and bombs. The enemy always had the initiative and element of surprise on their side. We had no clues as to the appearance of the enemy leaders. We knew their names but not their faces and only a few of the RIC could recognise the villains.

By the end of the year, that Home Rule Bill had finished its progression through the House of Commons, and on 23 December the Government of Ireland Act of 1920 was passed. It received the Royal Assent from George V providing for the partition of Ireland into Northern Ireland and Southern Ireland with separate parliaments.[7] Ireland however was still far from peaceful with deliberate acts of violence taking place on both sides. On 1 February 2021 for example, Captain Con Murphy from Co. Cork, was executed by British authorities, the first man to be executed in front of a firing squad since the Rising (in Ireland) of 1916.[8]

Neville writes:

> Early in March the Mayor of Limerick and his predecessor were murdered without any trace of their assassins. It was believed to be an outside job by some villains from Cork who had made the exhortation "Wake up Limerick!" Another curfew was imposed and the streets were patrolled by a searchlight party of sappers in a noisy lorry. Its only effect was psychological for it was incapable of surprise. During the funerals, the security forces were confined to barracks, lest they should provoke the rebels. O glory glory be, will politicians never learn that appeasement is the best of encouragements that villains can want? The procession was watched from every point on the walls of Ordnance Barracks. It was headed by a mass of school girls chanting from their rosaries, followed by the coffins flanked by pall bearers in Burberrys with their hands in their pockets, obviously armed with revolvers. Behind them marched a long column of men six abreast which, we surmised, comprised the Limerick battalion of the IRA. We fumed at being required to watch and waste the opportunity of putting the whole murderous gang into a bag, or even better into coffins.

Elsewhere in Ireland the violence continued. On 25 May the IRA occupied and burnt to the ground The Custom House in Dublin, the centre of local government in Ireland. Five IRA men were killed and over eighty captured by the British Army.[9] Neville was transferred with B company to Tulla in County Clare, where his platoon wanted his services in the company sports. Neville writes:

> The relief from city, bicycle and other patrols was immense. At Tulla there was soldiering to do. The company occupied the old workhouse, and it was fun travelling about our district in Crossley tenders, as guards to the RIC

Troops on foot and mounted on trucks with some children during the Irish Civil War. National Library of Ireland, HOGW 124.

collecting–of all things–dog licences[10].

Actually, the collections were a cover for keeping an eye on the inhabitants and villains on the run. The RIC at each point checked up on the presence of members of families. As policemen, they knew all the members and their occupations, and knew at once when a young man or woman was absent, and could, without giving offence, establish their whereabouts. I had the greatest admiration for the RIC during the rebellion. They were not trained to take on guerrillas any more than we were trained to take on police duties.

Early in June Neville's regiment was involved in a systematic military operation 'to drive the mountains of County Clare' in search of IRA men. The troops consisted of 17th Lancers Companies of 43rd, 55th and 93rd Highlanders, and Black and Tans. It was organised as a grouse shoot, with the cavalry acting as guns. 'Security was nil,' writes James in his usual black-and-white manner. 'The concentration of troops was known for miles around, and the IRA men on the run only had to follow the beaters (infantry) to be supremely safe. It was the Great War in miniature and totally useless, except as a means of keeping the troops fit. We drove from 0500 hours until noon, bivouacked, ate and then slept under the stars if the midges would allow. On one such manoeuvre, the Company lorry broke through the surface of a narrow bog road, and sat down like an old woman on a potty. We only got it out by removing the body of the lorry from its chassis and then towing it with another vehicle while all the men of the Company pushed like frenzied niggers.' (Neville was writing well before the 'n' word became unacceptable.)

The only success we had was fortuitous and unplanned by the Column staff. After three days of very early starts and long drives, the Column was given a day's rest. It was known that there were some rebels in the area because a patrol of the 17th had bumped a party of villains on hikes, who had opened fire on the Lancers and then vanished.

From another source Neville learned that there was a crowd of turf cutters on a nearby bog, named Coolregh, and that there might be some villains among them. The bog was surrounded and searched. It was triangular in shape with roads on two sides, and a deep stream about 20 feet wide on the third. The troops crossed the stream and about 20 folk who were cutting turves downed tools on spotting the soldiers and ran 'like hell' towards the apex of the triangle. There they ran into the 93rd and the Black and Tans who opened fire and stopped the flight in its tracks. The Irish were marshalled and marched at the double uphill to Feakle (a village in County Clare) Police Barracks where an RIC officer identified six men as alleged murderers, who were handed over to the 93rd for safe keeping. The remainder were allowed to go home. Neville was cock-a-hoop.

> Thus, without the benefit of a general, staff or operation orders, we who knew the country were able to collect six (alleged) murderers by using only 250 men. The operation commander had failed to arrest even one with 2,500 men. What this raid proved was that our forces depended on immediate action on receipt of information, and a grain of luck. Had we not been having a day of rest, the set-piece drive would have proceeded in its fatuous manner. And we would not have found anyone.

At this time, the army were given permission to shoot at any man seen running away on the assumption that he had either arms or a guilty conscience. The men Neville served with were reluctant to open fire on civilians. However, the new permission served to increase co-operation with the locals.

Neville says:

> Hitherto, the answer we always got when we asked someone why they were running away was always the same "I was scared of the military". But now people had to stand their ground, or risk being shot at. Those who refused to answer or did so suspiciously, were arrested and taken to the local police barracks for identification. If not wanted by the police, they had the pleasure of walking home. These tactics kept the IRA constantly on the move and the number of their safe houses decreased rapidly. They had to hide where they could find shelter and their presence became an increasing embarrassment to their hosts, who never knew when a descent by the military might be made on them.

They had about another three days of planned driving after the raid on the bog, over the hills between Kilameena and Glendree, but did not arrest any more villains. As it was the turf-cutting season, Neville's last days at Tulla were spent making sudden descents onto bogs in the area, but he did not repeat the success of the raid at Coolregh. By the middle of June he was back at Limerick, sad to leave Tulla as it was easily 'the happiest time in Ireland for me.'

Neville was then sent on an 'education course' at Newmarket, in England, which he enjoyed and which also gave him an opportunity to meet up with old friends in London and Bury St Edmunds. He also made a visit to Sloley Hall in Norfolk to meet his new half-brother, Richard, who was born to Reginald and Violet on July 15. But the only comments he makes refer to the new car he had bought—an open two-seater with an air-cooled engine—having sold Howling Herbert for £60 to a friend; and to the way his father's new wife, Violet, had decorated Sloley Hall—'execrable and pretentious'. Neville never liked his father's new wife and started referring to her in his diaries as 'the Grasper' or the 'Violent one'. Or even as 'the Witch'. So did his sisters.

While Neville was on this course, the government and the IRA came to terms and created the Irish Free State. The Irish Free State lasted from December 1922–December 1937. On the day the Irish Free State was established, it included the whole of Ireland, but as expected Northern Ireland almost immediately exercised its right to remove itself, and is still separate. The State came to an end in 1937, when the people voted to replace the 1922 constitution. It was succeeded by the sovereign and current state of Ireland, which is often referred to by its Irish language name, Éire.[11]

'It seemed,' Neville writes, over-optimistically as it turned out, 'that The Troubles were over.' But he goes on to point out that instead of the IRA shooting at the British Army, they started shooting at any Irish who did not agree with the stated aims of the IRA. Reluctantly Neville had to return to Limerick 'while the politicians wrangled'. At least his duties were now less boring and much less arduous. For the first time the 43rd was able to start the winter programme with individual training. The 52rd was quartered in County Tipperary and the regiments were able to meet and socialise. There were also plenty of opportunities for exercise—hunting, golf, dancing, football and hockey.

When he got back to London for leave again, he found a letter telling him that the examination for promotion to Captain was to be held on 10 February. He made a hurried visit to the booksellers Sifton Praed in St James's Street who were able to advise him—requirements included map reading, solving a practical problem, and writing orders on the problem. In between 'the odd hunt' with the Hertfordshire hounds, Neville got down to work on his map reading, compass and back bearings and judging distances. The exam was held in Shorncliffe in Kent and Neville stayed over at Sir John Moore Barracks, where his regiment had been due to relocate when they left Ireland, a move that was postponed. It was, he said, 'Very modern and comfortable after Irish workhouses.'

> The exam started with a tactical scheme. We were allowed to thrash out the solution in syndicates, which meant that the four of us from the 43rd (Jacko Pack, Basil Burt-Smith, Wykeham and Neville) were in the same team. I had worked hard at map-reading, so I went first and had to identify a distant target sited by a rifle on a tripod, then a back bearing. That was all OK, but then I was asked to identify the scale of a map from just a fragment and I was a bit stumped. I should have remembered that the Ordnance Survey maps show mileage figures on the main roads. From the distance between figures, the scale can be easily worked out.

Wykeham and Neville together wrote out their orders on the scheme, and at the end of the day, they were both told they had done very well, but that their answers were too similar for either of us to be sent up for a 'special'. With wry humour, Neville comments 'I think I could have achieved a special without Wykeham.' Anyhow, they all passed. And Neville was very 'relieved'. On his return to Ireland Neville was named in regimental orders to take over the sports and intelligence responsibilities (in Dublin). Gathering intelligence meant he was expected to pick up information by standing at street corners in plain clothes (as if that disguised him from being spotted at once as a British officer). He also found that it was impossible to mingle in a crowd because of his height (well over 6 feet). 'I was not allowed to be armed, which did not add to my enthusiasm,' he writes. 'It was a tedious business wandering down streets and alleys, unsure of what was expected of me. My weekly reports therefore contained little but hearsay.[12] I told Alfonso Powell that it was not my cup of tea and I believe Algy Sawyer, a very strong chap, and Jeff (Jefferson) a physical training instructor who knew jujitsu, took it on.'

Neville heard of a vacancy going at the depot in Oxford but did not get it. He was told that the Colonel wanted him to succeed Alfonso Powell as his adjutant. He could hardly believe this. He writes:

> In those days, an adjutant received 5/- per day extra duty pay. I joined the army in January 1916 as an ensign on 6/- per day which, paid into my bank Cox and Co, made £9 per month. My expenses of messing were £5.5/- per month, leaving me with £3.15/- for everything else. When my pay was raised (on promotion to Lieutenant) in January 1917, I got £10.10/- per month. On active service abroad I got a field allowance of 1/- per day and in Arctic Russia I got Arctic pay also but I cannot remember how much (except that I found an extra £400 on my return home, there being no way to spend money in the Arctic). After the war a subaltern's pay was raised to

(7 23 63) W5129—PP3583 7500 3/20 HWV(P747) Army Form C. 369.

REPORT on Officer or Non-Commissioned Officer attending a Course of Instruction at the School of Education { Newmarket. ~~Shorncliffe.~~

No. of Course 15 *Extending from* 24th June 1921 *to* 2nd September 1921

Rank Number and Name LIEUTENANT. J.E.H.NEVILLE.

Regiment Oxf: & Bucks.L.I.

Command and Station Irish. Limerick.

Permanent Address 1st Bn.Oxf. : & Bucks.L.I.

Subjects Studied { (A). Main Subject. ~~(1) Group A.~~ - History.
(B). Subsidiary- - English.
~~(2) Special~~ Subjects.

Proficiency in { (1) Knowledge of Subjects Studied (A). Very Good. (B). Very Good.
(2) Ability to Impart Instruction (A). Very Good. (B). Very Good.

Conduct and application to work in the School Very Good.

General Mark Awarded.*

PASS.

Remarks.

This Officer's work reaches a high mark, but it could be higher still if he would part company with some minor prejudices which do not allow his undoubted knowledge and ability to have their full effect in Educational Work. He appears to be not yet quite convinced that an Officer can and should be also a teacher, and that there is one diction for formal and another for informal occasions.

Date 2nd September.1921. H. S. Poyntz. Lieut.-Colonel,
Commandant, School of Education.

* Fail. Pass. Distinguished.

Neville's course report with some telling comments from the supervisor! September 1921.

John d'Arcy / NRO Nev 7/31.

£12.75 per month and with 7 years' service it went up again to £17.25 per month. I reckoned in 1922 I should be in clover as an adjutant earning £400 pa (about £33 per month). Moreover, an adjutant got a horse and fodder as part of the appointment, which meant that I should only have to pay for one of my quads.

By August the political situation in Dublin had cooled down (after the Battle of Dublin in June[13]) and the soldiers could go where and when they pleased in their spare time. Neville was ordered to take the weekly adjutant's drill, which he enjoyed though it was nerve racking at first. Alfonso had applied to get the job of training officer for Oxford University Officers' Training Corps, and Neville was expecting to succeed him as adjutant. But Alfonso did not get the job!

'I was depressed,' Neville writes. 'I had lost the chance of the depot job, and now the adjutant's job as well. Also hanging over me was the second part of the promotion exam for captain, including military law, King's regulations, pay and mess book administration (supply, accommodation and stores), imperial geography, and tactical problem on paper. All pretty formidable.' But at least he had the opportunity of going to the famous Dublin Horse Show with magnificent horses competing in the pair jumping from hunts all over Ireland. And Neville also enjoyed the 'immaculately turned out women' in toppers and veils. 'The pair of horses had to go round the course tied together with a length of string which, if broken, disqualified them,' he writes. 'The course was formidable - timber, fences, razor and flat-topped banks, and water. It was an exciting spectacle.'

Finally, in the middle of August Neville heard that the regiment was to move to Shorncliffe in September. He knocked off the days like a schoolboy with a calendar, and for once packing up was a pleasure. This time the move went ahead and on the evening of 14 September the 43rd embarked at North Wall. The regiment went to Moore Barracks where the officers' quarters were 'so luxurious' that the younger officers had never known anything like it. There was a large anteroom and a dining room, bachelor quarters above with two field officers' quarters (bedroom and sitting room) and several juniors' rooms. There were slipper and shower baths and servants' kitchens. Those soldiers with less than 10 years' service had never seen the regiment's possessions such as portraits, pictures, miniatures, trophies, silver, dessert plates and books. 'It was wondrous to see the regiment's heritage at last,' Neville writes. 'We hung the pictures in the ante room and Sandy told me the history of the silver and the trophies, won by our ancestors in far off parts of the Empire.'

Shorncliffe was a good station for Neville for many reasons. Not only was it well appointed, but it also had facilities for all kinds of sport—football, hockey, cricket, racquets and hunting. James brought over his two horses, Bankruptcy and Maureen, from Ireland, but he sold Maureen to Sandy Sanderson as the mare was not quite up to his weight. He bought a bigger gelding instead which he called Blue Ruin. This horse was 'a steady performer which never refused after I had schooled him. What he gave away in speed in a point to point, he made up in courage'. Fortunately for Neville his commanding officer, who was not a keen

The hockey team at Shorncliffe. Neville is sitting on the right of the central officer.
John d'Arcy / NRO Nev 7/33.

Neville's two horses, Blue Ruin and Bankruptcy.
John d'Arcy / NRO Nev 7/33.

horseman, never refused an application from his officers to go hunting on the basis that it was a good way to get an eye for the countryside and therefore also good training. But before Neville could go off and enjoy the sport, he had to sit his Part B of the captain's exam. He was 'completely foxed' by a question on the military law paper, but felt 'fairly happy' with imperial geography, military history, topography and the tactical question. He just scraped through.

Life in England was quite a lot more interesting than it had been in Limerick. Neville writes 'There were plenty of places to nautch[14], especially at weekends such as the Grand and Metropole Hotels, and there was no shortage of young women. There was a repertory theatre in Folkestone where plays were tried out before going on to London.'

Neville spent Christmas with the regiment again to avoid having to go either to Ecclestone Square or to Sloley Hall, and this time he took good care not to drink all the whisky on offer. After Christmas he sent Banko and Blue Ruin on ahead, and took off in his bull-nose Morris to Cowley with his servant Richard. 'Hunt ball followed hunt ball. Bicester, Heythrop, Old Berks, South Oxfordshire, and what fun we had. All the officers at the Depot were my good friends. Richard Crosse, George Naylor, Harry Vernon, Charlie Colvill, Jimmy Meade and Sandy also made Cowley their headquarters for their winter leave. These were the halcyon days of my service.'

In June Neville was promoted to captain, to his great surprise despite having recently passed the promotion examination. He was named to command the guard of honour to the Duke of Connaught when he came to Shorncliffe to open the Moore Memorial Hall and to unveil the statue to Sir John Moore (who had trained the famous Light Brigade at the Barracks). And finally, the following month he was nominated by Colonel Frank to succeed Alfonso as his adjutant.

This is the end of his memorial written when Neville was in his seventies based on his letters, diaries and memory. Now we are coming to the period in Neville's life when he made some profoundly bad personal and career changing decisions. It all started in 1923. And the following chapters tell some of his feelings.

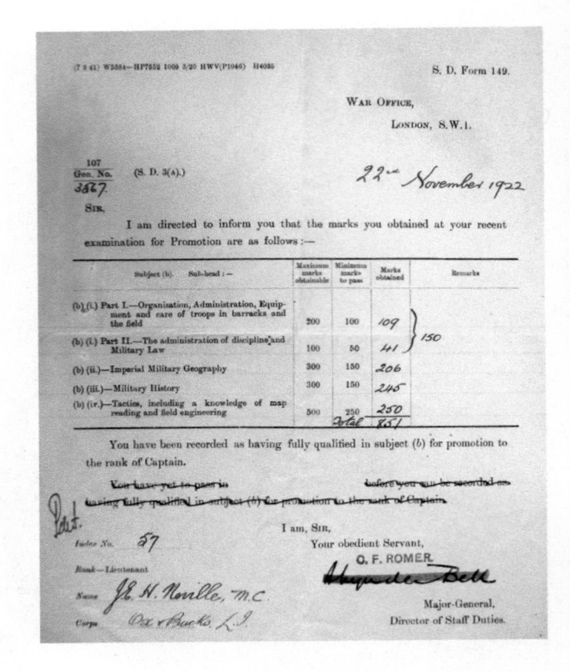

(7 8 41) W3384—HP7552 1000 3/20 HWV(P1046) H4035

S. D. Form 149.

War Office,
London, S.W.1.

107
Gen. No.
3867

(S. D. 3(a).)

22nd November 1922

Sir,

I am directed to inform you that the marks you obtained at your recent examination for Promotion are as follows:—

Subject (b). Sub-head:—	Maximum marks obtainable	Minimum marks to pass	Marks obtained	Remarks
(b) (i.) Part I.—Organization, Administration, Equipment and care of troops in barracks and the field	200	100	109	150 (Parts I and II together)
(b) (i.) Part II.—The administration of discipline and Military Law	100	50	41	
(b) (ii.)—Imperial Military Geography	300	150	206	
(b) (iii.)—Military History	300	150	245	
(b) (iv.)—Tactics, including a knowledge of map reading and field engineering	500	250	250	
		Total	851	

You have been recorded as having fully qualified in subject (b) for promotion to the rank of Captain.

~~You have yet to pass in before you can be recorded as having fully qualified in subject (b) for promotion to the rank of Captain.~~

I am, Sir,
Your obedient Servant,
C. F. ROMER
~~Haynes de Bell~~
Major-General,
Director of Staff Duties.

Index No. 57
Rank—Lieutenant
Name J. H. Neville, M.C.
Corps Ox & Bucks L.I.

Neville's Promotion Captain report 22 November, 1922.
John d'Arcy / NRO Nev 7/33.

Notes

1 Ireland and World War 1, Wikipedia, February 2018, and www.bbc.co.uk/history, British History in depth: Ireland and World War One, February 2018.

2 In early 20th century parlance, that means 'horrible', not 'wonderful' as in teenage 21st century language.

3 Wikipedia, February 2018. Churchill even defended their activities by saying they enjoyed the same freedom as police in Chicago or New York in dealing with armed gangs.

4 Wikipedia, February 2018.

5 The R.I.C. was the main police force in Ireland from the early 19th century until partition in 1922. Then it was disbanded and replaced by the Garda Siochana in the south and the Royal Ulster Constabulary in the north. The Black and Tans, so-called because of their uniforms, were feared by the locals because they frequently used violence to punish local people for perceived misdeeds. The Black and Tans and the IRA were sworn enemies. Walsh, M., *Bitter Freedom, Ireland in a Revolutionary World, 1918-1923*, Faber and Faber, 2015.

6 21 November—Bloody Sunday: The IRA, on the instructions of Michael Collins, shot dead the "Cairo gang", fourteen British undercover agents in Dublin, mostly in their homes. Later the same day in retaliation the RIC opened fire on a crowd at a football match in Croke Park, killing thirteen spectators and one player and wounding 60. Wikipedia, February 2018

7 On 7 March 1921 Michael O'Callaghan, a former Mayor of Limerick, was subjected to a particularly violent and brutal raid at his home. At 1am in the morning Black and Tans men wearing goggles and with their coat collars turned up and hats pulled over their eyes, forced their way into O'Callaghan's home and shot him dead in front of his wife. About 30 minutes later, similarly-disguised Black and Tans called at the home of Clancy, O'Callaghan's successor as Mayor of Limerick. Having forced their way into the house they shot him dead. Mrs Clancy, in struggling with the murderers, was shot through the arm. While Neville is usually correct, on this occasion he got the wrong end of the stick. Cottrell P., *The Irish Civil War 1922-23*, Bloomsbury, 2008.

8 Wikipedia, February 2018.

9 Wikipedia, February 2018.

10 These were required by law until 1988, though the requirement was widely ignored by dog owners.

11 Wikipedia, February 2018.

12 For many who had fought in the First World War or seen colonial service, the war (in Ireland) often seemed no more than a nuisance, albeit a tedious and sometimes deadly one. ... amongst officers, the belief was prevalent that the conflict required either a political solution or else a more substantial military effort under the full cover of martial law. Sheehan, W., *A Hard Local War* p. 48, The History Press, 2011.

13 The Battle of Dublin marked the beginning of the Irish Civil War in 1922. Walsh, M., *Bitter Freedom, Ireland in a Revolutionary World, 1918-1923*, Faber and Faber, 2015.

14 A fashionable word at the time for "to dance", though during the Raj in India a nautch girl provided other services as well as dancing.

The Affair 1923

This is where it all goes horribly wrong for Neville. He strikes up a close friendship with the wife of his Commanding Officer, Captain Douglas Speed, then falls deeply in love with her. Despite realising that this is a dangerous thing to do, he fails to bring his feelings under control. Eventually he and Myrtle Speed decide to run away together and Neville resigns his army commission.

Between October and December 1923 Neville's diary is full of stories about Myrtle. These are the only months of that year for which there are entries, and there are only a few entries for January 1924. Much later, in 1952, Neville described how he consigned his diaries of that time to a bonfire. The memories were clearly much too painful for him to retain.

Beginning on 9 October his diaries tell how he helped Myrtle and her sister out of a car accident as they were on their way to join the East Kent Hunt near the barracks at Shorncliffe. It seems that Myrtle's husband did not enjoy very good health and did not ride to hounds, so meeting at the hunt was an opportunity for her and Neville to get together alone without arousing suspicion. In fact, because of the captain's health, the Speeds had decided to sell both their horses, so Myrtle usually borrowed one of Neville's mounts—Blue Ruin. This gave Myrtle, who was unhappy in her marriage, some kind of debt of gratitude to James, and it seems it was perfectly acceptable for the two of them to eat dinner together at hotels such as The Grand at Folkestone, even though, as Neville comments, it made *him* feel 'like a guilty boy'.

He writes:

> We discussed practically every subject (over dinner), and I have come to the conclusion .... that I should like to marry one of her breed. Thoroughbred, she has such an excellent wit and humour, and yet as seems to be always the case in life, she is beyond my reach. She told me she thought I had a very large heart .... I suppose I do. She advised me to marry a widow if possible, to avoid the early difficulties which personally I don't think one ought to shun. I can't imagine anything more gruelling than to fall in love with a married woman, so perfectly hopeless and yet they are far more attractive than girls.

Neville spent a great deal of time during this period behaving like a lovesick teenager and emotionally that is probably exactly what he was, despite having been in active service for the last two years of the Great War and elsewhere. He relied on fellow officers, especially Toby Sturges, to advise him and help him through difficult times. Another officer, Alphonso, was already married and he and Toby used to talk about the difference in Alphonso's behaviour. Home in Sloley was no longer the source of comfort and consolation as it had once been, now that both his sisters had married,

Blue Ruin.
John d'Arcy / NRO Nev 7/33.

Officers' Hunting Season 1923. Neville is third from the right on his horse, 'Bankruptcy'.
John d'Arcy / NRO Nev 7/33.

and his father had remarried. As Neville has already recounted, the new wife did not get on with the children. His father had promised to come and visit him on his way back from Antwerp (where Angela was living) but failed to make it, and his sister Angela was still breast-feeding her new baby Patrick. Neville felt very sorry for himself.

He got an invitation to go to dinner with the Speeds and he was delighted. His mood swings were marked at this stage, as is so often the case during an infatuation. One look, glance, a telephone call from the beloved can change the whole tone of a day or a week! It was not a dinner *á deux*—there were eight guests—but Neville did sit next to Myrtle and found the evening wonderful —he was loath to return to the barracks.

The following evening was the Charity Ball in Ashfield. A small group consisting of Neville and an unknown lady friend, Captain and Mrs Speed and six others, assembled at Horton Priory first for dinner which was 'excellent' and then on to the Priory for dancing. 'Greatest fun in the world' writes Neville, 'but we were dragged away soon after 21.30 to go back to Horton for supper. I offered Myrtle a mount for the opening meet of the Drag and we talked and laughed a lot, and then we are going to have a party at the Grand when D (Douglas Speed) goes to Scotland to shoot.

> Lie still there, little flutterer. I wish she was not married. I would have popped the question by now, I really believe. ... the married state is the real one .... Though bachelordom means freedom.

At the end of the month Myrtle was due to ride Neville's mount Blue Ruin to the drag hunt, but the horse had a cold and a cough and was not fit. Neville worried in his diary that Myrtle was simply leading him on, but in the meantime he was also corresponding with PooBah, a long-time girlfriend who had married someone else. It seems that at this stage he was doomed to be smitten by women who were not free to commit to him, a pattern that dogged him throughout his twenties.

November started with another invitation from Myrtle to go to dinner at the Speed's house after hunting to make up numbers as one of the male invitees had dropped out. Neville considers this 'extraordinarily kind'! By now Blue Ruin was better and Neville was able to offer Myrtle the horse as a 'thank you' for the dinner invitation. The only trouble was that Ruin was liable to rear up on his hind legs! There was no fear in Neville's mind that he would refuse fences, but he was worried that Myrtle might be thrown backwards, even though she was clearly an experienced and talented rider. Neville had taken to putting his prayer book under his pillow at night which was said to help a person dreaming of the future spouse!

The Drag went well, through Dibgate to Bangore Wood, over to Oak Banks and then across the Training Area. Afterwards Neville went back for dinner.

He wrote:

> I thoroughly enjoyed it all and M was as wonderful as ever. We sat in a private car at the end and talked of life

Opening Meet, East Kent Foxhounds, Elham, 5 November 1923.
John d'Arcy / NRO Nev 7/33.

> and of the things that make one lose one's temper and we came to the conclusion that the parental mania had a very ill effect! It certainly has on me – I am like a bear with a sore head as soon as I step inside what is officially called home.

And yet another invitation from Myrtle the following day! Neville had spent the day at a very dull Court Martial and Myrtle had been out with the Mid Kent Stag Hounds. They got together in the evening at The Grand in Folkestone where they danced and talked and drank cocktails for hours. Neville got the impression that she had not had an easy life, nor was her life at present as an army wife much better. And again the following day, Sunday 4 November, they spoke on the telephone, this time Neville calling her and inviting her to ride on Monday. Neville says he knew it was a risky move to see her again quite so soon but he 'could not help it'. Things became far too intimate that day. Myrtle got soaked to the skin by a downpour of rain and returned to Neville's barracks for tea in Sandy's room (Sandy being a fellow officer). Myrtle took off her wet blouse and put on a shirt belonging to Neville, and Sandy said that he wished she (Myrtle) was not married as 'Neville would make her a much better husband'. Neville does not record her response to such a comment though he does say that he felt the same!

The next day Neville records in his diary that he wrote a few letters in the evening but really, there was only one person he wanted to write to. 'It is the very Devil,' he writes. 'If I only knew whether there was some reciprocation, I should not feel quite so much that I am making a bloody fool of myself. I suppose there is no doubt about that.' It is understandable that Neville should be afraid of rejection and this is clearly why he takes so long to declare his feelings for Myrtle. But there is no mention of concern as to how all this will affect Douglas Speed and their son, Myrtle herself and his own career in the army. Neville frequently mentions that he knows this affair is risky, but risky for whom? He seems unable to see the bigger picture.

Neville made a trip to London half way through November where he met up with PooBah at the Carlton Club. It was a painful encounter. PooBah told him that he 'was absolutely nothing to her', though it seems she meant this only in the romantic sense. Neville says that it hurt rather but was also a relief to know where he stood. They remained friends.

Then Neville visited his other sister Jane on the way back to Shorncliffe, who was expecting another baby in January. When he got home, he found a letter from Myrtle inviting him to dinner the following weekend. He enjoyed the evening and writes some revealing remarks in the diary afterwards.

> Sunday November 18. Extremely parky all day. Read in the afternoon after writing a letter to PooBah. I wish I felt a little less anxious about her. Of what value was my interest? Nix, and that is why I suppose I feel rather sad about the whole thing. It means that all, or practically all, that hectic passion was thrown away. (He means the deep feelings between PooBah and her husband). Because I have pretty strong ideals about marriage. And yet were I in the same circumstances what should one do? I know myself well enough to be certain that I should say yes.

It is a little hypocritical of Neville to say that 'I have pretty strong ideals about marriage', when he is an adulterous relationship with a married woman. Sometimes he will not see the beam in his own eye, as the Biblical saying goes. About a week later Neville decided to call Myrtle to offer her a horse for the following day. He had not realised that Douglas Speed was in the same room as Myrtle while they spoke until he (Douglas) started speaking to Myrtle while she was on the telephone. Neville says he 'felt like a wolf in sheep's clothing!' There is no question that Neville knew what he was doing was wrong.

> He goes on:
>
> I suppose he does not mind, or dare not. I don't understand quite how one could act under the circumstances. Personally, if M was my wife, I should feel exceedingly jealous if anyone else offered mounts to her ... My God, I wish she was not married! The very sight of her makes me feel such things as I have not felt for many a moon and she – well, what does she care? It would make it slightly easier if I knew that I was a bit more than a common friend.

The following day, 20 November, they went out hunting together and afterwards had tea in his room which he says felt like the old days at Eton! He took her home in his car and Myrtle invited him in for dinner, only to find DS (Douglas Speed) was at home. Douglas had just returned from London where he had seen a specialist about his heart. Apparently, the heart was weak which brought on fainting fits which may not be ideal for a soldier. Neville slunk away disappointed.

There was a letter waiting for Neville when he got back to his barracks from his father who announced that he was standing for election again in South Leeds. Neville was astonished! His father constantly complained of having no money yet was prepared to 'throw away' thousands on a campaign and maintaining a house in London. He saw later, on 27 November, that he had indeed been nominated by the Conservative Party for his old constituency.

At the weekend he got together again with Myrtle. 'We had quite a cheery little dinner,' he writes. 'And did a copious amount of dancing (at the Grand). But more talking! I learnt a good deal and she was highly amusing over her married life. She told me that she had an understanding with D, that if ever she wanted to go off—it should be done. That she expected that he would go off one day. That he could not understand the little things of life, having always had them and she could not unburden herself to him because he had no or little sympathy, in other words, she is not happy. I reminded her of Byron's essay on friendship where he says that a man to whom he has no one to unburden his soul, is miserable, and she replied that she was miserable indeed. Her hands have more lines than any I have ever seen. And she tells me that she is to be married three times and have two children. That the next child must be her next husband's. She was amazingly candid and said that I made her so!!! D is apparently going to Switzerland, and leaving her behind and she said that she would love to come up to Oxford and have a hunt there, and we arranged to go to a show in London.' It seems clear from these words that Myrtle, like Neville, had visited a fortune teller who had 'read her hands'. It was very fashionable at the time.

The conversation stirred up in Neville what he called 'the toils', by which I suppose he means that his mind churned round and round this information all night. He formed the impression that Myrtle was deeply unhappy in a marriage to a cold-hearted man who did not understand her, and whom she had wed when she was too young to understand what marriage really meant. Neville did not know what he should do, though deep down he makes it clear he ought to end the relationship. The last quarter of November was extremely cold and the ground was too hard for hunting. Neville mooched about at the barracks worrying and thinking about Myrtle, until he was forced to the dentist's chair for a tooth extraction which rather took his mind off things.

The start of December saw a sudden thaw in the weather. It rained heavily on Sunday 2 December and going to church was made voluntary which meant, as Neville put it 'no-one went at all.' The general election was in full swing with the Conservatives expected to get back in with a 'good majority'. Neville heard nothing from his father that week but was not surprised as he understood that he would be very busy.

Neville was still fretting about Myrtle but at least the thaw meant that hunting could start again and he, rather tentatively offered her Bankruptcy as a mount. He was worried that the horse would throw her and that he would never forgive himself if that happened. More importantly he was churning over and over in his mind about what to do – should he break away and tell her he could not see her any more? Or should he just carry on and hope for the best? He worried that Myrtle had failed to see that he, Neville, was really in love with her and hoping for more than friendship and that, if she had, she was totally blind to his feelings. Not a good sign.

On Tuesday, 4 December, they rode to hounds, Myrtle handling the horse 'brilliantly'. Afterwards they had tea together in his room at the barracks, and Neville showed her a picture of PooBah. To which Myrtle said 'I should like to see you in love!' Neville records that this was a 'priceless remark and that he had thoroughly enjoyed it all – and she seemed to like coming to tea with me too.' The conversation came even closer to the bone later as Neville took her home in his car. 'I think you will make quite a good husband,' said Myrtle. 'Soft!' replied Neville. 'I'm not a confirmed bachelor,' and they both laughed. 'What sort of girl would you like to marry?' Myrtle continued. Neville described Myrtle to herself but tried not to portray her too obviously.

Myrtle said she was going up to London the next day so Neville invited her to lunch at his club, and afterwards to a show—'*The Little Minstrels*'. A few days later Neville heard that Myrtle had had a row with her husband because she had stayed out too late and used the car too much. This made Neville feel a bit guilty but still he could not bring himself to bring the affair to a conclusion.

'What am I to do?' he writes. 'Blow off steam to her? I don't think I shall be able to pen up my feelings much longer .... And yet what good can it possibly do to tell her, except spoil our friendship? ...If I want her I shall have to leave the army and I would do that and more, but where to find a job? If she cares for me at all, the fat will be in the fire good and proper. I wonder, oh! I wonder. This sort of suspense is the very deuce and all his confounded angels. I shall just tell her simply how I feel, and trust to a merciful Providence and hope she won't laugh.' He does not, of course. As usual, he prevaricates and asks PooBah for advice even though all the waiting drives him mad with anxiety.

In the meantime, the election was a disaster for the Conservatives and his father lost by 4,000 votes to the Labour candidate. 'There goes £1,000 down the drain!' Neville wrote. 'This evening there are 213 Conservatives, 150 Labour and 150 Liberals, as well as other odd parties.'

December dragged on and Neville made little progress. He attended dances and balls, shooting weekends and hunting meets, met other girls and thought only of Myrtle, got advice from PooBah to tell

Myrtle everything then ignored it, had a couple of wonderful evenings with Myrtle at The Grand but failed to open his heart to her. He was miserable, then elated. Every time he tried to speak his truth, his tongue 'froze in my mouth'. He spent Christmas at the barracks and resolved, for the umpteenth time, to tell Myrtle what he felt on Boxing Day when they were due to hunt together—but yet again, though countless opportunities presented themselves, he backed out.

Finally, on Wednesday 2 January Neville does actually declare himself, with a strong prompt from Myrtle. 'Then after dinner we sat in front of the fire and talked,' he writes:

> She told me that she had already told D. that she would leave him, and said that she was married only in name. I fooled about with Shot (the dog) and my tongue felt very sticky until eventually I plucked up my courage and asked her not to laugh at me if I told her something. A still voice—oh! it was so still that I can hear it now—said very kindly "Of course I won't." And then I managed to tell her that I was more fond of her than I ought to be. And she, bless her heart, replied "And so am I". My heart thumped until I thought it would burst. But still we both felt that it was unfortunate that it had been said in D's house. From that moment we told each other all that the past had meant. And I told her that I had tried to bottle it up but could not. And then we discussed the situation and I said that I was quite prepared to chuck the army if she wanted me. She, Myrtle of my heart, was too glorious for any words to describe. Never, as far as I can see, has she been told that she is good at anything. A more humble person I have never met and I wonder how many words of encouragement she has ever received from him. She said she did not know that I cared for her, and yet I thought it was so painfully obvious. And so the evening wore on and we talked so that I can't remember what we said, though there was that vague feeling of shyness all owing to my conscience and the feeling that I was betraying a man who had been kind to me. And yet what claim has he on her, except only in the name of husband. And just as we were going up to bed, I asked her to kiss me and she said 'No' at first, and then with an impulsive movement we kissed each other and the ecstasy of that moment will live long in my life.

The following day, after hunting, Myrtle backtracked a little saying she felt uncertain which frightened Neville rather. The uncertainty continued well into 1924, but eventually they decided to make a go of it together. Six months later they were on board a ship heading for South Africa. It was nothing short of a disaster.

Starting Over

Neville and Myrtle had eloped to South Africa where he hoped to buy land and set up a farm. It did not work out and it seems another man, unnamed, followed them and Myrtle transferred her affection to him. Neville returned to Norfolk a broken man, to try to start again. Eventually he found work as an inspector on a cotton-picking scheme in The Sudan.

1925

January

Sadly, there is no diary for 1924. I am sure that Neville kept a diary for this year as he refers to it occasionally in 1925, saying that it made him 'feel sick' to read it and that it ought to be destroyed. It is most likely that this is what he did, before handing over all his papers to the Norfolk Record Office, date unknown, but a few years before his death in 1982.

1924 was a chaotic year for Neville. Despite the loss of the diary for this year, he left enough clues in his 1925 diary for a reader to work out what happened. As we saw, Neville declared his feelings to Myrtle in early January 1924, and then he had to wait while she made up her mind what to do. After several months of indecision, she finally said 'Yes' to leaving her husband and going off with Neville, who put in his notice to leave his regiment. The pair ran away together to live in South Africa, buying land to work as farmers.

But the affair went wrong. Another man, referred to by Neville as 'the traitor' or 'The T', whose name appears to be Toby, (possibly Toby Sturges) travelled out to South Africa to visit the couple, and came to live on the farm. M abandoned Neville for him. Neville knew T from his army days and mentions later in 1925 that he was chauffeur for T one evening in Shorncliffe. Neville was understandably distraught when his affair with M came to an end after just a few months, and with no reason to stay in Africa, he returned to his family home in Sloley in Norfolk the same year, very much with his tail between his legs. He was very afraid that his father would want nothing more to do with him because he had caused a scandal, but Reginald was a kind family man and said of course his son must come home.

Neville now had no wife, no job and no prospects. His career with the army had come to an abrupt halt as he had committed the ultimate sin in stealing the wife of his CO. He tried to get back into the army, but was told that this would not be possible. Finding another job was very difficult. His father, an MP and a London barrister, tried to help by asking around at a high level what his son might do and where he might go, but to no avail. Everyone Neville senior spoke to said they would look into possibilities, but the wheels turned very slowly and very often his enquiries came to nothing after a long wait.

The year 1925 began with Neville staying with Jack and Jelly (Angela) in Avenue Elisabeth, Antwerp. He was very unhappy, regretting all that had passed in the previous 12 months, and wondering how he would ever be able to face the world again and get another job.

He wrote in his diary:

> I feel utterly finished. I sweat when I think of what the future will be, of the hell that has got to be lived through during this very year that starts today. If only the earth would open and swallow me up. If only I could go somewhere where I should never meet anyone I knew, I could live in a

> certain amount of peace. But that would be cowardly.

Neville turned to the occult in the form of spirit writing,[1] which was very popular at the time, to try to get some answers and perhaps also some sense of certainty when everything else in his life had fallen apart. 'In the evening we did spirit writing. I asked some questions such as, '1. Will T marry M? A. He will. 2. When? A. Very soon, in March. To my reply that that is impossible, it wrote 'You have heard the result'. 3. After the divorce is through? A. He will. So begins the New Year. How will it end?'

The following day he got a letter from Pony, a friend in Natal, asking him and M to come and stay and to ride their polo ponies. Pony had evidently not heard that he and M had parted, and the letter 'turned my insides out.' Again, they consulted the spirits in the evening which said he would 'find peace through war', but did not say which war. And he dreamt 'feverishly' of M that night, when she said that she could not come back to him now 'having waited all this time, and done all this'.

Still in Antwerp, he mused on the possibility of returning to army life for a short while and then going off somewhere completely remote as a soldier, where no-one would know him or what he had done. Perhaps there he would die of malaria —but if he lived, he might save enough to pay back his father the money he owed.

But:

> Here I am building castles in the air again as ever! When shall I learn that dreaming brings disappointment! We walked along the dunes this afternoon, in the teeth of a bitter wind and a banked-up sky of red gold. I could not help thinking how M, one and a half hours ahead of us in time, was spending the afternoon, probably at tennis at the country club in Parktown (an upmarket residential suburb of Johannesburg), and drinking iced drinks and lolling in a glorious sun.

With Jack and Jelly he visited art galleries and the cathedral in Antwerp, went to the theatre and to the cinema, and took French lessons. His days passed quite pleasantly—he read *The Times* and wrote letters to his family - but he complains of feeling 'mouldy and depressed', worried about the loss of his good name and how people would turn against him and gossip about him.

One day a letter came for him from Toby in Durban, which enraged him. Neville confided to his diary, 'He said that if I thought he had interfered between M and me, I was accusing him of the most despicable thing that one man can do to another, who is his friend. I consigned it to the fire, which is the best place for such balls. I cannot imagine how he expected me to be anything but highly incensed at receiving such utter tripe.' A second letter from the T, in answer to one of his own, asked him to bear no ill will. Neville was understandably scornful, particularly by T's remark that Neville 'would find something congenial to do'. 'The thought of him still makes me shiver with fury,' he writes.

By the middle of January, Neville had gone on to Paris with Jelly. Jack could not go with them. They visited the cathedral but found the station and many of the houses bashed about as a result of the war. But there were positive signs. 'Houses are patched up and still look half destroyed but the progress is astonishing.' he writes, 'when one comes to think that it is only six years since the war finished. We reached Paris at 5.30 and came straight here and got rooms at the Hotel Burgundy. I am sadder than I've felt since I came over here. What is the cause? Why does M haunt me tonight more than usual? I wish I could go somewhere where I need never see another blasted woman. I am still feeling most frightfully depressed. At the back of my mind is the thought that this would have been so much fun with M. I am in a state of ghastly suspense, waiting for news of her. I am also afraid of running into someone that I know. The feeling will not leave me.'

By Monday 19 January he had had enough and was more than ready to go home and face his future, however difficult that may be. The trip, he says, 'is having a most depressing effect on me. A year ago, I was as happy as a king because I thought

Notre Dame from the Seine, 1925.
National Library of France.

she loved me. She had said so often by now and like a fool I believed her.'

At one point it does seem that the army, indeed even the 43rd, would take him back if he could guarantee that he would not have anything to do with M in the future, an assurance that he confides to his diary that he would be happy to give. Two days later he arrived in London to stay with his other sister Jane in Harley Street. 'I rang up Moore Barracks and the Colonel said it would be quite convenient for me to go down this afternoon. At 1pm I was in a train once more for Folkstone and we rattled past all the well-known country. It was rather terrible passing Staplehurst where we finished a magnificent Stag Hunt—past Headcorn and Pluckley and all the familiar roads down which M and I used to hack home from hunting. Luckily there was no-one about and I saw the Colonel. He said that before he recommended me to Hanbury-Williams (Major General Sir John Hanbury-Williams, Military Secretary to the Secretary of State of War), he wanted me to guarantee that there would be no scandal as far as the regiment was concerned, and that I would have nothing to do with M in future. I gave it willingly.'

The following day he spent most of the morning with the Colonel, who demanded to know the whole story before he could recommend him to Sir John. So Neville told him everything. Once all was on the table, the Colonel said that if M ever wanted him, Neville ought to go back but that it would not be necessary for him to live with her and that he should feel 'an infernal shit' if he did not do that, adding that he saw no reason why past possibilities should stand in the way of his career, so long as he gave her his name and supported her; that until she remarried, he was practically unable to marry himself. After lunch he saw Sir John who was 'very nice'. He said he would forward the application to the Military Secretary and write a private letter to Worthington Evans. It looked as though he might resume his career after all, and he felt 'much better'. 'Also I have made up my mind - as M used to tell me, I shall never look back and I shall never see her again.'

Neville learned that his sister Jane had had severe reservations about his affair with M from the start, to the extent she thought that T had even made an advance arrangement with M before he came out to South Africa. Neville disagreed with his sister, thinking that M was incapable of such behaviour, even though Neville knew that he was not her first lover while she had been married to DS. 'What a fool I was ever to think that I should be any different from the rest,' he writes. 'For there is no denying that

Worthington-Evans, served in Stanley Baldwin's second government (1924-29) as Secretary of State for War.

Library of Congress, LC-DIG-ggbain-37099, public domain.

she is a flirt'.

But on the last day of January, while Neville was back at Sloley in Norfolk, he got a letter from the army. He writes:

> Oh God, the blow has fallen, Jane rang me up and said she had opened a letter from Banbury. The letter came from Worthington Evans. And it said that he had seen my application and had considered it, and as there was no precedent for re-instatement it could not be done on any account. The whole question had been exhaustively thrashed out some years ago. I have been a fool and I suppose in my vanity had begun to bank on a return to the army. This is No 1, and how many times shall I be turned down in the future? Molly has got onto her friend Home[2] and is going to see him on Tuesday and the Gov'nor and I are going to see Worthington Evans, but I don't suppose anything will come of it now. It is fate again, standing with a drawn sword. It has been an awful day. I took the Gov'nor into Norwich and waited outside the club. I could not face people today. The bottom has fallen out again and left me high and dry. I feel hopelessly tired and forlorn and my courage has ebbed a good deal. Perhaps Worthington Evans will re-consider it if the Gov'nor sees him and if Molly can get Home to intercede. But I think it is hopeless now. My vocation must change though I know I am a soldier at heart and pine for the old life. Oh M! What a legacy you have left me. What an uphill grind!

February

Neville woke the following morning at Sloley Hall with the old feeling he knew so well of repressive gloom. He had felt so much better when he thought there might be a chance of resuming with his old regiment, despite having to face many old friends and colleagues with the failure of his elopement with M. By keeping busy all morning - unpacking his things from the loft of the stable, hanging up a few pictures in his room (some of Shorncliffe and two small prints of Eton)—he managed to keep the worst of his thoughts out of his consciousness. Rather bravely, he also put up the four hunting prints M had given him the previous year, and which had hung for two months in their sitting room on the farm in South Africa. But he complained to his diary that a few of his favourite items seem to have been removed to other parts of the house; a reading lamp which Bobbie had 'nipped' for her bedroom, and a little writing table Jane had given him now resided in the governesses' room.

Next day he and his father got the train to London where they called on Hanbury together and gave him copies of Neville's application to re-join the army. Hanbury's advice was simply 'Keep on trying' but that was about all. From there they went to the War Office but the Colonel was out. The following day Neville was having lunch with his sister Jane when their father rang, to say that he had seen Worthington Evans, who had not seen the application but promised to do 'all he could' if Peyton, the Military Secretary, could be squared by precedent.

Neville writes:

> Jane and I sought feverishly for an army list and eventually bought one from the Stationery Office. We found a soldier called Henry Briseby, who had resigned in September 1920 and had re-applied successfully in January 1922. Later I dined with the Gov'nor and found another example. But it seemed to me that Hanbury, WE and Peyton were playing some kind of horrible game. Peyton had told the Colonel that if WE was OK, then all would be OK. Now WE says the same of Peyton.

No-one seemed able to take responsibility.

His dear friend Molly rang him to say she would see Lord Home the following day, and she hoped he would be able to help. Neville was not exactly expecting anything to come of all this maneuvering, but he was still 'vaguely hopeful'. But as before it all came to nothing, or very little. 'The Colonel was very kind but when I rang for advice, I was told that my case had been turned down by everyone,' Neville writes. He went off to meet Molly and she took his papers to show Lord Home, but she returned very quickly to say that he could do nothing and that he had been trying the same thing for another man, who had also been turned down. Neville was shocked and wounded all over again by this second refusal to consider him. 'I must try for something else,' he writes. 'But what? I feel rather beaten and cowed not knowing what to think, and my head feels tired and my mind wounded. For I have banked on this and now that my reinstatement is impossible, I'm damned if I know how to compete with the immediate future. This is a bitter blow and has robbed me of much of my courage.'

But there was worse to come. Back at Sloley, Neville found a stinging letter from his close friend PooBah. He had written to her, advising her not to leave her husband for another man, but had clearly overstepped the mark for this is what PooBah writes in return:

Dear Jim,

> I've just got your letter and I think we had better not meet if you are going to take up this attitude. Just because your woman has let you down, you need not tar us all with the same brush. I have forgiven you a lot in days of yore, and I've always been ready to help and sympathise, and take your part and generally be your well-wisher and supporter, and I see no need to be rude now, if you don't approve of my behaviour. We had better stop being friends, PB.

Oh dear! Poor Neville had lashed out in his pain and fury and upset a dear friend, who understandably, did not like it one bit. 'I did not mean to be rude,' he confides a bit pathetically to his diary. 'But I suppose it must have sounded rude. I am always doing that these days. As for forgiving me of old, I think the boot is on the other leg. She had more need of my forgiveness. It is however not worth worrying about and she does not want to be my friend now. Perhaps I am well out of it. She is not my type now.'

Once again, Neville took to unpacking all his kit—vests, pants, a few books, his helmet, his highland kit, fishing reels, officer's suit of uniform—to try to take his mind off his worries. Sadly, he could not find his mother's letters, which made him remember all over again how much he had lost when she had died. But he got a nice letter from Jelly in Belgium which cheered him up. On his last day at Sloley Neville finished all the unpacking, oiled his tools and repacked them, and stowed away all his kit.

Neville and his father went back to London on Tuesday 10 February. Neville had decided that idling around at Sloley in Norfolk was no way to find another job, so he went back to his father's chambers, where to his utter astonishment, he found waiting for him a letter from M.

My dear Jim,

> This is the promised letter and just to say goodbye. I hope all goes as well as possible with you, and you will make a great success of life. Also find real happiness 'ere long. You were rather previous in your congratulations as I have not the slightest intention of marrying again for years. I hope to go and stay with my uncle in Europe in about six months' time and then possibly go on to America if I cannot face England. Good luck, old boy, never look back, forget and forgive, marry soon and be happy. You won't hear from me again but I wish you the best of luck. Yours ever, Myrtle.

Neville's response was outrage. 'Marry soon!' he explodes onto the page of his diary.

> Forsooth, I shall never marry now, not after today. Why did she write, what has happened? Has she found T out? What is it all about? She doesn't say how she is. My God! What a legacy that woman has left me. Every day it gets worse and worse. I suppose she will go and stay with the Minister at Bucharest who is a relation of hers. P'raps her family has persuaded her. It was all T. I will never speak to him again.' But Neville was frightened by the letter as well as angry. 'Of course,

> I am not going to answer her letter. It would be madness. Jane advises me not to open any future letters but return them unopened or burn them unread. The whole letter has frightened me, that she wants me to take her up again, but is too proud to say so in as many words. I don't really care now. I may have changed, but the enormity of the crash she has brought to me is just dawning on me and I do not want her fruit.

A couple of days later, Neville rang his father to find out if he had seen Amery or had an answer from WE. To Neville's disappointment, he had done nothing—seen no-one, asked nothing. He had not seen Amery in the House. He *had* seen WE but not spoken to him. 'He does not seem to realise that I want to get a move on,' Neville complains. But to his credit, he realised that he had to stop relying on other people to do things for him, and get on with it himself. He started fishing around for jobs, trying the Colonial and Foreign Offices. He was told Palestine was full and no vacancies were likely to occur, but he was given a pamphlet and saw that he could apply for a soldier's job in West Africa or a Police, Administrative or Secretariat job in The Gambia. There were jobs in Sierra Leone, the Gold Coast, Nigeria, Kenya, Nyasaland, Tanganyika, Zanzibar and Somaliland. The Foreign Office told him about Sudan which 'went by selection', and while he might be a little old, he would be allowed to count four years' war service.

But still he was mourning the army:

> I shall gradually lose touch and the regiment will merely be an episode in a useless life. How I loved the 43rd, nothing engrossed me so much, took my attention, until this woman came along. Never again shall I hear Charlie blow at Reveille. It is awful and she platitudinously wishes that I shall make a success of my life which she did her best to bitch and has succeeded in bitching. I feel just hopelessly indifferent to everything and everybody.

His comments are all a bit rich really, considering how he moaned in his diary only a few months previously about how boring army life was, especially in Ireland. And he never seems to consider how he made M's husband, Douglas Speed, feel, nor their son. Nor does he take into account that it was his own decision to leave the army. Neville had lunch with his father and showed him the leaflets he had acquired from the Foreign and Colonial Offices. He got the impression that his father was not that keen on any of them, but would prefer his son to quit England and stop all the embarrassment. The pair then walked to the House where Neville senior was given a letter from WE saying he would like to meet him at 4.15pm on Friday. Neville had the impression that this would only be to tell him more about the reasons why his son could not be reinstated.

While they were there, Neville told his father he had heard from M to say she was planning to return to England. Neville senior was alarmed. 'Why doesn't she stay where she is?' he said. 'Is she mad, insane, what is the matter with her? Is she coming to patch things up with you and then leave you again?' Neville said he had made up his mind on that score—he would never see her again—and had given assurances to the Colonel, and was going to stick to that plan. Neville met PooBah at Harrods for lunch. PooBah had written him a short note saying she would still like to be friends after all. Neville discovered that she had decided not to break it off with her husband, even though he had been in India for the past eight years (five of which PooBah had lived there with him).

And he got a nice letter from the Colonel saying he was sorry that Neville had failed to get into the army. He was summoned to a meeting with his father, Peyton, WE and the Colonel, which made him 'sweat in every pore' as he waited in the lobby outside the meeting room. Neville was called in and tried to produce the precedent of Harry Brisely but he could see it was no good. Peyton 'made the excuse' that at that time, 400 officers were needed. But he did promise that he would try to help get Neville into the Sudan Defence Force and that he would write to the Sirdar[3] in Khartoum, and WE said he would write too and recommend him strongly.

Both the Nevilles, father and son, were much happier as they left that meeting. Neville junior said that he knew he was not out of the woods yet, but he could not help feeling excited at the thought of earning a living again. But there was going to be another long wait. Amery told him it would take a month to get a reply from the Sirdar. Amery's letter would be to the governor of the Sudan, Sir Godfrey Archer, and he in turn would have to speak to the Sirdar. But he was pleased that he had real grounds to hope this time and he wanted to get everything fixed up before the possibility of M's return. James was still staying with Jane and Reg (his sister Jane had married Reginald Vick, a doctor in Harley Street), but confessed to his diary that he missed having no home of his own, such as the regiment had been. And for once Neville empathises with Reg, saying it must be awful to come home from work to find someone else sitting in a chair, just as Neville had found the T on the farm. So Neville decided he would go back to Sloley to wait for news, even though he never felt wanted there, even though it was no longer really his home and even though he no longer had many feelings for the people who did live there. He rang his father to ask if it would be convenient for him to go there on Friday, and his father said he was going there himself on Saturday. By chance Neville mentioned he had seen Amery, and to his dismay, his father said there was a 'hitch in the Sudan business'. It appeared that General Peyton had written to him to say that a Foreign Office nomination was necessary, as only Active Officers could be employed.

Neville was frustrated. Peyton had practically promised that he could get him in. It seemed to him that 'these wallahs' did not know what they were doing or what promises they made only to be broken when convenient. 'The fact is that they do not really know what they offer,' he wrote. 'I shall lose heart if I am not careful and buzz off abroad and go to hell.' Neville was invited to go to the Depot at Cowley, to help edit the regimental journal. He was frightened to go because of what people might say about his botched elopement, but Sandy, Jimmy and Robin were there and were kind. Nevertheless, it was painful for him. He could hardly bring himself to look at the horses, and he discovered that Sandy had improved the mess to make it look more like a gentleman's home and had also started a museum. He and Sandy talked about the journal a good deal and Neville agreed to go back later to do some editing.

Back at Sloley he met his father who said he had spoken to Austen Chamberlain (Foreign Secretary and half-brother to the future Prime Minister Neville Chamberlain) who in his turn had said it was 'nothing to do with him who went to the Sudan, but was in the gift of the WO (War Office)'. 'Pon my soul,' Neville wrote. 'I do not understand it. The FO says WO and vice versa and between the two of them, they do not understand whose the responsibility is, and there we are and there we remain indefinitely. I started on my photographs, all the regimental ones, but they made me feel sick. God! What a lot I had, and what a little I have got now. My future and my career—all gone! Why did she do it if she knew it would all go wrong? Today we have been parted as long as we were together. Years it seems since September 30th, since I sailed to that bloody country!'

March

Back to Sloley on the train, and to a long conversation with his father. At least, Neville senior talked while his son stuck in photos or wrote underneath them in an album. The relationship between them seemed to have softened slightly, and Neville was content to let his father chat on about 'the petty jealousies of constituents in villages, and that he was the only really good candidate they had ever had! He is a dear, but such an alarmist, obstructionist, and a slow mover and prejudiced. Anything new is bad to his Tory mind—society, politics and progress. However, all this is a matter of opinion. He is very good to me and I must try and repay him somehow.'

Neville senior went off to London the

The three children in Reginald Neville's new family—Richard, James' half brother in the middle with Michael and Rosemary Hunter on either side.
John d'Arcy / NRO Nev 7/32.

next day while his son stayed at Sloley which these days, he said, he greatly enjoyed, if only he was not in such constant pain, and did not feel such a fool. He also began to wonder if his father might leave Sloley Hall to his new son Richard (by Bobbie), cutting his older son out of his will. That prospect depressed him still further as he had begun to appreciate how much he loved the place. Later in the week his father wrote to say he had no news, nor did he expect anything till the letters to Egypt had been answered. But as things stood, Neville was in the dark as to whether anything could come of it. So he went off to Cowley, where he got to work editing the Regimental Journal. Everyone there was talking about the point-to-point and Colonel Bayley's wonderful command which saddened him as it made him realise, yet again, what he was missing.

Neville senior was making little or no progress on finding out about the Sudan, or even if that would be possible. Neville returned to London to stay with Jane and reported in his diary that he really did not care anymore 'except that I am bored stiff with doing nothing at all.' Bobbie (the new Mrs. Neville senior) was also in London, staying at her husband's chambers, and relations between her and her stepson were deteriorating rapidly. Neville does not report her exact words, but it seems she made it clear she did not want him at Sloley Hall any longer. The one redeeming feature in his life was PooBah, who had decided not to leave her husband and she and Neville had arranged to dine together. He also says that he had been thinking a good deal, and much more coherently.

He writes:

> Life is gradually becoming easier and I can face people a bit better. The more I think, the more I realise that M never cared for me beyond a passionate craving. There was nothing deep in her affection, and had I not been blind as a bat, I could have seen that she was hopelessly exotic and spoilt selfish. Nothing stable in her. But she was devilishly attractive and now I see that had I sacked the T from the farm and held her by force, my only chance of keeping her lay in that. But I was damnably weak. I ought never to have let her go until she was sane.

When he dined with PooBah, he heard news of M:

> She said she thought I was the wrong person to do what I did, because I am blessed with a conscience and she had expected that if it went wrong, that I should be the offending party. She told me a bad bit of news, in that little R (M's son) was always asking where his mother was and missed her tremendously. That cut me to the quick. That DS had got rid of the Dower House, sold the furniture and had gone to live at Knowlton with his family. My God! It is awful, the wreckage that I have caused, and that boy robbed of the love of his mother. I don't deserve to live anymore.

But time was passing and it was already nearly six months since his affair with M had ended. Everywhere Neville went, there seemed to be something to remind him of what he had lost—the weather turned to spring and with the change, came the pangs of spring the previous year. When he went for a walk with PooBah, it was along a road he had walked with M, and he remembered how she had asked him if he would want a baby at once, after they were married. When he went for dinner at Claridge's in London, he sat at the very same table he and M had sat at the previous year.

> My hat! I miss her sometimes so much that it does not seem worth while

> trying to go on without her, and yet were she here now, I should know that if she was not actually loving me, she soon would be loving someone else. PooBah told me that she (M) was very unbalanced and has had that reputation in Kent. I wonder how she is living these days in Jo'burg.

With no news from anyone about his prospects, Neville fretted away his time, sick of the inactivity and lack of purpose. What he really hoped for was a job in the Defence Force and 'a scrap', wondering if the British Empire could remain peaceful for much longer. He longed to hear the crack of a bullet and the rattle of a machine gun again. He was not immune to the irony that death was often granted to those who loved life, but refused to those who just wanted it all to end. On 29 March Neville reminisces that it was exactly a year ago that the 'foul business' with M was fixed up. Looking back, he realised that by the last Sunday in March of 1924 things had gone so far between them that it was all out of his control.

> It all stands out so vividly in my mind. Indeed it will do forever I fear. The restlessness within me gets worse daily, I think. I don't know really what I am hoping for. It is a funny thing and yet I do still hope for something to turn up sometime.

The wait went on... and on... and on. Neville began to feel it was hopeless to expect a job out of the government and his father seemed as powerless as anyone, despite all his powerful friends. Being an MP had not helped his son at all. 'They all kowtow to their bloody parties and get nothing except the bird,' he complains.

> The Labour Government could not have been worse. All hope of ever getting back to the Regiment has gone. Look M, at your handiwork and be proud of it. Robbed of the other half of my life. The light of my life, you robbed me of that and how!

On the final day in March, Neville went to his father's chambers. Neville senior was 'pretty angry' with Worthington Evans and told his son he was 'going to tackle him' over all the confusion. Neville junior went on with his father to the House where he met a director of a syndicate in Sudan, saw the private secretary to the Colonial Office, then to the War Office where the Colonel offered to write him a testimonial. Finally, at dinner he met Ernest Levin, who had friends in high places in the Sudan, who said he would 'write'.

But still nothing definite. Neville was suffering wild mood swings, one minute thinking the wait would be over soon and full of optimism, the next back in the depths of despair. He had now been back a full six months and as he put it, was 'no nearer a job now than then'. He heard from his friend Tyger Wyld who was going to take up sheep farming in South Africa. 'Be of good cheer,' Tyger said in his letter. 'But what is the good?' Neville replies. 'No progress at all, I am struck down with all this business. The woman will haunt me everywhere. She would never worry, for without doubt she will still get someone to marry her.'

April

1 April was a bad day for Neville, even though no one played any practical jokes on him. He woke up feeling like he was back at the start of the past six months, and had achieved nothing in that time. His father had told him he could do no more from his position in the government and that Worthington Evans had actually got angry with him as he had asked too often for news. WE added that he had never known anyone who had left government service, and then returned. His father privately expressed his view to Neville that everyone who might once have helped now knew the facts of his case, and had turned against him, in fact were intending to block anything he tried to do. His father even suggested that he would be as well farming in South Africa as doing anything else, and suggested that he should go back there, making his son feel as though he was not wanted in Sloley. Neville began to see that his father had been embarrassed to ask ministers and powerful friends to help. Later in the day it got worse, as Neville saw General Asquith who told him the Sudan was hopeless. They had made regulations about age and Neville was really too old.

They were looking at men of 18–24 and Neville would find himself having to take orders from men both younger and less experienced than himself, which would feel irksome.

The one optimistic note was that the staff in Brazil needed to be expanded and he would know more in May, but could not make any promises. He wanted to know when Neville was at school, what games he had played, what war service he had, and what he knew about cotton; had he been to Swaziland, for example. Neville began to think that he was adversely affecting his prospects by getting all this influence. 'People don't like influence for it shows that a man does not rely entirely on his merits,' he said to his diary. 'It becomes daily worse and more trying and I can't see any daylight ahead. It seems an age since I had anything to do.'

But there were also some enjoyable social events to enjoy. Though he felt he could not really afford it, he made plans to go to Holland to stay with Jelly again, and to the Grand National and Henley boat races with Jane. Coming out they met their cousin Herbert Neville-White, who came back for tea. 'He was a "great success" with the ladies,' Neville writes, 'And he was in the Near East in the '90s. It is sad to think of what he might have done for he was a friend of the King and accompanied him on his tours of India. But his career has been "bitched" by a bloody woman. He could have been anything if he had divorced that useless human being'.

Then Neville went over to chambers to see his father and said that he had donated all his furniture at Sloley to his sister Jane. He also commented that Jane very much wanted to see him, as she had begun to feel abandoned by her father. At that point Bobbie answered for him saying that he was so busy that there was not time for such things as 'family visits'. When his father had gone, he and Bobbie had an unpleasant row. 'After hawing for some time,' he writes,' she said "What do you want out of Sloley?" I replied "Only my own furniture." Bad tempers flared on both sides. "That will mean that I shall have to buy more to replace it," said Bobbie. Neville "The stuff that was in my room should go back into my room." Bobbie, "But I like the rooms to look nice and it is the only dressing room left." And so the argument went on. She was so offensive; I could have hit her. But I am determined to get all my goods and belongings out of Sloley. If Jane won't have them, I'll put them into store. Everything I have, and then there can be no more bickering. I will never go there again, and that will suit that whore of a woman and me.'

A week later he was in The Hotel Victoria in The Hague. The weather was glorious. Their boat got in at 6am, and he and Reg and Jane had a full English breakfast together at the hotel. Angela arrived a bit later. Neville liked The Hague at once, commenting on its clean appearance and good state of repair, and the weather was even warm enough to sit outside. But things quickly began to spiral downwards. Jane and Reg had spent a full 20 minutes deciding which room to have in the Hotel Victoria, only to discover that it was too noisy. So the whole group moved to another hotel—in fact, not even a hotel but a pub—which was admittedly nicer but also more expensive.

They spent the day sightseeing, looking at Dutch Old Masters such as Rembrandt and Vermeer, then on to a museum to see a display of torture instruments. Then over dinner they got into a fierce discussion about ideals and war, during which Neville was 'shouted down' as he puts it, for saying that the war was inevitable and it was better to face it when they did, rather than wait and go it alone. But all the others said Britain had gone to war to protect Belgium. Neville then commented that if there was another war, men would again come forward to fight, and was shouted down a second time. Finally Neville put his foot in it a third time by asserting that no one did anything without a degree of self-interest. Jane flew at him and said there was no self-interest in having children, which her husband Reg refined further by saying that married couples had children because they wanted to enlarge the human race. At that Neville laughed loudly and Reg got angry. Neville added in his diary that he had never heard 'such balls'.

At yet another hotel in The Hague, they all set out to see the famous tulip bulbs which Neville said was certainly 'wonderful —ultramarine, cobalt, pink, orange, sky blue, maroon, mauve, crimson, yellow, blood red, and his favourite, salmon pink.' Then on to see azaleas and hydrangeas. But poor Neville spent most of his time wandering round these brilliant multi-coloured gardens on his own. He and Jane, usually such good friends, could hardly say a civil word to each other, and the two sisters Jane and Angela seemed to have formed a tight little twosome.

'Whatever I say is ridiculed,' Neville confides mournfully to his diary. 'I can do nothing right for Jane. It was a weary day. But the journey back gave us a wonderful view of the hyacinth fields on each side of the railway. They looked like carpets and I longed to be able to paint it somehow.' But 'Dinner was pretty bloody. I put my foot in it again by saying something quite inoffensive. Such idealistic crankish balls annoys me more than I can say. We arranged to go to the Island of Marken (North Holland) tomorrow to see the national costumes.' Their little group spent a day at Delft. Though the churches were all locked, Neville found the streets pretty and the spires impressive. However, he was worried about living in a house where the front door abutted onto a canal! He would really like to have gone on to Antwerp but felt he had better be on the spot in case anything turned up.

'Maybe I could go to Ceylon and plant tea and bury my ambition,' he wrote. 'The Gov'nor is right, I am not fit to be employed at anything. What a fool to have chucked up a career for a woman, no woman would have done what I did, they are too clever and have too good an eye for the main chance. The women take everything as a right, blast them! But what does it matter, what does anything matter these days, but a job far away from the sight of a white woman.'

He was also a bit worried about how much this was all costing, and since he had no income, he was drawing all the time on savings. He announced his decision to return to London, and got it in the neck from the others in his travelling group. 'Angela took it very well.' he writes. 'But Jane took it personally and attacked me and wanted to know how much money I had, and how I had spent it. And if I was as low as this, why did I come at all? I said I had thought £15 would be enough, and it was not my fault that I was low. She said all this haggling made it very difficult for her and Reg. Then she said she did not understand me, that she had been as kind as she could be and had had me on her hands all this time and here I was behaving very funnily. That rattled me. God knows, I know that I have lived at her house, and sponged on her, and I have always intended to pay her back in kind or in something she wants. I shall have to pay her as soon as we get back.'

Back at Fig Tree Court, Temple, Neville was able to pay back Jane and Jelly what he owed them, but he hated having to depend on friends and family so heavily for a place to stay. Added to this he recorded that 16 April was a terrible anniversary—it was exactly a year ago that he and M made their ill-fated decision to run away together. The only news on his return was bad. The Colonial Office had written to say it was not able to offer him a job. Rather reluctantly, Neville made his way back to Sloley, where he made the mistake of reading his diary from 1924 in bed:

> It nearly made me sick to think what I did last year and I threw it away. I think that diary ought to be destroyed and yet I do not like to do so because it may come in useful and one never knows.

And it was not long before Neville fell out with Bobbie, over some post of hers that he inadvertently destroyed. He describes it as a 'proper hick boo' and indeed it does sound as though they would really have liked to punch each other on the nose.

> "This is my house," Bobbie started. "And so is chambers, and don"t you forget it."
>
> Neville; "I am sorry".
>
> Bobbie; "You never told me you were going up to London."

Neville; "I realise only too well that there is no place for me here, that I am a stranger—lock stock and barrel and I will never come here again. If this is not to be my home, I will clear out everything. I hate being dependent and when I get a job, you would have no more cause to complain."

He continues in his diary:

I am heartily sick of her and all her machinations, she is a grasper and I shall always call her that. Money and possessions are all she cares about, she takes all she can get fairly and pinches the rest. A damnably, dangerous insincere woman. Tonight she showed her colours and I have hoisted mine. She can have her bloody possessions, but none of mine. Not one, if I can stow them elsewhere. I may have been wrong in destroying her post, but I can do no more than apologise.

One thing led to another and there was a further row the following day over not enough deference shown to her. His father seemed powerless to intervene and stop the row. They had a long chat before he left for London during which Neville tried to tell her that he had nowhere else to go, that he had stayed away in the past, that he had not been there for the past two years and that he did not want to be here but in the circumstances there was nowhere else to go. Bobbie for her part said she had tried to treat him like a brother and was genuinely fond of him, which rather surprised Neville, who commented finally in his diary that 'She is utterly and hopelessly insincere, a bit of a liar, and of course a grasper *de luxe*.'

By the middle of April the weather was warm and inviting, but Neville was in despair at ever getting another job. He idled away his days at Sloley while life went on around him, occasionally getting into arguments with his father about war, but keeping out of the way of Bobbie, as far as he could. But on 28 April when he took 'the two Gs' (the Gov'nor and the 'Grasper') to the station at Worstead, he stopped to buy a paper. He must have been anticipating it slightly because he turned to the divorce pages and saw that he had been cited as the other party in the case of Speed v Speed.

Today it came, the news of absolution. Luckily it was among 143 others, so it was less conspicuous than it might have been. What will she do with freedom, I wonder? Who will she wreck this time? Had things been different, I might now be rejoicing. Prepared for the happiness to come. She had said "In six months' time, we shall probably laugh over this." I expect she is laughing now, but she will feel outcast at the same time as I am outcast. Even if she marries again. To what end our joint sacrifices?

On the same day, he received an application form from the Metropolitan Police. Neville's immediate reaction was 'Do I care?' But he decided to fill in the form and send it off anyway. His sister Jane said she thought it would be a good idea, get him used to living in London, even though Neville really preferred country life. But he knew that the chances of finding work near Sloley were 'remote'.

May

May began with another terrible anniversary for Neville—this time, a year since he and M left for South Africa. And he wrote another rant in his diary about how betrayed he felt, how stupid and mad he had been to believe anything she said, how utterly hopeless and selfish all women are.

But at least he was at Sloley on his own (while his father and Bobbie were in London) and he was able to do some practical work in the garden for his father, starting with a fence which needed fixing. As he worked he talked to Mike, the odd job lad on the estate, who said his ambition was to be Prime Minister. Neville quickly tried to talk him out of politics, saying the best career a man could have was in the army. By the end of the day he was feeling fitter and happier, as manual labour generally does help both body and mind. He was brought back to his immediate problems quickly however. Firstly, there was a letter from his sister Jelly, whom Neville says had begun to despise as she and his other sister Jane talked exclusively and at length about babies and underclothes and house interiors. And secondly there was a form of application from the Sudan Office for him to complete. The following morning a third letter arrived inviting him for an interview at the Colonial Office. The interview went well and the officer seemed to say that there were jobs going in Nigeria, Tanganyika and Uganda. Neville was told that he would hear by the end of the month.

Back to Sloley to continue work on the fence, and on the Saturday he was joined by his father. But relations with his step mother deteriorated further. Bobbie was rapidly removing as much furniture as she could to Neville's chambers in London, as Neville senior had said that all the furniture in his chambers, should go to her on his death. Neville was saddened by this. As he says in his diary 'I have known (the furniture) there all my life'. Later in the week all three went to a tennis party where Bobbie was disappointed in her standard of play and started fishing for compliments from the other players, which she usually got. Neville confides in his diary, 'that is all she thinks about, how good she is so that people can tell her that she is good. It helps to swell her head.'

Then a letter arrived from the Sudan Government, asking if he was still serious about a job and if so, to appear for another interview on 10 July. Neville determined to say 'Yes'. At the end of the month (30 May) Neville saw in the paper that Captain Douglas Speed, the former husband of Myrtle, had remarried, a woman called Nicola Blake. Nicola and Douglas had been close friends and she had sometimes played the piano to accompany his singing at Christmas parties. And Neville's reaction? 'I am delighted and wish him all the happiness in the world,' he writes. His father wondered whether the whole thing had been a set up —namely, that Speed had wanted to get shot of his wife and had encouraged her to go off with Neville, who would then carry all the blame, while he quietly remarried.

June

Neville took his father and Bobbie to lunch, and then on to a fete at Westwick. All went well until he tried to drive the car between a tram and the curb in Magdalen Street in Norwich, and hit a lamppost. His father accused him of driving too fast—25 miles an hour was the limit, in his opinion! And so Neville was obliged to go no faster than that for the rest of the day. It was only when they got back to Sloley that his father told him that the car belonged to his stepmother, Bobbie. 'I guess I have driven it for the last time,' he writes ruefully. 'I fairly wrecked the running board.'

Sunday 8 June was 'A certain person's birthday, a thing of no importance these days. I sweated all day on the typewriter without ceasing and felt fagged at the end of it.'

The summer weather was good. Neville spent much time playing tennis and cricket and swimming, both in Norfolk and in London with friends. In the evenings he played bridge. Life was good, very good despite a continuing sadness that he was no longer in the army and still had not found another job. But then on Saturday 13 June a letter came to say that the Sudan Government wanted to see him at 11.30am on Monday. 'It looks as if there might be a job going', he writes. 'I can hardly believe it.'

A friend, Tiger Wyld, arrived back in England from South Africa and Neville met up with him. 'I don't think he will find it so easy as he thinks to get a job,' Neville comments, 'especially with a wife and child.' Tiger also applied for a job in the Sudan, but was offered nothing. Then Neville was interviewed at the Rembrandt Hotel in London the following Monday, and to his delight and surprise, was offered a job in the Sudan working as an inspector at the Gezira Cotton Picking Scheme, and given a day to decide. His first reaction was to tell his father, whom he found at the House of Commons. 'He did not sound very pleased and I think he really feels that he does not want me to leave the country,' Neville writes. 'Much as I love him, I realise that my presence in England is hopeless and I must quit for the good of all. Also the Grasper has her eye on Sloley to go to Richard (her son by Reginald). The joy of having an offer counter-balances practically everything'.

Neville senior then mentioned a 'brewery job' to his son, which he had not done before. The son was a bit baffled, since he had lost confidence in his father's ability to swing anything for him with political influence. Neville senior even offered him enough money to put into a business—anything it would seem to stop his son from going abroad again, despite all the differences and problems there had been at Sloley. But James made up his mind saying he must earn some money to save for the future, and accepted the job in Africa. He was medically examined the same afternoon and was told he would sail on 10 July, so there was little time to prepare. All the following week he would start learning Arabic, and there was a certain amount of shopping to do, as well as packing up at Sloley. But with new prospects and a permanent job, he felt 'quite different.' He dined with an army friend called Woolley in Soho, and had a cheery evening.

The garden at Sloley, on which he had worked so hard while out of a job, was in full bloom with foxgloves and herbs filling the air with perfume, and the strawberries were fruiting. Nevertheless, he says, 'I am pleased to be leaving, though I am exceedingly loath to leave Bilgey (his dog). Woolley shall have her.' The Arabic lessons turned out to be fun and Neville quickly picked up the habit of saying 'Thank Allah' instead of Thank God. He also greatly enjoyed the shopping sessions buying two pairs of breeches, a polo saddle, shirts and a pith helmet. He was able to buy most of these goods through a purchasing agency, saving 10 per cent overall.

With all this activity, the pain of his loss of Myrtle and his career in the army receded. He comments rather bitterly however that:

> The Traitor will probably go down the old-fashioned drain where he will be appreciated, by the parasites who dwell there. I wonder if the One is regretting it. After all, she has lost everything now and her husband obviously did not care an imperial damn. It is her cushion and she can sit on it. Her pride will be injured and she has nothing to satiate it with now. She has not even got me off whom to score. Poor M, she is down the drain now, hoist with her own petard. I expect the Traitor is feeling distinctly tired these days and I should not be surprised to hear that he had given up farming, in favour of professional dancing. Much more his line where he can talk balls to women till Kingdom Come. I am out of that now, thank Allah. Here's to the future in a country where white women cannot live.

Notes

1 Automatic writing or psychography is said to be a psychic ability which allows a person to produce written words without consciously writing; according to aficionados, the words arise from a subconscious, spiritual or supernatural source. The earliest reports of automatic writing as a spiritual practice was reported by Hyppolyte Taine in the preface to the third edition of his De l'intelligence, published in 1878. Georgie Hyde-Lees, the wife of William Yates, also claimed that she could write automatically.

Automatic messages may take place either by the writer passively holding a pencil on a sheet of paper, or by a 'ouija board'. In spiritualism, spirits are claimed to take control of the hand of a medium to write messages, letters, and even entire books. Automatic writing can happen in a trance or waking state. The author of Sherlock Holmes, Sir Arthur Conan Doyle, in his book *The New Revelation* (1918), wrote that automatic writing occurs either by the writer's subconscious or by external spirits operating through the writer. Some psychical researchers such as Thomas Jay Hudson have claimed that no spirits are involved in automatic writing and that the subconscious mind is the explanation.

Alleged cases of automatic writing have included the notorious English occultist Aleister Crowley, the American psychic Jane Roberts, the American research psychologist Helen Schucman and the American author Neale Donald Walsch.

Needless to say, scientists consider all this to be highly questionable. Sceptics consider automatic writing to be the result of the ideomotor effect (a psychological phenomenon where a subject makes motions unconsciously). In 1927, psychiatrist Harold Dearden wrote that automatic writing is a psychological method of "tapping" the unconscious mind and there is nothing mysterious about it. According to investigator Joe Nickell, a prominent American investigator of the paranormal, "automatic writing is produced while one is in a dissociated state. It is a form of motor automatism, or unconscious muscular activity." Neurologist Terence Hines has written that "automatic writing is an example of a milder form of dissociative state."

It is possible that Neville was indeed in a 'dissociative state', grieving as he was for everything he had lost—the woman he had intended to marry, the dream they had together of buying and running a farm in South Africa, and the British Army. Wikipedia, February 2018

2 Possibly Lord Home of Yarmouth though I cannot find any reference to this name.

3 The rank of *Sirdar* was assigned to the British Commander-in-Chief of the British-controlled Egyptian Army in the late 19th and early 20th centuries.

The Sudan
July 1925–December 1926

Working in The Sudan sounded like an adventure, but Neville quickly found the country and the work tedious. The work meant supervising local people and since he spoke little Arabic and did not understand the culture, it was extremely difficult. There was little to do outside the job except drink whisky, play polo or bridge, and Neville did not get on well with the other ex-pats. Most disheartening of all was the constant threat of disease, particularly malaria which Neville suffered badly from. He lasted 18 miserable months, then returned to England.

July

It was only a week now before Neville departed yet again from his family in Norfolk and from all his friends in London. There were a few last minute loose ends to tie up —he gave his hunting kit and saddle to Woolley and shifted his furniture into the stables at Sloley—then it was time to pack his bags. His sister Jane was expecting a second baby so he made a last visit to see her and Reg in their new home south of London, and had a tearful last lunch with them realising that her children would be quite big by the time he saw them again—if he ever did.

Then there was a round of inoculations and vaccinations, before a final farewell at a party thrown for him in London with all the uncles and aunts attending. It was not a jolly affair. 'The reception was cool to say the least of it,' he writes. 'Aunt A was cooler than ever, the frost sticking to her very hair. Aunt R gave me arctic conditions!'

And finally, the day came on 10 July when he had to board the train at Victoria. Neville's father was, this time, showing emotion openly. 'He was genuinely cut up,' writes Neville. 'His voice was breaking and great big tears stood in his dear eyes. I found it hard to control the lump that flew to my throat. He stood facing me and begging me not to break my heart. He said, "For God's sake, do not break your heart and become embittered with your fellow creatures. Be gentle and kind and don't take offence. Do not steel yourself against your friends." Neville later recalled how he leaned out of the window of the carriage and waved and waved to his father until he could no longer see him, the great lump of emotion in his throat threatening to explode into fits of crying. And finally, Neville pulled the window shut.

He was travelling with another young man called Ponsonby. Ponsonby's aunt met them in Paris and escorted them across the city to pick up another train, this time to Marseilles, on the south coast of France. Neville did not get much sleep on the second train as he had no pillow and he complains in his diary that the train stank of Gauloises and garlic! They boarded the boat at once on arrival in Marseilles, and sailed at noon. Neville comments that it 'seems only a moment that I was coming home (from Africa) but it was such a six months, that I hope I shall never have to spend again. I am not sorry to be off, whereas poor Ponsonby is feeling pretty miserable (as he is leaving behind a girl whom he hopes to marry on his return to England in 2 years' time). I know how he is feeling!'

The boat, the SS *Herefordshire*, turned out to be a comfortable vessel, with cabins quite a lot larger than the Ehrman packet steamer which had transported Neville to and from South Africa 18 months previously. Most of the passengers were bound for the Sudan, Ceylon (now Sri Lanka) or Rangoon (then the capital of Burma, now Myanmar).

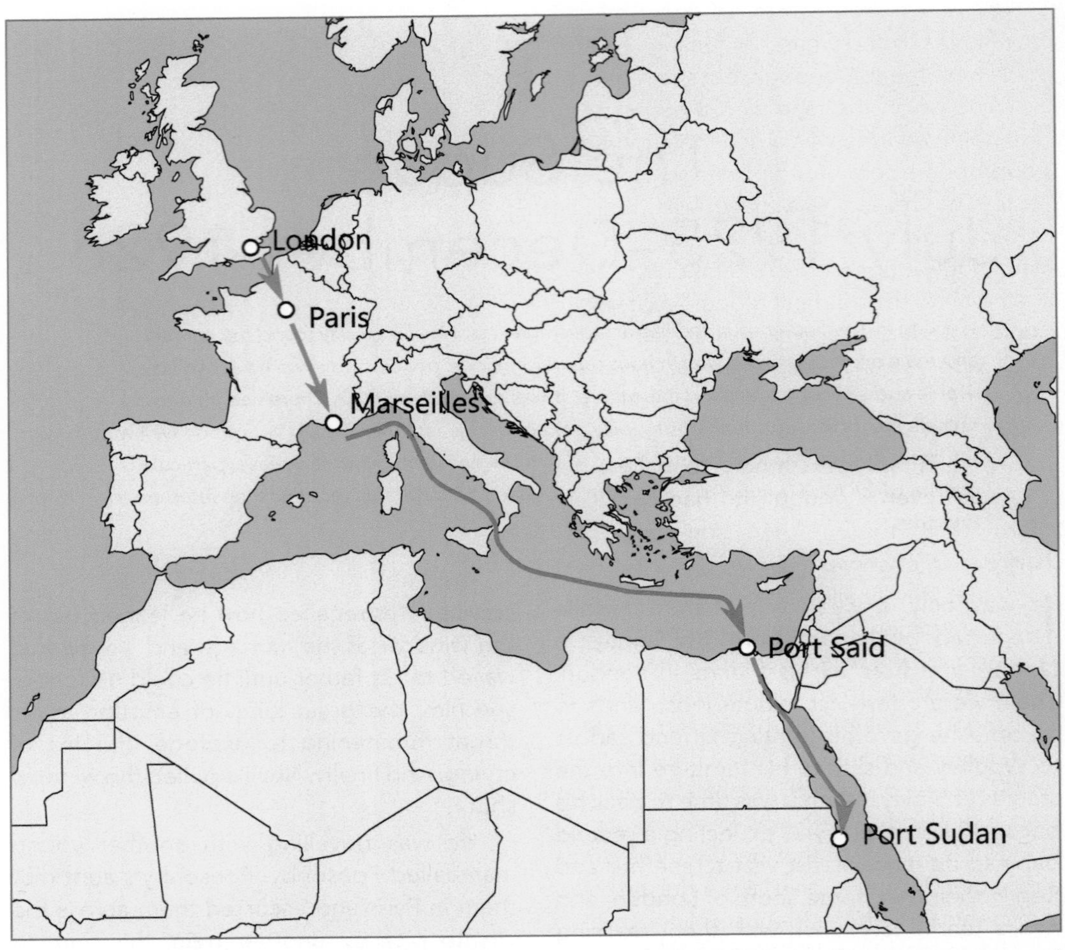

Map showing Neville's route to Port Sudan.

Neville bumped into at least two people who were either teachers or former students at Eton, so he was able to gossip over bridge about hunting and rowing. Then there were deck games such as quoits, identifying the various landmarks such as the volcano Stromboli on the Italian coast, and a number of islands such as Crete and Sicily. Dinner was at 7pm after which came dancing and Neville chatted to the ladies about art and antiques. He could be very charming when he wanted.

They stopped at Port Said where passengers were allowed to go ashore even though the temperature was in the 100s. Neville said it was hard to describe the place. 'Wherever we went, these nasty dagos followed and wanted to make us buy dirty postcards,' he writes. 'Small boys kept shouting "English books, pretty post cards, very pretty!" Then there were the usual bum boats hanging round the ship, selling carpets (made in Birmingham!), beads, shawls, silks and so on. There were men and boys diving for coins as at Madeira. They swam like fish!'

Once through the Suez Canal into the Red Sea there was a cooling following wind, though the temperature did not drop. Neville noted that a ship, the *City of Singapore*, passed the other way going north to Rotterdam, having been pulled all the way by two tugs from Adelaide. 'Some tow!' he writes. He was detailed to play in a skittles team on the side named Khartoum, a tournament which lasted over two days. His team was beaten in the finals, but 'It was good fun'.

He writes in his diary:

> The worst part of a sea trip so often is that one meets ripping people on board, and never sees them again. However, it is a long time before I shall have another trip, at least I hope so.

On Sunday 19 July he arrived at Port Sudan and took a train via Atbara to

Khartoum. His first thought was that it was 'Devilish not being able to speak a word of the language' and the second that the heat in the middle of the day was pretty bad.

> As we were having lunch it came up off the ground and hit one slap in the face. I sweated profusely the moment I stepped ashore... ...The country is very like South Africa but there are not even the bushes that exist in that drought. Here one occasionally sees a camel and the stations have neat little flat roofed houses dotted about.

His train was extremely comfortable however; even though it had no air conditioning, the sleeping compartments were as large as the cabins on the ship, and he could open the windows and let in a cooling draft. The train was due in at Khartoum at six that evening, and by nine pm he was at the Garden Hotel. 'Even though I have taken no exercise and have done nothing all day, I am feeling absolutely dog tired,' he writes. The following day Neville was given a whistle stop tour of the city by two ladies whose husbands were posted in Khartoum. He took them for 'ripping drinks' followed by lunch and then tea. Neville wrote to his family and then dreamt vividly of his sister Jane giving birth to a boy, and subsequently of 'The One'. The following day Neville and Ponsonby boarded yet another train for Bakarat (headquarters of the Gezira Board about 72 kilometres south of Khartoum) and again the day after that on to Remitab, his final destination another 35 kilometres south west.

A narrow-gauge railway had been constructed in the early 1920s specifically for the Gezira Scheme, transporting staff such as Neville from the coast to the fields of cotton, and the end product—freshly picked cotton—back to the coast to be taken to England to be woven into fabric. As the size of the project area increased, the railway was later extended and by the mid-1960s it consisted of a complex system totaling 716 kilometres. Neville does not say so, but it sounds like he had a bit of a shock when he saw where he was going to work. 'The country is as flat as a pancake and not a sign of a tree anywhere, with here and there a village of round straw houses and a roundel to each holding.'

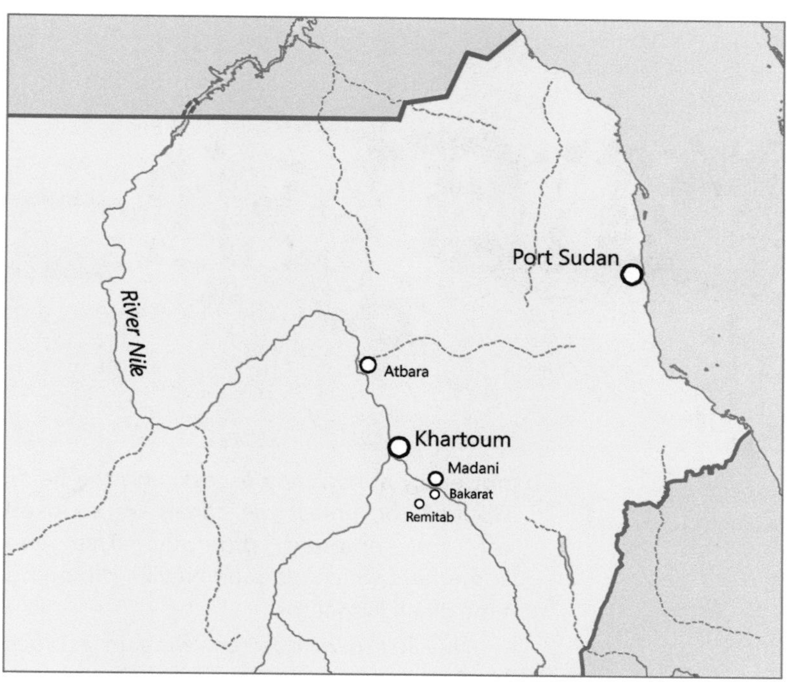

Map showing Port Sudan, Atbara, Khartoum, Bakarat and Remitab and Madani.

The Gezira Scheme consisted of an area of about 300,000 feddans (309,000 acres or 483 square miles) situated between the Blue and White Niles, and was one of the largest irrigation schemes in the world. It was operated in the form of a triple partnership —the Sudan Plantations Syndicate Ltd (a British-based company), the tenant cultivators (in other words, local natives) and the Government of Sudan. The Government provided water from the Sennar Dam, and also paid for the pumping stations and the construction and maintenance of the canals. As landowner, it rented out the land to the tenants at 10 piastres (about 10 new pence) per feddan per annum. It also took 40% of the profits, the tenants took another 40% and the remaining 20% went to the Syndicate, for which Neville worked and was paid a salary. Neville's duties as an inspector included the direction and control of the tenants. The tenants had to make sure the pumps and sluices were operated to ensure the cotton had just enough water to thrive but not so much that the plants were swamped. It was important that the flow was steady throughout the day and night. During the rainy season, it was especially difficult to manage the water, as the heavy clay soil did

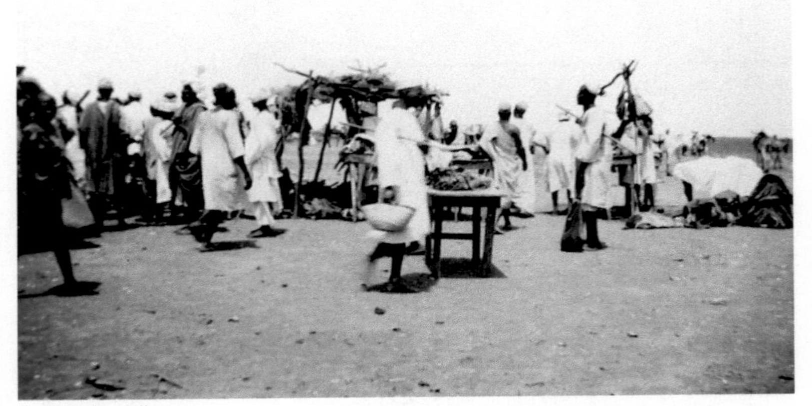

Butcher's stall at Gedidim Suq.
John d'Arcy / NRO Nev 7/34.

not easily absorb any excess, and the fields would flood unless the canals were closed off and emptied promptly. This was something which plagued Neville during his time as an inspector.

Neville's own quarters were in a block hurriedly erected by the British in cement. 'My block inspector's name is Austin,' he records in his diary:

> I was allotted a little room full of scorpions. Then we went out in Austin's car for a while and met other workers and inspectors.... It is a truly vast show, canals, dykes, ditches everywhere and as the water has only just started under the summer damn (*sic*), many canal banks are breaking. Later we went out on horseback—well, ponies really—to look at the plot I am to take over, about 800 feddans. All the (*black*) workers flocked round me like flies and I felt an awful fool not being able to understand a word. I hope it will come in time.

One local man, from Neville's description a tribal elder, said that he, Neville, would 'get' Arabic in under a month!

Camel 'Jehu'.
John d'Arcy / NRO Nev 7/34.

Madani was the nearest town of any size which could only be reached by car, so they had to wait for the rain to stop, otherwise the car would become bogged down in mud. Neville thought it 'not a bad spot' and was able to buy a few things including some trees for his garden. He also sent a cable to Jane as he was anxious about the forthcoming birth of a new nephew or niece, and opened a bank account. On another visit to Madani a few days later he saw in the paper that his sister Jane had had another girl and records in his diary that he was 'disappointed!'

His first reaction to his new circumstances was quite positive however, he writes:

> I am quite comfortable, I am amazed at myself being here at all. If I can save all my private income for 10 years and perhaps add a few pounds now and again, I ought to be fairly well off at the end of it. If I can put away £400 a year for 10 years, I shall have quite enough to live on from the interest. (*At the time interest was around 5%.*)

The inspectors played polo in the evenings with tournaments at the weekends, there were little tea parties where the wives or servants provided sandwiches and poured whisky, and plenty of bridge. There were also duck and crane shoots. Neville had a small garden in which he grew a variety of vegetables to supplement the rather boring, meagre diet of tinned food from the shop, which was expensive. There were very few European women who were unattached and the local women were rarely seen at all. On the down side the climate was either unbearably hot—over 100 degrees in the sun—or it rained so hard that the roads turned to mud and were impassable. One night soon after he arrived there was a storm during which two and a half inches of rain fell, accompanied by several deafening claps of thunder. A bit later the rain turned to hail. Neville recalls:

> The noise of the hail on the veranda roof was like an engine letting off steam and I had to shout to Austin in order to make myself heard. There were hail stones as big as starlings' eggs and I fully expected the veranda roof to be pierced. I don't see how the canals can hold all the water.

It did not take long for Neville to start whingeing again to his diary:

> As far as I can see, I shall never have a house to myself here and the prospects of promotion are very small. I am so much older than all the fellows. None of them went to the war and I feel a generation older than them all.

Leave is a long way off but that is an expensive business and I shall have nowhere to go unless I sponge on Jane and Jelly. I shall just have to spend it in the country which is cheapest to live in.

And then soon after this small outburst, it was back to full-blown depression. He moans:

My estate gets worse and worse and I shall probably get the sack soon. If I got the sack from here, I should go out in the sun without a helmet and finish it all. I still wonder sometimes what my aim in life is. There is none at the moment. Will there never be any? I'm damned if I know. Here I shall remain until they find out my complete incompetence and then God knows. The future holds nothing for me still. True I am happy enough here, as far as happiness in me lies these days; it's been a month tomorrow. I shall never realize my ambition to make a name for myself and distinguish myself. All the men senior to me would be my subalterns in the regiment.

There was a selection of stinging insects and reptiles to be wary of such as scorpions, snakes and spiders—Neville always had to check his shoes and his bed before putting them on or getting in. He kept a daily tally and, for example, on Tuesday 6 July, 1926 he killed 35 scorpions in the house having found four in his hat the day before. Another day he 'met a tarantula on his doorstep.' He was rarely stung, though he does record one sting in June 1926. 'Had a putrid night,' he confides to his diary. 'Could not get to sleep and so pulled my bed into the south corner, and pulled up the blanket. A bloody agrab (Arab word for scorpion) stung me and gave me absolute hell. I never want to be stung again.'

And then there were the butterflies—black with white spots, brown with yellow spots, red tipped, painted ladies, some as large as a man's hand, some as small as a British blue. But by far the most pernicious insect was the mosquito, its bite loaded with the parasites which cause malaria. Neville succumbed quickly. He had his first dose in October 1925, just a few months after he arrived. But far more severe was the second in March 1926 when he was hospitalised for several weeks. The first thing he noticed was that his appetite disappeared. Then his temperature went up. One morning it was 101 and he wrote in his diary that he did not feel too bad, but by lunchtime he started shivering and felt as if he was going to freeze to death even though he covered himself with blankets and coats. He took his temperature again and it had gone up to just over 105—dangerously high.

I felt perfectly and unutterably bloody for the rest of the day. Harvey came by and offered to take me to Medani (to the hospital) but I refused as the idea

Cars with Jamieson (driving), Pearson, Milne, Rudd and Austin, getting ready for polo.
John d'Arcy / NRO Nev 7/34.

Neville's servant Abdul with his two horses.
John d'Arcy / NRO Nev 7/34.

of a journey in the car was not good.

The fever left him at sundown, and for the next two days he stayed in bed feeling 'weak as a lamb'. Then the headache came, a reeling, splitting headache which did not respond to any painkillers. To add to his woes, there was nothing to do but work, and his office was as hot as an oven. He and two others were trying to get the accounts ready for inspection, but Neville had to retire early to bed with the shivers.

> I woke in the middle of the night with a start, convinced that I could find all the numbers in one place. I searched under the chair, cushions, papers, table, everywhere for the numbers. Then I sat down on the bed and realised suddenly I was raving!

This transition from feeling OK one minute and delirious with fever the next continued for several more days, until finally one of the inspectors insisted Neville went to hospital. Here a nurse, Miss Poyce, cared for him, piling on the blankets when he had the shivers and filling hot water bottles for his feet, then removing everything when he had a fever. She gave him tea to drink but he brought that up. She also took a blood test which confirmed he did indeed have the malaria parasite. Oddly his main thought at the time was that he had not written to his father recently and that Neville senior would take offence. The only remedy in those days for malaria was quinine which Neville was given in large quantities. Quinine prevented the attacks of shivers but could not kill off the parasite which lives on in the liver. (It remains in use to this day as the first line of defence against malaria in parts of sub-Saharan Africa where modern drugs are not readily available.) Thus, Neville could expect to suffer further attacks of malaria throughout his life, though the attacks would be less severe as his body developed a natural immunity to it. Every European working in the Sudan cotton business at that time expected to get malaria at some point. The mosquito which carries the disease likes to live and breed near stagnant water, and there was plenty of that in the canals.

Pearson looking very thin after a dose of dysentery, January 1926.
John d'Arcy / NRO Nev 7/34.

He was also given arsenic, which was used in small doses, to quell fever where quinine had proved ineffective. Since arsenic is well-known as a poison, Neville might have been frightened to take it but he records no adverse feelings towards it and no ill effects. After a week of rest and doses of quinine, arsenic and iron, Neville was feeling better, but still weak and still with no appetite. 'Last week was a nightmare,' he wrote in his diary. 'I never want to go through that again. It is a terrible life this, dull, hazardous to health, poorly paid and hardly worth sticking—but what else is there?'

He was in hospital for about a month, during which Eid al-Fitr (the end of Ramadhan, the Muslim equivalent to the Christian period of Lent followed by Easter), was celebrated and this caused Neville to rant in his diary.

> A hideous noise the blighters made all day, beating drums incessantly, till I could have gone out with a machine gun and slaughtered the lot. The drummers did not tire till late in the night.

There were other serious diseases to contend with. His boss Austin regularly went down with dysentery and the toilet facilities were primitive and very smelly. Their clerk contracted typhoid. He was taken to hospital, sent back out to work after 10 days still with a fever. He became delirious and went back to hospital where he died. Austin told Neville that he thought it was 'a stout effort' of the man to return, and he had only done so for fear some of the higher-up bosses would suspect that he was shamming. In the heat every slight cut or abrasion quickly went septic. 'I am going rapidly bad,' he wrote on 14 February, 1926:

> Wherever I have an abrasion the wound goes septic and my hand and arm are bound up. I shall have my face in a sling soon as a razor cut went bad

Pearson's Bungalow, Heweiwa House.
John d'Arcy / NRO Nev 7/34.

in the night and an old razor cut under my chin has also gone bad. I am a nasty sight. It is not want of green food and my bowels are open enough.

A few days later he records:

The doctor stuck me with manganese for the sores and said I should not feel it, but I did. My backside has hardened up as if I had had an injection of concrete.

Apart from matters of health, Neville found his old-school attitude and bullying temperament did little to endear him to anyone. All the inspectors had servants in the house to keep it clean and prepare food, and tenants to do the work in the cotton fields. Neville quickly became unpopular with his staff. This is an extract from August 6, 1925, not long after he arrived.

A most amusing day all told. First of all it was pay day and all the New Tenants came in to have loans advanced to them for watering and sowing. I had a few words with Khalil my servant re my old fishing boots, and in English I called him a "bloody fool" for he had broken the keeper strap. He understood me and said that at the end of the month, finished. I said "Good". He said "Am I not good?" Then he said in English, "You sorry." I told him to clear out at once. After lunch Austin saw him fighting and kicked his bottom. In the evening he asked me for his reference and I said. "Why are you going so soon?" "Because the boss hit me." I replied with "O la la". 'After sundown I asked Austin to ask him why he was leaving. He said because I had called him a bloody fool and I had hit him. Austin told him to stay for 6 days and he refused. So Austin said "You must be a bloody fool." At which he said "Thank you, thank you". Austin then upped and sloshed him one and he ran like a hare. Later Austin's servants reported that he had eaten all the eggs, pinched enough flour for 4 loaves, a bag of potatoes and fat. We went out and found him and Austin ran him through the mud to the tin storehouse. We could do nothing but laugh. He refused to go into the tin store because it was full of scorpions.

To be fair to Neville, at the beginning he did at least try to be a good boss:

I have the blues here sometimes. I shall probably be a rite (*sic*) bad inspector. I can't figure out how to get the truants to work at my word. I must be just. I don't want to hit them. They want leading and treating firmly.

But it quickly degenerated into Neville

Neville sitting in a planter's chair on the verandah of his bungalow, October 1925.
John d'Arcy / NRO Nev 7/34.

treating the servants and tenants as badly, if not worse, than all the other inspectors. On Thursday 4 March, 1926 for example he wrote in his diary:

> First I found the tenant who should have been taking water, sitting in his house. Later I found two more tenants lazing about. One said there was no work and the other that the sun was hot!!! I ended up hitting one of the men. He refused to mount a donkey and go to Ramitab and said he was ill.

And again on Tuesday 9 March, 1926 he writes:

> Had a … row with Ibrahim (his servant), who refused to try and mend a fishing net and said it was not his business. So I kicked him out of the house. Later Ooman came along and interceded for him and I told him straight that I did not want the boy, but that as the rest of the household seemed to want him, he had better stay. He's a disgruntled boy and I am in a vile temper these days.

On February 24 he says that:

> I met Harvey late. He said he was receiving complaints that I was too hard on the tenants and that I was frightening the women. I shall have to go steady, an excess of zeal on my part to get the stuff picked. Harvey was very nice about it and said he understood the difficulty but also he did not want a complaint to go into Barakat or the Government.

The most exciting part of Neville's week was to receive letters from home, and he would seize upon them when they arrived like a man parched of water.

> Mail Day! Thank God! Letters from Jelly, the Govn'r, and PooBah and much news. Apparently, Jane was taken very suddenly and the baby had started to come before the doctor appeared on the scene. Jelly watched the whole thing, said it was very interesting. The Govn'r was full of questions and news, the Palace Garden Party and his presentation to the Queen as a member of the Royal County. But he is angry that the government has given in to the miners (who were threatening to strike).
>
> PooBah said in a PS that she had heard that Douglas Speed had begged Myrtle to come home but she refuses. That was news indeed, for I had expected her to be home by now. The other news I saw in the paper that Wilko Radclife has had twin sons and Bollocks Lowndes is engaged to the daughter of the *charge d'affaires* of Luxembourg. He would have to marry into that sort of clan. How the 43rd will laugh when they see that.

In February 1926 Neville got another letter from PooBah who was ski-ing in Wengen (Switzerland). A girlfriend with the surname of Hardy who lived near Shorncliffe, was in the same hotel and she had told PooBah that M had returned to England 'to live with her people' (i.e. her mother and father). 'I am constantly meeting her in Ashford,' the Hardy girl had said. 'Apparently she is quite happy and pleased with life.' PooBah continued that M's former husband DS had remarried to Nicola (Blake) and the pair were 'very happy' and that Nicola was 'devoted' to the Speed's son Richard.

'M still calls herself Mrs Speed,' PooBah wrote. 'She gave Maurice Speed (her former father-in-law) a lift in her car the other day, and chatted away as if nothing had happened. I admire her. I should think it must have been awful for her but she has been brave and brazened it out in her own county. It needs some courage to live within 30 miles of her ex-husband'.

To add to all his woes, Neville genuinely was very lonely and frequently dreamt of his jolly days in the army where he had friends to laugh with. Christmas Day was especially bad even though he received a special parcel from his family. A polo tournament on 26 December and bridge at Jennings' house on the 27th failed to revive his spirits. But on Monday 28 December he was delighted and rather proud to find his first vegetables had come up—radishes! He also had a 'good mail' including two letters from his father. Rather wistfully he records that snow is lying on the ground in Norfolk and a nearby pond had frozen over so the family, gathered at Sloley for Christmas, had been ice skating.

His final entry for the year 1925 sounds like a man who is trying his hardest to make a go of things, but who for one reason or another, continually fails. Thursday 31 December.

> The old year lies a 'dying. It is 6pm and I shall soon be off to dine. The last five months here have gone quick enough and I am not sorry to be saying "Goodbye to 1925". It has been a lively year by my getting this job—but all the same I wish I had someone a little nearer than 3000 miles. I thank all who have been kind to me in the past year, the Govn'r, Jane, Jelly, Reg, Jack, Milly, PB and all my army friends, Woolley, Sandy and the Regiment in general. I can never repay some of them. A long hot year lies ahead of me, but I must not think of its length. I wish I was a bit happier here in this block. I want to try and get things right, but they don't do at all. Things are going wrong and I worry and I dream about water and dry cotton and picking forever.

1926

Still in the Sudan

Water was a constant problem. It had to be regulated to irrigate the cotton crops regularly, but not flood them. The equipment was so unreliable that Neville often found himself out all night trying to either open or close the gates. So it was on Tuesday 5 January 1926. Neville writes:

> A very long and tiring day. There is hell's own work to be done these days....water is a constant trouble. It gave me a bloody night for at 6pm I found the water butchering at my sud (overflowing the canal). I opened all lubia (*sluices*) and rode to Harvey. He was out but I managed to get him on the phone. He said he had got the water cut off. I came back to dinner at 7.30 and went out again at 8.15 till 10.45 by which time the water had not abated. However, there was nothing else to be done and I went to bed dog tired.

He also got told off by Harvey a day or two later as he opened a particular sluice. In the morning he found Harvey at his house, livid with rage because the railway (*canal*) had been watered. Harvey said it was Neville's job to get rid of it somehow and told him he had to open one lubia. 'But I had never told the ghaffir to open that lubia,' Neville whinged.

> Harvey said it was my business to see that the railway was not watered. Why was the end so empty? I said there are only two pipes to take all the water. Then you must open cotton (*canal*), a thing I had thought was a great crime. Then he said I must stay on 38 SW, till it was drained. So I did from 8.30am till 4.45pm, without breakfast, lunch or tea or a drink of water. My ghaffir told me that the head ghaffir came at about 8pm and told him to open 38SW. But I have not told Harvey. No matter what I do, it is wrong. If I don't open lubia, the end fills and seeps to hell. If I do open and the canal breaks, and the land is watered, then there is hell. So whatever I do there is hell to pay.
>
> And I am getting a little tired of it. He said Paunton had been down at 11pm one night and found the sud empty which was as Harvey said I must have

> it. Well, I suppose he is paid to raise hell over everything, but his order one day is wrong for the next, and I don't know what to do. If I hold water I am wrong, if I get rid of it I am wrong, so I can't just compete with this business. A little more and I shall quit. They can find someone else to take on the job. The water is never constant and one never knows when it is coming for the last two days it has started to rise at sundown.

By Friday 16 April 1926 he was fed up confiding in his diary:

> I shall take things easier and not worry so much. I have not been able to sleep without aspirin for three nights, and I dream about this infernal cotton. After all it does not matter all that much and though I am bored stiff with the monotony of the work, yet I hope better days will come soon, when I get a car and can go off and see other people.

Soon after that he had a chat with Harvey and discussed his future. Harvey advised him to hang on until they knew whether the Syndicate was to have the new concession. If it was refused by the Sudan Government, then it meant he might stagnate there any number of years and never get any promotion. There were many men younger than Neville who were already senior to him in the Syndicate, and he felt he could never make up the time. 'If the Syndicate does not get the concession, I think I shall have to chuck it and I shall have wasted 18 months,' Neville writes. 'I shall also have earned a name of not being able to stick at anything. It is rather an awkward situation. Harvey said he thought Junior Inspector's salaries would reach 700 (*pounds sterling a year*) as a maximum limit, but one cannot save the hell of a lot out of that.'

His birthday on 5 July was a happy day when he got a letter from all the family wishing him many happy returns of the day. 'It is rather amazing to be 3000 miles away and yet get a letter exactly on the right day,' he mused in his diary. 'Damned nice letters too. Also, one from Harvey thanking me for my work in the winter, and saying that though he had found fault, he had appreciated my work and hope I would benefit in future. A damned nice letter, begorrah.'

Life continued in much the same way

The Mahdi's tomb is located in Omdurman. The tomb was seriously damaged by naval gunfire on Lord Kitchener's orders following the Battle of Omdurman in 1898. The tomb was reconstructed in 1947. Here we see it in 1936.

Library of Congress, LC-DIG-matpc-17358.

until Christmas 1926 when he and a few friends went to Khartoum by car on 23 December. Leaving Gezira around 3pm they got into Khartoum around 7.30pm and managed to get rooms at the Grand Hotel. Sadly, there were no young ladies around for them to chat to or dance with, but there were some 'splendid cocktails'. Neville was astounded that the cocktail mixer was a local man. 'I never knew one of these natives could do anything so useful.' They had a fine time in the city—went shopping for suits which were cheap and plentiful, to the races and a 'riotous evening'. On Christmas Day Neville and a friend strolled in Khartoum Zoo in the afternoon, then had a good lunch followed by a siesta. Again sadly, the Governor of Khartoum was giving a ball, which meant that again all the young women were at the high society event, not at the bar in the Grand.

The following day they went sightseeing mounted on ponies and saw the Mahdi's tomb[1] and the Khalifa's palace[2]. And on Monday 27 December, the party came to an end and they drove back to Gezira.

Neville was hoping for leave to return to England. And on Sunday 27 February 1927, he finally set off on what sounds to the 21st century mind like a dream trip—via Khartoum, across the Nubian Desert to Abu Simbel, then Luxor, Cairo, on by boat to Venice, by train to Paris and finally arrived in London on 18 March.

Notes

1 Muhammed Ahmad bin Abd Allah (August 12, 1844–June 22, 1885) was a religious leader in the Sudan who, on June 29, 1881, proclaimed himself the Mahdi, the messianic redeemer of Islam. The Mahdi led a successful military campaign against the Turkish-Egyptian government of the Sudan, culminating in the Battle of Khartoum, which had been held by the British General Gordon. He died unexpectedly on 22 June 1885, a mere six months after the conquest of Khartoum. Wikipedia, February 2018.

2 Khalifa or Khalifah is a name or title meaning "successor", "deputy" or "steward". It most commonly refers to the leader of a Caliphate, but is also used as a title among various Islamic religious groups and orders. His palace was extremely fine. Wikipedia, February 2018.

PooBah—1927

In this chapter Neville picks up the threads of his life with his former girlfriend PooBah, now married, and falls in love with her again. She has to leave for a while to be with her husband in India, and Neville pines for her for months until her return. When she does finally get back, it seems she does not really love him but is using him as a backstop for affection while she and her husband separate. Again Neville is badly hurt.

Home at Last 1927

There are many blank pages at the start of the diary for 1927 but by the end of April Neville had started to make a few entries while he was on holiday touring France by car. He covered a great distance, including the countryside and main cities of the south west of France, ending by going over the border into Holland on 5 May, to visit Antwerp where Angela was living with her husband and family. There he stayed until 21 May, enjoying picnics and days out with his nieces and nephews. But finally, the time came for him to say goodbye.

> Felt quite bloody all day at the thought of leaving Angela and the children. Took the children and Jelly down to the Grand Bazaar and said "Goodbye". It was very painful. I wish they lived in England.

He got back to Dover the following day feeling 'rather miserable as all the fun lies behind me and the thought of the Sudan ahead of me is perfectly bloody.'

Neville met up with PooBah and they went to the Chelsea Flower Show together. He heard from his father who had been offered a baronetcy. And finally, he returned to Sloley in Norfolk where the garden was looking 'wonderful, very clean and tidy!'

When he got back to London, he heard from PooBah that Myrtle was now running a millinery shop in Beauchamp Place in London—with lots of boyfriends willing to date her. Toby[1] (from the South African adventure) is recorded as being in the Malay States, but intended to marry Myrtle later on.[2]

Neville wrote:

> It all sounds like a romance. I should dearly like to know what the secrets are. I am sure they would be detrimental. Joan Pape told PB that she often wondered if Myrtle realised what she had done to me. Nicola (*the new wife of Douglas Speed*), is going to have a baby. I hope they are happy.

Having talked things over with his father Neville decided to resign from his job in the Sudan giving his 'ruined health' as the reason. Then suddenly, without any preamble on 4 June, Myrtle makes an appearance in his diary. Neville, Jane, PB and Jean Bagby, went to Eton for the Fourth celebrations, taking a picnic with them. Neville records that

> (We) split up at about 4pm when M and I hiked off through Windsor Forest to Bagshot and Camberley, then on to Basingstoke where we had tea. M took the wheel to Yeovil where the crowd was as thick as dust. After dinner I took over and drove to Honiton, puncturing on the way. Quite a nice day.

I find it truly extraordinary that there is no indication of bad feeling between them, and no grumbles from Neville about Myrtle's apparent lack of understanding on how she has 'ruined' his career. They appear to be good friends, even staying the night in the

opposite: PooBah (no date).
John d'Arcy / NRO Nev 7/32.

Postcard from the period: Boscastle, the harbour.
Poppyland collection.

same hotel and continuing the following day to Exeter and Oakhampton. They enjoyed a walk along the beach together in Bude and M told him stories about people she had met, including one about a man who had tried to physically carry her off when she was at Grangemouth. Perhaps Neville was actually a man who forgave easily, though according to his diaries, quite the reverse is true. It is more likely that he had no idea how to confront her.

They continued their break in Boscastle, Tintagel, through Wadebridge and Bodmin then across the moor back to Bude. There is just one telling remark from the diary.

> This morning M told me that Helen had told her that she would have married me if I had asked her. Thank Gawd I didn't.

Nevertheless, they went and sat on the breakwater after dinner and watched the sun set into the sea. 'Such a lovely spot,' Neville wrote. 'Just the place for a honeymoon!' It is all a bit extraordinary. From being deeply in love with M, and admitting that he never actually asked her to marry him, to being a friend, good enough to go on holiday with, without any discussion about the past! No recriminations, no tears, no angry shouting match—Neville was indeed an odd person. On 17 June he and M went shopping, then they joined Jane and PooBah and other friends for a 'riotous' dinner where everyone 'laughed long and loudly from dinner time till 4 in the morning.' Again on 19 June he rang her and drove down to see her at Ferring (West Sussex) between Worthing and Littlehampton. Again they went on to the coast for the afternoon where they fell asleep behind a groin out of the wind. All very amicable. Later they went back to M's flat where Neville received a telephone call from Chris Foster who knew of a job vacancy in a firm of stockbrokers which might interest Neville.

On June 21 Neville went along to see the firm, Glissen and Co, where he met a man called Traub, a Brit but with origins in Turkey. Neville recorded in his diary that he 'could not understand him'. Neville's father promised to 'find out' about the firm.

Another possibility was to work in a firm called Leon Brothers. He met a representative of the firm called Simon who said it could be arranged that he should come into the office and learn from the bottom without pay. Simon also said that Neville should see Sir George Leon. Neville duly met Sir George and agreed to start the following Monday, July 4. Even Neville's father seemed to think it was a good idea.

Edwardian England[3] was very fond of games after dinner. While Neville and other

Postcard from the period: Tintagel.
Poppyland collection.

guests played bridge after dinner at The Hoo in Kent at the home of Molly and Jock, the rest of the party played musical bumps in the library, to which the hostess Molly objected as the sofa covers were all new. 'Molly asked them to play some game in the drawing room, and they all trooped in and kicked up hell's own noise just so that we could not play,' wrote Neville in his diary. 'It was a vile exhibition of bad manners. One girl, Ruby Atkinson, wanted a good smacking.'

On his first day at the offices of Leon Brothers, Neville was given a vast list of figures to add up which 'made my head whirl' and then he did a continuous ledger with Peter Leon. 'All very strange, and I felt a complete fool,' he wrote. 'But all the clerks were very nice to me.' PooBah met him after work and presented him with a wonderful pipe to replace one he had lost. 'Truly a royal gift', he said. The following Saturday Neville went to Lords for the cricket and was not a little embarrassed to meet Douglas Speed at tea, with his new wife Nicola.

On Neville's 30th birthday, 5 July 1927, he spent the evening with PooBah. He was 'simply amazed' when out of the blue, PooBah mused that she would probably be Mrs James Neville by now, if his family had not so obviously disapproved of her. Apparently, Jane had talked to PooBah about her brother James and noted that 'he always seemed to make the most unfortunate choice in women.'

Neville wrote in his diary:

> PooBah had an opportunity then of saying that she would have married me, if it had not been for that remark and Jane's attitude generally. They (*my family*) certainly did treat my friends very funnily indeed, and damned badly. She said that even now she did not think she could live up to my standards, which hurt me a good deal, and that she had seen me looking surprised at her. And yet of all the women I have ever known and wanted to marry, she is the only one whom I regret not having married.

Another job offer came in. A friend in high places wrote saying that Lord Plummer wanted an ADC non-regular (ie. an ADC who was not in the Regular Army) to go out to Palestine where Lord Plummer was governor. Neville confided in his diary that he would 'look into it', but was not sure now that he wanted to go back into the army. The job turned out to be for a year only, and would lead to nothing more. Neville decided against it. Neville and his father had a truly terrible argument over a flat that Neville wanted to rent. Neville had fallen in love with the one-bed apartment in Central

London. It had a bath, geyser and basin, gas fires and a gas oven and was in good decorative order. But his father advised him against it on the grounds that it was 'not in the Temple' and that a bath was unnecessary! The two men insulted each other at the front door of the London club where they had had dinner. Neville senior called his son a 'woman' and 'childishly prejudiced'. The son retorted that he might call a man a shit or a bugger, but never a woman. By the time Neville got back to the agent, the little flat had been taken. (Did his rather Victorian attitude mean that shits and buggers ranked higher than women?)

There is a long gap before the next entry on Tuesday 1 November, 1927. Neville had mentioned in his diary, *en passant*, that PooBah was soon to go back to Calcutta, East India. And Neville found himself utterly distraught with her disappearance from his life.

He wrote:

> The one person who has never changed towards me in all these years has gone for a term of six months. I am more than desolated. The agony of it is appalling and I am still feeling sick. I wonder how she is feeling, poor little mite, in a cabin of 30 others bound for a land she loathes.
>
> I shan't hear from her for 10 days—whether her tummy is better or whether the soldiers have come (the 52nd was also due to sail for East India). I am now in bed and still feel sick. I wonder how she is feeling. She will be in her wretched bunk feeling as lonely as I.

Some weeks later a wire arrived at Neville's club. 'Arrived safely with the soldiers—missed post from here—all love'. Neville wrote that he was tremendously relieved, and also jealous of all the people 'buzzing round her' when he, Neville, 'had the right to buzz. The greatest regret of my life is that I never married her or rather that she would not have me, for I would love her to be the mother of my children.'

His job was not going well:

> The office is superbly bloody. I get no orders to execute and there seems little or no chance of making any money at half commission, and I shall be a clerk for the remainder of my days. So I must try and write, and make a few pounds that way.

He also reflects on M. 'I know now what it must have been like to be M in the old days when I disappeared from her, and no wonder she thought me a shit.' This is new information about 1924, and it sounds as though, furious at the interloper of T on the farm in South Africa, Neville went off on his own when perhaps he should have stood and fought his ground. On Saturday 5 November Neville had a row with his sister Jane over her treatment of M, which put him a bad mood for the rest of the weekend. He wrote to M and asked for her opinion. 'I really don't see,' he confided to her, 'why the minutest errors of mine should never be forgotten, while Jane and my family incidentally were the cause of all my troubles. If they had received you kindly in the beginning we should have got married and there would have been none of the troubles of 1924. True, we should have been pretty miserable at the beginning, but a little knocking about would have done me a power of good and if I had not broken your heart and spirit in the first year, we should be happy now I know. At the beginning it would have been awful for I was a bloody pig and a disapproving shit, but then again – that was the influence of my priggish family.'

Every day Neville called in at his club to pick up mail. Most days he was disappointed, but on November 14 there was a letter, 'quite a fat one', written between Marseilles and Port Said. Neville was overjoyed:

> She said she had a bloody journey down with all the windows shut, and that a woman with a child had pinched her berth and she was hunched up like a sardine and supremely miserable. Though her letter was unhappy, it filled me with relief and made me come over all queer with its suddenness. How I wish I was with my own beloved sailing down the Red Sea, warm at least instead of miserably

and damnably cold.

He recorded that he went to a party at the Colts where he saw a few old friends, but 'the whole time felt terribly lonely. I imagined PB (*with me in Paris*) dancing and laughing and standing with her arms folded, in a characteristic attitude.

Neville wrote in his diary.

> Too damnable. A mass of humanity on board and one Mundo McLeod suggests that she (PooBah) should share his cabin as he was alone, but she pointed out that the ship's officials might object and "you too—though you would have no cause to." Then on Thursday it began to blow and she was terribly sick and the ship lurched and rolled and wagged her tail and was generally bloody. I went to the Anchor Line office and found out that they are due in at Bombay on Tuesday 15 November, and she will be in Calcutta on Friday. It was just heaven getting a letter.

Another letter arrived from Suez on Thursday 17 November in which PooBah asked Neville 'not to love anyone else while I am away,' adding 'but I don't think you will because I think you belong extra specially to me.' Neville was overjoyed. To add to his joy he won at cards that night.

Monday 21 November, a cable arrived from PooBah saying she had arrived safely in Calcutta the day before. Neville was delighted and said in his diary that he felt very close to her. By now Neville was very depressed again and was on the verge of taking a room at Number 174 in Pimlico, in which 'he could do penance for my very existence'.

> It is a pokey little room, vilely furnished. Perhaps I can gain merit from the Gov'nor who I hope will never come to see me there. However the landlady, Molly, is a nice kindly woman and it does not matter where I live, and the Gov'nor cares still less as far as I can see. I could go and stay with Jane, but I don't think I could curb my tongue another time if Reg called me an outrageous shit. And besides if he does not know that I am a shit, his perspicacity must be very undeveloped. I can put up with anything in the hope of a home when she comes back.

Neville does not elaborate, but it does sound as though he is hoping that he and PooBah can be married when she returns from India. The following day he describes his loneliness, and how a 'black pall overhung the city all day, and we worked by lamplight'. He goes on in horribly racist terms. 'I expect she is being feted and much attention paid her in Calcutta. Bless her, but I am jealous of every soul who speaks to her. Why should black men be honoured with her very presence when I am denied it?' He spent the evening writing a long letter to her. He also dug out some old letters from PooBah and made himself thoroughly miserable by realising that he had wrecked their relationship a long time ago.

In his usual dramatic style he recorded:

> O! thrice damned fool that I am! Why oh why am I such an untrusting jiggins and so cruel? But by God I have paid to the last farthing since!

It seems that before PooBah married, Neville had been extremely rude to her friend Chris (a man), but that 'he had forgiven Neville'. PooBah had then told Neville to be 'courageous', which made him want to cry. Neville fell foul of his brother-in-law Reg by sending Jane a letter saying he was going away on Saturday—which Jane, by then pregnant again, was terribly upset over. A few days later she started bleeding badly and passed out. It does not quite make sense that an unthinking letter should do so much damage, but Reg accused Neville of 'causing the miscarriage'. I only repeat the incident because it does seem as though Neville had a terrible way of upsetting people, both intentionally and also without malice.

At the end of December he met PooBah's friend Chris. Neville told Chris that he was living in Pimlico in a pokey, vile room of which he had become quite fond. Neville also commented that Pimlico was where 'the tarts live' and Chris seemed surprised that Neville was not living with one! So 1927 at least ended with a joke.

Notes

1 This is probably Toby Sturges, a good friend of Neville from army days. Neville does not say so, but losing M to a good. friend hurt him deeply, far more than if he had lost her to a complete stranger, as one might expect.

2 Although 'Edwardian England' ended 17 years earlier, many of the customs persisted.

3 The Federated Malay States (FMS) was a group of four states in the Malaysian Peninsular—Selangor, Perak, Negeri Sembilan and Pahang—established by the British Government in 1895 and lasting until 1946. Two years later the Union became the Federation of Malaya, and finally Malaysia in 1963 with the inclusion of North Borneo, Sarawak and Singapore. Wikipedia, February 2018.

More PooBah—and then Kay

The affair with PooBah continues but towards the end of the year, Neville meets yet another married woman, Kay, who is considering separating from her husband. Unbelievably Neville repeats the pattern of the past five years and becomes involved for a third time with a woman he cannot have, hoping she will settle down with him.

1928

January

Sunday 1 January was bitterly cold, cold enough for the pond at Wickmere (near Cromer in North Norfolk) to freeze over. Neville records that he fell more than ever while skating but they cleared enough snow away to allow for a spot of ice hockey. He lunched afterwards with Alphonse and wrote his first letter of the year (probably to PooBah). Apparently, a friend, Woolly had been turned down by the girl he asked to marry him, and was distraught.

As soon as he could, Neville made for London where, at his club, he collected a letter from PooBah, still in India. She was being very sociable—dinners, dances, lunches, polo, but she complained that she longed for 'a quiet dinner at the Raj'. Her tummy was very unsettled and Neville was worried about the possibility of dysentery. Neville meanwhile, was still in London pining for her and complaining that he was 'in the bad habit' of dining out at the club, which cost him 17/6 per week. In a subsequent letter she revealed that while she was having a great time with 'dinners, drinks parties and all manner of gaieties', she and S (her husband) were 'all wrong'.

'The politeness is getting on my nerves,' she wrote to Neville. 'He is betting Rs100 on a horse (equivalent to about £1000 today) at the races but had not got me a Christmas present. All the affection I had for him is in the past, and if S would just say an affectionate or friendly word, it would be fraudulent.' Neville's reaction was this: 'She is being starved and methinks she must turn somewhere else for the affection that is her life's blood. It is a terrible cry and one passage has frightened me. She says that she is not tired of me nor has she stopped loving me but that I would understand. It is a bad thing to read between the lines, but I seem to feel that she would just say that without reason.'

There are awful echoes here of what he wrote in his diary when he and M were 'dating'. PooBah is also a married woman 'starved of affection' and looking for a shoulder to cry on. But Neville does not seem to see the pattern. It got worse. A letter Neville had written to PooBah for her to receive in Bombay did not arrive in time, and was forwarded to their address in Calcutta where S opened it. Neville records that the letter was really very indiscreet and says that she 'is the only woman he had ever loved'. S was angry and told someone that if it were not for B (their child) that he would 'free himself, but it is anyway all over between them.' 'They never speak to each other except in front of other people,' Neville wrote. 'She seems to think that S is laying a trap for her to fall into. I can't believe it. It has knocked me utterly sideways and I am miserable. I can't even write as I would and say that I am falling for her.'

By March there was only a week until PooBah returned from India and Neville was full of suspense and doubt. On the 15th, Neville received a wire from her saying she had contracted pleurisy and was unable to sail. He was devastated and 'anxious as hell' and feared he might not see her until May.

The torture for Neville continued until March 26 when a friend rang to say she had had a cable from PooBah saying she was much better and hoped to sail 'next week'. The agony came to an end about a week later when Neville got a cable telling him that she had sailed and would he meet her in Paris! Neville readily agreed to meet her in the French capital. He even bought her a gift, a pale aquamarine brooch which looked like clear water.

Finally, confirmation came that PooBah was on her way home. He received a cable from Port Said saying she would meet him at the Ambassador Hotel in Paris. They arranged to meet on 19 April. Realising that PooBah would find the weather in Europe very cold, he decided to take some of her warm clothes with him, including her fur coat. Neville arrived in Paris on Friday 20 April at 10pm and got a taxi to the station.

'The Marseilles train was just pulling in as I arrived,' he wrote in his diary. 'There seemed to be many, many people getting off, but no sign of PooBah. I was quivering with excitement and walking slowly up the platform. For a moment, I thought she must have missed the train—and then suddenly I caught sight of a hand waving. It was PooBah!

'(At first) I was speechless,' he wrote. Then 'How we talked! Gosh, I can't believe it even yet. The poor lamb has the beginnings of a cold.' Indeed, PooBah soon had to retire to bed in the hotel, coughing and wheezing while they shopped in the Champs-Élysées. Neville spent a lot of time searching for chemist shops for medicines and then they lunched at the Café de Paris. But she said that she felt rather depressed, and hurt Neville by saying that she would never marry again. From Paris they went on to Bruges where they saw a play, *The Trial of Mary Dugan* which Neville greatly enjoyed, but he saw great big tears form in PooBah's eyes. He thought she must be tired and feeling insecure as she had now no home to go to.

Back in London they went house-hunting for PooBah, found something in Belgravia and then went on in 'glorious hot spring weather' and picked primroses in Guildford. PooBah gave Neville a beautiful bedspread in embroidered silk which touched him deeply. But still she was not well and Neville recorded that she really ought to be in bed for a week. They met up with an old friend of PooBah's (another man) and Neville quickly realised that he was not the only man in her life. He recorded:

> I am not jealous, strangely enough, but I am afraid that I am living in a fool's paradise if I think or even conceive of her being mine. It's going to be a long strain, and I'm afraid at the end of it I shall only find a gap more awful than any in the past. But it is worth risking that gap in case ...

In May a doctor confirmed that PooBah had laryngitis and confined her to bed for a week. During that week Neville spent at least one whole day with her at her new flat in Ebury Street while she read her letters, one of which was many pages long and from her ex-husband. It was either so nasty or so unbearably emotional that she passed out while reading it, and Neville had to bring her round with a cold sponge, a glass of whisky and smelling salts. Her health did not improve. She stopped sleeping, was depressed and anxious, and contracted asthma. Neville, naturally enough, became worried and tried to persuade her to go to Norfolk where the 'good air' would help her recover. By chance Neville discovered what was troubling PooBah. Apparently two mutual friends, Esme and Reg, told her that Neville was living in the hope that she would marry him—and she had already decided that she would never marry again.

Neville felt sure that if PooBah married the right man—himself—she would no longer want 'to philander up and down the world', as she had had it put to him. Neville recorded in his diary, rather forlornly, that he 'was bidden not to hope—ever!' Understandably, Neville felt pretty miserable. He realised that 'I am running my head into a brick wall ... but I can't help hoping. I must hope for something in this life and I can't hope for anything better than making a home for her one day.' There followed a deal of confusion for them both. They spent time together and PooBah was often 'sparkling company ... just like the old days', but she said that Neville was frightening her by appearing not to hear that she did not want to marry again, and Neville could not bear to let go of his case.

Finally, PooBah wrote to him, setting down in black and white her feelings for him which were friendly enough, but she repeated over and again that she would never marry him, not even if he was a rich man (rather an inappropriate comment since he so obviously was!). The reason she gave was that he tended 'to put her on a pedestal and she could not live up to his expectations'. Neville was cast into the deepest gloom—but still he would not let go, recording that 'faint heart never won yet and I can't give up now just when my chance has come which I have waited 10 years for.' But PooBah persisted and finally Neville was forced to accept the reality—she was fond of him, but nothing more.

From an observer's eye—mine—it would seem that Neville allowed himself to be used by these women, all of whom were married, and who simply who wanted a handsome man to escort them around town, all the while whispering in his ear that her marriage was unhappy and might end soon. It was misery for Neville who wanted to get married and start a family, and who was in effect, strung along. It is a pattern that occurs three times altogether. I want to give him a good shake, but at the same time I feel so sorry for him. For the second time in 5 years he had given himself, heart, soul and mind, to a woman who only wanted to use him as a crutch. The awful thing is that he could, at times, see this. 'I suppose I shall just ache my heart out until it becomes so hardened that no-one can touch it again,' he confided in his diary. 'I thought that last time.'

The following day he and PooBah were on their way to watch a cricket match, when she told him that she was 'pining for TB and was very sad that she could not meet him again.' Neville was shocked. She went on, 'Perhaps it would mean happiness for me if I could take up with him again.' 'Gosh, the agony,' Neville wrote:

> I have been so wrong (*in thinking we could marry*). All is so changed that I hardly like to suggest anything at all. I think and think what I can do to please her, and I am signally unsuccessful. Before she was so full of sweet little sayings to me, which made me bubble with joy. Now I can hardly raise a smile. It is so cruel.

Despite all these good intentions of friendship but nothing more, their romance struggled on. Neville still did not accept that his case was hopeless. At the start of June, he was round at her flat cleaning it out while she went off to lunch with a new boyfriend.

> I put all the books away and swept the floor and polished up the furniture and had everything practically clean by the time she came back, I was determined that she should have nothing to do … I had no lunch … but I cannot eat these days and I told her why—that I am devilishly anxious about her. She only laughed and said I was silly to fuss. I said that no-one had fussed over her before and she replies that S had always complained that she was always ill, and he had poopoo-ed her illness. She now has a backache which she says is a return of the bladder trouble. I am wholly consumed with anxiety and can neither eat nor sleep. As a matter of fact, it is more than that. I am more deeply in love than I have ever been with her and she is not with me. In fact, she is rather sharp sometimes.

All this time Neville had been trying to persuade his father to help him financially so that he could 'live like a gent'. Neville recorded in his diary that 'he was not prepared to go on living like this very much longer.' He spoke to his father's second wife ('the grasper') on the telephone and got the news that his father was 'perfectly willing to help him', but Neville had heard this so often before, and nothing had ever materialised. He determined that he would write it all down this time, and try to keep his father to it.

Things went from bad to worse with PooBah. Neville wrote in his diary:

> I think she cordially dislikes me now. She snaps at me when I do my very best. I can understand the reason, but it makes me so very shy and it is so just

> like M was that I fear it is the beginning of the end already. I am playing a losing game these days ... she is right. She will never be mine and it makes my head swim... She is just fond of me but never will be in love with me again. ... And last Sunday when she talked of Tom—ugh! It is a repetition of the M affair complete in every detail as regards facts. I shall be quietly broken in time and suppose I shall go abroad again, and next time for ever. God, I wish something could end this ghastly barrier. I am writing this while she is in the room! She does not know how much I love her and want her. She keeps me at arm's length and all my patience has to be exercised.

There is one extraordinarily sad story during this period. Neville says that he bought her a light with a lampshade from Italia House for her room, and smuggled it in without PooBah knowing. Later on, she mentioned to him that this light had appeared, and asked him if he was responsible. At first, Neville refused to admit it was him but finally he owned up.

'Eventually I told her,' he wrote in his diary. 'And I won my kiss—which she never gives me nowadays voluntarily. I suppose I am still comparing these days with last year, which I must not do, when she wanted to lie in my arms, and was "in love" with me. Now I feel she tolerates me and I am terrified of making mistakes.' Poor Neville! Fancy having to go out and buy something in order to get just a kiss from the one you love.

Later in June she took up with her old set of friends – Roz and Pongo and Sam – and Neville became really quite unstable, not knowing how he stood with PooBah. Was he just a friend? Was he more? Why did she treat him with such disdain? His friend Chris said he would try to find out from her why she behaved as she did. Neville recorded 'I have a feeling of suspense always in the pit of my stomach, that a blow is coming and if it is I would far rather it came in one crash than in my being quietly shelved without a word.'

The agony continued, day after day. They went to Eton for the day for cricket, but PooBah spent little time with Neville, constantly 'buzzing off between stumps', as he put it in his diary, to see relatives leaving him to wander alone and he wondered if she did not want to be seen with him in public too often. The constant anxiety was starting to affect his health and he developed very bad earache. The following day, also at Eton, Neville had an attack of some kind and PooBah said she wanted to go home. Neville wrote in his diary, 'I am very definitely out of favour and if only she would say so and execute me quickly, I should suffer far less. I could not sleep and am utterly miserable.... It is not her fault but being left to guess is hell. Last year it was always "When shall I see you again?" She kept all weekends free. Now it is the reverse and O! such hell!'

On Sunday (July 15) Neville went round to her flat to discover that she was just getting up, around 12 noon. Apparently after she got home the previous night Pongo had rung her, they had gone out for a carriage ride round Regent's Park and then to a night club until 2.30am. Soon after Neville arrived, PooBah went off for lunch with Sam. She and Neville went to see the cricket, but she did not speak to him or look at him, and announced that later that evening she was going swimming with Sam at Shepperton. 'I am not jealous', he wrote in his diary. 'Just wounded to the core and I don't know what to do about it. It seems I am being told politely without words that I am not needed any more.'

On Thursday (July 19) Neville was expecting to dine with PooBah, but she rang to say she was ill with cystitis (a bladder infection). Neville had an early supper and then went round to look after her - scratched her head just the way she liked it, smoothed her back, listened to her moaning about how ill she felt, and then went home.

The following day Neville dined with Kay Oldham. This is the first mention of yet another woman in Neville's life who is destined to give him more heartache. They discussed soothsayers which interested Neville a great deal. 'She is most awfully nice and a discerning woman and pretty withal—but rather hard. I feel that I can't get to the flesh for the skin, whereas I wear my heart on my sleeve.'

The impasse with PooBah continued for a

few more months. They talked openly occasionally about their feelings for each other which gave Neville cause for more hope, but finally on 17 October 1928 PooBah confessed to Neville that she was 'in love with S.B.' Neville was devastated, even though, as he admitted to his diary that he 'knew this blow was coming and it was only a question of time.'

> God, it can't be happening again. Oh Christ, what have I done to deserve this. It must be a third punishment for some sin committed.... Alone, alone in this howling wilderness with no support, no help, no companion.

He rang his new friend Kay and asked her if she would go with him to a soothsayer, but Kay had just been and did not rate her services. Neville eventually caught up with Kay on 19 October and they had dinner at '*Napoleon's Josephine*'. 'She's a dear', Neville wrote. 'But rather cynical.' He heard from his sister Jane the same afternoon who asked if 'something awful' had happened on Tuesday as she had felt 'simply ghastly' for no reason.

Neville sank into another deep depression, similar to the depression he had experienced after his affair with M had ended. He and PooBah talked occasionally and PooBah repeated her refrain that Neville 'was the only man she could really trust and rely on', from which Neville took some hope. However, he began to see that his 'darling PooBah' wanted the best of both worlds—someone a bit dull to rely on, and someone else more exciting to give her a good time—and, as Neville put it in his diary 'This is rather at my expense.'

Despite Neville's rather *prima donna* expressions of another broken heart, he at once started to see more of his friend Kay. They had lunch together, shopped together and even went back to a soothsayer together. Kay said she was 'much disturbed' when the soothsayer, a Mrs C, insisted emphatically that Oldham (Kay's husband) was going to die, and she did not know what to do about it, whether or not to go to China.

On November 2, PooBah invited Neville round saying 'she felt depressed'. Neville did not go. 'Here endeth that episode in my life and henceforth she must do without me,' he wrote. But he was presumably much encouraged by 'A wonderful party with K.O. (the same day) and then to the *Café Anglais*.' Kay rang the following day to say she could not come with him to the Chelsea Theatre that night, then M rang up to say she was going in to hospital to have an operation on her foot. The only person who did not contact Neville that day was PooBah!

Neville was starting all over again with his third married woman. And again, he started with a 'fever of expectation and suspense'. 'The only thing I know is that K is worth 100% of M,' he confided in his diary.

> I've been tortured by M and I'm sure K is not the torturing sort. She has had it herself, poor dear.

Neville saw K on Tuesday 6 November when he took her to a party at the house of his brother-in-law Reg. He danced all night with her, and only her, then took her home and they sat by the fire talking until 3.30pm. Neville wrote:

> Gosh! It has made all the difference in the world to me! Then I remembered! Mrs C had told me that the woman I should marry would have two children and her husband is going to peg out. All the time I thought she meant M, and it was really this. I can hardly believe it. It is too wonderful!

The following day was the same, only this time they went out to dine on half a dozen oysters followed by roast partridge, then home to talk until 3.30pm. 'I am completely light-headed and joyful!'

This went on all through November. 'I feel so sure and certain and so happy!' Neville wrote again and again. 'She knows I am vain, proud and conceited and still she cares!' The only slightly less-than-happy moment came when Neville got tight one evening and Kay was 'terribly upset'. As a result, Neville felt 'a complete worm' the following day. But she rang him and told him not to be too miserable over it. On 22 November Kay heard that her husband was on his way home from China, where 'his services had been dispensed with by the concession.' But nothing seemed to come of this. There is no further mention of Kay's husband, and she and Neville continued as before.

More Kay and Finally a Bride!

Still with Kay (the third married woman) but very unhappy, Neville publishes his book 'The War Letters of a Light Infantryman'. At the end of the year he finally meets a lovely woman, Marie-Louise Pierson, who is able and willing to marry him!

1929–1932

By now Neville was 32 years of age and just starting on another affair with a married woman who thinks she wants a divorce but is not sure. I have to confess to a certain frustration with the man and I began to wonder in this stage of his life, how often he would have to repeat this mistake before he understood himself.

Sadly he got used all over again. He spent a huge amount of time with K, even taking her to Sloley for the August Bank Holiday weekend where he took her out on the Broads in a motor boat. At dinner K argued about how she hated a boy shooting or hunting—a bad mistake in front of a family rooted in the Norfolk countryside. 'We all jumped down her throat, poor dear,' he wrote. 'But her construction was that we were all intolerant.' On the Monday the family, including K, all went to the Barton Broad Regatta and then to dinner with friends at Dilham, a nearby village.

During this period Neville seemed to do very little paid work and was often short of money as a consequence. He never mentions in his diary any projects he was involved with at the office, nor any office gossip. He spent all his time going to the cinema, or to the theatre, club, or to visit K at her flat, or at a party, or playing bridge or poker. His diary is full of meaningless gossip, though he does mention that he was pleased that his former lover M was miffed that Neville was no longer there for her to fall back on.

K was often in a bad mood and regularly used foul language, taunting Neville for being either 'niggardly or poor'. As before, Neville seemed to get on her nerves easily, quite probably because he seemed to have nothing else of importance to do other than look after his girlfriend.

He wrote:

> Like all the others she has taken to cursing me and hurting me, and I am afraid I hurt back. This evening was terrible—she never said what she wanted to do, and I am sure that whatever we had done, it would have been wrong in the mood she was in. Then she accused me of being a beast but would not tell me how.

All this time K was saying that 'she may get a divorce, or she may not,' which made their relationship very tense.

In September K went off to Le Touquet, the fashionable French seaside haunt of the rich and famous, for a little 'gambling break' and wrote to Neville that she had lost his mother's pencil. 'At this time she could have done nothing more stupid,' Neville wrote in his diary:

> I feel it is a very, very bad omen. It's like losing an engagement ring, only this was far more valuable to me. It was the most valuable thing I had and she couldn't take care of that. I am terribly upset and not a little angry for she lost it at that bloody Le Touquet place ... just the sound of the name makes me fume.

But K returned to England on 30 September and the couple made up.

November 6 that year was their first anniversary and the day did not go well. They struggled on through the following

opposite: Outside the Oratory after the ceremony, April 5, 1932.
John d'Arcy / NRO Nev 7/32.

year (1930) with row after row after row. They seemed to be supremely unhappy but neither could bring the relationship to an end. 1 January, 1931 should have been a day of real achievement for Neville. He had been working for some time on editing the letters he and his father and sisters had written to each other during the war but he had failed to find a publisher. He had decided to pay to have it published. But he seems to take little pleasure in its final appearance.

He wrote:

> My ruddy book (*The War Letters of a Light Infantryman*) came out yesterday. I am going to lose money on it. No-one will buy it and why should they? There are a good many bad mistakes in it and some were never altered.

He had also been asked to write the history of his regiment, The Oxford and Buckinghamshire Light Infantry, though this was also a voluntary effort. It must have been an honour to be asked to compile this history, but he sounds churlish in his diary. 'The history will take all my spare time and will give me no time to read anything but the Chronicles,' he recorded. There were endless parties, dinners, theatre and cinema visits, sometimes with K, sometimes not, but the relationship remained rocky and frosty. On 22 February, for example, he wrote, 'I don't think the time is far off before she transfers her affections back to the old love'.

[HAY WRIGHTSON.

MISS MARIE PIERSON,
only daughter of Mr. and Mrs. Pierson, of Flesk, Burnham, Somersetshire. Her engagement to Captain James E. H. Neville, M.P., was recently announced.

Announcement in the newspaper of the engagement.
John d'Arcy / NRO Nev 7/32.

On Sunday April 19 he wrote:

> I showed K the review of my book in the *Times Lit Sup*. She was not impressed and made no comment. But it is good to know that the critic thinks more of it than she does, for she is a rather cruel critic and thinks she is a master in English so that I hardly dare write to her now for fear of making a solecism which she will notice.' He was also involved with the Territorial Army and mentioned that he was going to do the LDSI[1] course. He got a 'raspberry proper.' '" Damn and blast your bloody territorials," said she. She doesn't seem to like them much, and probably less because I like the job very much. She is probably jealous of the job.

By contrast K was spending a lot of time with a man called Croesus (it is not clear if that was his real name, or a nickname which Neville had given him on account of his fabled wealth). Neville did not like this much but K was happy to ignore his feelings and carried on regardless. The word 'cuckold' makes an appearance in his diary. They seemed to argue about everything—politics, relationships, and very often, how valuable was an education for girls. 'K did not like my remarks at supper that to send a girl abroad in these days was a complete waste of time and money,' he wrote. 'This is because she learns nothing useful, only extravagance. In a woman's market (the marriage one), it counts for nothing. A man does not know nor care whether a woman has been to Switzerland or not—it's all balls, this so-called finishing.' By this time—the middle of 1931—'the sight of me gave K pain and sickness'.

Finally, on Thursday 19 November, there is the first mention of his future wife, Marie-Louise Pierson, the sister of a well-known golfer. Neville writes:

> I met a perfect little pet, Marie Pierson, tall and dark with limpid eyes, and a beautiful figure. Rather like PB to look at except for the nose. She works in a shop in Brook Street. I was very smitten though one must not be beguiled by a pretty face. I took her and her brother home to Cromwell Road.

Two days later Neville rang Marie-Louise and they arranged a date for the following Wednesday. Neville reports in his diary that:

> I really did feel rather excited when I went to call for my new lady. We dined at the club and went to *The Anatomist* (a popular dark comedy by James Bridie) at the Westminster Theatre. Marie-Louise has very light eyes and is definitely pretty and vivacious .... Her light blue lace frock was as pretty as she. She seems to go to the theatre every night!

Predictably it was the end of the road for Neville and K, whom he now describes as

The six bridesmaids, from left; Ida McCartney-Filgate, Sarah Vick (both nieces of the groom), Mary Emmet (goddaughter of the bride), Marigold Wilson, Heather Flower, and Ann Miller. The pageboy was Christopher McCartney-Filgate (the groom's nephew).
John d'Arcy / NRO Nev 7/32.

'neurotic', though he adds that he very much does not want to hurt her.

There was a small shock in store for Neville however when he discovered on Sunday 6 December over supper with Marie-Louise that she was a Roman Catholic! And had been educated at a convent school in Bruges! Neville was taken aback, fearful that this 'damned religious business' might scupper his chances with her. There was a bit of a hiatus, but on December 23 Neville reports that he had lunch with MLP—and gave her a gift of a pair of silk stockings. And on 28 December Neville got down on one knee and proposed. MLP accepted him the following day. We have to assume the following months leading up to their wedding were busy and happy, as Neville does not record anything in his diary about this period.

Nor does he record what his family, especially his father thought about his choice of bride, but I think they must have been pleased. Marie-Louise came from a good family with money, she was physically attractive and both her daughters confirm that she had a lovely temperament. At least three announcements of their engagement appeared in the press and they were married at London's Brompton Oratory on the afternoon of Tuesday April 5 1932, with a reception afterwards at Ennismore Gardens. The bride wore a 'classical white satin dress and a white satin train lined with chiffon. She carried a sheaf of Madonna lilies and an upstanding wreath of orange blossom (on her head) holding in place a long tulle veil,' according to a press report of their big day in The *Times* on April 8. The six bridesmaids

Guests outside Brompton Oratory.
John d'Arcy / NRO Nev 7/32.

wore long dresses of white net with turquoise-blue sashes. Best man was Captain HEF Smyth.

Neville himself was 'thrilled'. He wrote a touching poem to his new lady-love which he had enclosed with the silk stockings. And here it is.

And what have women that men have not too,
Save hosiery, save silken hosiery?
And what art thou, thou glossy hosiery?
What kind of make art thou, that ladder'st least

From English hands or those of Germany?
What are thy holes? What are thy takings-off?
O hosiery! Show me but thy mark,
What is thy sole? Of silk or crushed pulp?

Art thou aught else but sleekness, strongly wove
Creating fervour in the hearts of men?
Wherein thou art less envied, being worn
Than they in weaving.

What has the Boche, instead of English shine,
But sheenless texture? O be sick, fair wench
And bid thy shop girl give thee English hose.
Think'st thou thy purchase'd treason will not out

With English legs encase'd in German silk?
Will it give place to flexme and low bending?
No! it will ladder straight from heel to knee.
And so encompass thy discomfiture.

Let not thy wayward fancy search the shops
For foreign goods that English men can make
'Tis not the scent, the powder and the buff,
The silken hose, the shoes, the voile de soie,

The fabrics, purchas'd from a foreign land
That can to English homes bring back prosperity.
Therefore to thee, I give these English hose
In protest of thy purchases confess'd;

And pray that if they will not fit thy case
Thou wilt return them whole to Peter Jones
And ask for others in the given's name.
So fare thee well.

Notes

1 LDSI – List of Territorial Army Divisions, Wikipedia, February 2018.

Postscript

After his marriage to Marie-Louise, James settled down living first at a house called Coleraines in Essex, and then at Frankfurt Manor in Sloley where he ran a farm. His daughter Janie described his activities as a farmer with some scepticism, saying he was a 'bit of an amateur'. Fortunately for him and his family (Rosalind, known as Lindy, born 1933, and Janie, born 1935), Marie-Louise had money so they did not starve. James' half-brother Richard (Reginald's son by Violet Hunter) inherited Sloley Hall. Richard never married and the Hall then passed to Simon Gorton, James' grandson by his daughter Lindy. He and his wife Babs ran it as an up-market bed-and-breakfast establishment. It is now run by Simon's son Peter Gorton and his partner Jodie.

James continued to keep a daily diary and there are some 60 volumes of his journals in the Norfolk Record Office, along with the typescript of '*The War Letters*', and some short stories under the pen-name Gaid Sakit, and many documents of family papers. He maintained an on-going interest in the British Army and was responsible for writing five volumes of the history of his regiment. Between 1931 and 1946 he was re-employed in the 12th London Regiment and was put in command of the Light Infantry Training Centre during WW2.

James loved the high life and was delighted when he was invited to become Master of the Bowyers Company in 1936, and in 1947 was elected to the court of the Worshipful Company of Fishmongers. He succeeded his father to the baronetcy of Sloley in 1950 when Reginald died, becoming the 2nd Baronet. His other interests included being a member of his local District Council (Smallburgh), a founder member of the highly-regarded Norfolk Churches Trust

Neville with his two daughters, Lindy as a toddler, and Janie as a baby.

John d'Arcy / NRO Nev 7/32.

(whose patron is King Charles III) and a Governor of the well-known public school Gresham's at Holt in north Norfolk.

Marie-Louise died in 1981 after suffering some years of ill-health. James remarried the same year to Betty Cowell whom he had known for some time. He died in 1982.

Neville with his wife Marie-Louise and niece, Sarah Vick, 1997.

Janie Neville.

Bibliography

The Great War

The Three Emperors, Miranda Carter, Penguin, 2009.

Great Britain's Great War, Jeremy Paxman, Penguin, 2013.

Queen Elizabeth the Queen Mother, Sara Barton-Wood, Hodder and Stoughton, 1999.

The Battles of the Somme, Martin Maris Evans, Phoenix, 1996.

Grandad's War, First World War diary of Horace Reginald Stanley, Juliet and Heather Brodie, Poppyland Publishing, 2007.

The Baker Brothers, Diaries from the Eastern Front, 1914-19, Brenda Stibbons, Poppyland Publishing, 2018.

History of the 43rd and 52nd Light Infantry in the Great War, JEH Neville, Naval and Military Press, reprinted 2008.

Russia

The Murmansk Venture, Major-General Sir C Maynard, Naval and Military Press, 2010.

The Day They Almost Bombed Moscow, Christopher Dobson and John Miller, Atheneum, 1986.

Churchill's Crusade; the British Invasion of Russia, Clifford Kinvig, Hambledon Continuum, 2006.

Ireland

A Hard Local War, William Sheehan, The History Press, 2011.

Bitter Freedom, Maurice Walsh, Faber and Faber, 2015.

The Irish Civil War, Peter Cottrell, Osprey, 2008.

General

Evolution of the British Electoral System, Martin Pugh, The Historical Association, 1988.

Great Manifestos 1900-97, Iain Dale (ed.), Routledge 2000.

The Story of Sandhurst, Hugh Thomas, Hutchinson, 1996.

Original sources

From Norfolk Record Office, Neville papers – Nev 7/3a (Reginald James N Neville), Nev 7/8 and 9 (Angela Neville), Nev 7/10, 11, 13, 14, 15,16, 17, 18, 19, 20, (Marie-Louise Neville), Nev 7/18, 19, 29, 30, 31, 32, 33, 34, 35, 36, 37, 38, 39, 40, 69, 70, 71, 72, 73, 74, 76, and Nev 11/ 61, 62, 64, 65, 82, 83, 84, 85, 86, 87, 90 (JEH Neville).

Websites

American-historama.org

Butterfly-conservation.org

BBC.com

Encyclopaedia Britannica

Eton College

Firstworldwar.com

opposite: Neville in 1953 in full dress Oxford and Bucks uniform as Gold Staff Official in Westminster Abbey on the occasion of the coronation of Queen Elizabeth II.

Janie Neville.

History.com
Historylearningsite.co.uk
Ireland and WW1
Imperial War Museum
Lt-Col Sir JEH Neville, 2nd Baronet
Militarywikia.org
Official British Army blog
Royal Military Academy Sandhurst
Stoke House School
Spartacus Educational
Saint-petersburg.com/museums
Sir Reginald Neville, 1st Baronet (1927)
Wikipedia
Who's Who
Wellcome Collection Online

Index